Ethics

ROYAL INSTITUTE OF PHILOSOPHY SUPPLEMENT: 35 — note: include supplemental subtitle

EDITED BY

A. Phillips Griffiths

CAMBRIDGE
UNIVERSITY PRESS

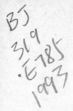

Published by the Press Syndicate of the University of Cambridge
The Pitt Building, Trumpington Street, Cambridge, CB2 1RP
40 West 20th Street, New York, NY 10011-4211, USA
10 Stamford Road, Oakleigh, Melbourne 3166, Australia

*A catalogue record for this book is available
from the British Library*

Library of Congress Cataloguing in Publication Data

Ethics/edited by A. Phillips Griffiths
   p. cm. —(Royal Institute of Philosophy supplement: 35)
   Also published as a supplement to Philosophy vol. 68 (1993).
   Includes bibliographical references.
   ISBN 0–521–45764–5 (pbk.)
   1. Ethics, Modern —20th century. I. Griffiths, A. Phillips
II. Series
BJ319. E785 1993
170—dc20
                  93–27332
                   CIP

ISBN 0 521 45764 5 (paperback)

Origination by Michael Heath Ltd, Reigate, Surrey
Printed in Great Britain by the University Press, Cambridge

Contents

Preface

The essays in this volume are based on lectures given to the Royal Institute of Philosophy at 14, Gordon Square, London in the session 1992–93.

'Given', that is, in every sense: the Institute, as a small charity, depends on that of its speakers. We are most grateful.

The Institute owes a particular debt of gratitude in this instance to Professor Singer, who came all the way from Wisconsin for the sole purpose of giving his lecture. Not for the first time: he made a special visit in 1986 to give his lecture on Value Judgments, printed in the Institute supplementary volume *Key Themes in Philosophy*; and he arranged and conducted the 1984–5 lecture series on American philosophy, editing the subsequent supplementary volume.

To the Institute, he is by way of becoming an institution: though not in the sense in which he is interested (see p. 229). His original, stimulating and, it is to be hoped seminal, paper included a number of scrupulous acknowledgments to people, sometimes named and sometimes not, whom he suspected of having contributed to his thought on this matter, which high-handed editing has suppressed. One was to a Director of the Institute who knows, as well as any of them, that the development of this distinct branch of ethics is entirely Professor Singer's own.

Objective Prescriptions*

R. M. HARE

I offer no apology for presenting a simple paper about what is essentially a simple subject: the objectivity of moral judgments. Most of the complications are introduced by those who do not grasp the distinctions I shall be making. I am afraid that they include the majority of moral philosophers at the present time. These complications can be unravelled; but not in a short paper. I have tried to do it in my other writings (see esp. Hare 1981: chs 1, 12 and refs).

The term 'objective prescriptivity' was introduced by John Mackie (1977: ch. 1). Mackie thought that not only some misguided philosophers but even ordinary people think that when they use moral language they are uttering objective prescriptions. Hence his well-known 'error theory' of ethics. According to this, when we utter a sentence containing a word like 'right' or 'wrong' we all think, both that we are saying something prescriptive, i.e. action-guiding, and that we are stating some fact about the world; and we are always mistaken, because there are no such prescriptive moral facts existing in the world. I agree with Mackie that, in the sense in which he used that expression, there can be no objective prescriptions. That is to say, if by 'objective' we mean 'factual', in the sense of 'merely factual', a prescription could never be that. An imperative like 'Shut the door' does not state any fact about the door. And a statement of fact like 'The door is locked' cannot be used to tell somebody to do something. It only becomes a guide to action when conjoined with some general prescription like 'If a door is locked, do not try to open it'.

The idea that there are no moral facts has a respectable history in philosophy, going back supposedly to Hume and even to Protagoras. Its re-emergence in recent times has been a cause of *Angst* and anguish. If one had thought that there were moral facts, especially if one had thought that they were established by God's command, and then came to see that there were not, it might seem that the bottom had dropped out of one's moral world: 'God does not exist, therefore everything is permitted'. Even if one had not

* This lecture was also given at a conference of the Sociedad Filosofica Ibero-Americana in Gainesville, Florida, in 1992.

1

believed in God, but only in some ruined but romantic moral temple left over from his demise, one might be, as many would-be good boys have been, led into bewilderment, despair, even suicide.

All this makes me think that the belief in objective prescriptions is not just an error. For many centuries since the beginning of recorded history people have been using moral language, or more primitive precursors of it, and thinking that they meant something by it that was sometimes true. It is hard to believe that they were simply mistaken all that time. Of course there are examples of such mistaken use of language. For much of the world's history until recently people have talked about witches. Now we know (though in some other parts of the world they do not) that there are no such people as witches, in the sense of people who *really* have magical powers as opposed to *pretending* to have them. So the people who talked in past times about witches, and even burnt women to whom they attached the name, were mistaken in thinking that the word picked out a property which some women really had. And according to unbelievers the words 'God' and 'the Devil' were like this too. But do we have to believe that words like 'right' and 'wrong' are the same?

I shall be arguing that we do not, and that all the time, when people used words like 'right' and 'wrong', they were saying something that they did want to say, and which it was useful to say, and which was even in some sense (which I shall explain later) sometimes *true*. There was a mistake, especially on the part of some philosophers; but it was not the mistake that Mackie thought he had detected. Mackie thought that people all along were using the words which they thought picked out properties that actions done in the world really had, and that they were mistaken in this: there are no such properties. I shall be arguing, in contrast, that they were mistaken in thinking that *that* was what they meant. I shall call this mistake *descriptivism*. Whether most ordinary people committed this mistake, I doubt; but many philosophers certainly did. I think that the ordinary people who thought it, thought it only because they had taken a wrong *philosophical* path in trying to explain what they meant, no doubt led astray by philosophers, clergymen, and others. Left to themselves, they could have used the words quite happily without ever asking what they meant, like the centipede who can go on walking quite happily until someone asks him how he does it.

The words 'right' and 'wrong' did, and do, serve a purpose in language; they have a use, as Wittgenstein might have put it. It is a task for the philosopher to explain, if he can, what this use is. Before I give you my own answer to this question, I am going to discuss some other, as I think mistaken, answers. Nearly all of these are motivated by a desire to do something for the bewildered and potentially suicidal good boys I mentioned earlier. They actually made the good boys' situation worse, as we shall see. What these well-meaning philosophers were after is often called the 'objectivity' of moral statements; but for lack of an understanding of what this means one can go sadly astray, and indeed land up in the very position (sometimes called 'relativism') that these people were trying to avoid.

At this point I must say that I do not intend in this paper to take issue with the people who call themselves 'moral realists', because I think that might be a waste of your time. What is called 'moral realism' purports to be an 'ontological' view, as it is called—a view about what exists or does not exist *in rerum natura*. But I have found it impossible to discover what the view is. In another paper (Hare 1985 = 1989: 82) I have explained why 'ontological' ways of putting the dispute between so-called realists and anti-realists lead nowhere, except into a conceptual enquiry about the meanings of the moral words and how they get those meanings—which is where we ought to have started. The only clear way of formulating this dispute is as a dispute between descriptivists and non-descriptivists, who have opposing views about the meanings of the moral words. We should also have to take into account another conceptual dispute, about the meaning of the word 'exists'. All ontology comes down to this conceptual question in the end. But that I shall leave aside, since I have already discussed it in the paper referred to. I will confine myself to some rather polemical and perhaps provocative remarks.

The only way, it seems to me, in which a realist can pretend really to be doing ontology and not just conceptual analysis is for him to hold a crude correspondence theory of truth. According to such a theory, for a moral statement to be true would be for there to be, out in the world, some solid entity called a 'moral fact'. Because I do not think that there are any solid entities called 'facts' out in the world (moral or any other sort), and do not even know what it would be like for there to be, I cannot discuss such a theory. The world (contra Wittgenstein in the *Tractatus*) consists of things, not of facts, as Sir Peter Strawson pointed out long ago (1950).

There is of course a very big question about what it means to say that *any* statement, moral or other, is true; and to this question I shall be recurring later. But I do not think that you will wish me to discuss the crude correspondence theory I have just mentioned, because I should be surprised to find anybody holding it who understood the issues. Probably what realists are most wanting to maintain is that moral statements can be true or false. This is sometimes, in introductory ethics lectures and even elsewhere, said to be the view of people called 'ethical cognitivists'. That too is misleading. An 'ethical cognitivist' ought to be someone who thinks that one can *know* that moral statements are true. So he must at least think that some moral statements are true, and also therefore, presumably, that some are false. Since I myself think, both that moral statements can be true or false, and that we can know them to be true or false, I get extremely cross when people classify me as a non-cognitivist. Such people show only that they have not understood the issues, as will shortly, I hope, become clear. We need to say *what it means* to call moral statements true or false, and *what it means* to say that we can know them to be true. I shall in what follows give some hints on what I think about this. But that is all I have time to say about cognitivism and realism; I come back now to the question of objectivity, confusions about which it is my main purpose to clear up.

The most common mistake of would-be objectivists is to treat the word 'objective' as if it meant the same as 'factual'. This mistake I have mentioned already. It is tempting to make it, because it looks as if the problem would be solved if we could show that moral statements state something objective in the sense in which ordinary matters of fact are objective. This amounts to the claim that moral statements are like many other kinds of statements (statements about the colour or shape of objects for example) in being *purely* descriptive of the world. Establish the moral facts, the idea is, and then all moral doubts will be at an end. But since that kind of purely factual objectivity or pure descriptivity is incompatible with prescriptivity, as we have seen, this claim amounts to the abandonment of the idea that moral statements are prescriptive. That is, they stop being guides to our actions. One can think that something is wrong, but then go on to say 'Yes, it is wrong; so what?'. This is one reason why this way of solving the problem will not do. Since the whole point of calling actions right or wrong is to provide a way of deciding whether to do them or not, if you abandon the prescriptivity of these moral statements you might as well stop making the statements. A non-prescriptive moral language has lost its function, except in so far as non-prescriptive uses are parasitical upon the prescriptive uses of other people, as where we call an act wrong, meaning no more than that it is the sort of act that people *call* wrong.

I hope that nobody will raise the tedious objection to what I have said (which I have answered often before) that purely factual statements *can* guide conduct, as in the following example (which I expect you have heard before): the tyrannical mistress says to her cleaning lady, 'The stairs are dirty', and this guides the cleaning lady to clean the stairs. The point is that it would not do so unless there were an assumed 'standing order' in that house that when the stairs are dirty they are to be cleaned. This 'standing order' is a prescription, and of course it, together with the factual statement that the stairs are dirty, provides a guide to action; but the factual statement by itself does not do this. Many examples of this type are put forward by descriptivists, but the answer to them all is similar—and similar, too, to the point I made about the statement that the door is locked, which can guide actions, as I said, only when combined with a prescription.

That, then, is the first trouble with this proposed solution: if moral statements were purely factual they would not guide our actions. A second one is that there is going to be a difficulty about how to determine whether the factual claims allegedly made in calling acts right or wrong are true or not. There are two standard alternative ways of determining this. The first is to say that we are all, if we have been properly brought up, able to recognize these facts. Let us call this way *intuitionism*. So, it is claimed, there are some acts which everybody will agree to be wrong. These deliverances of our moral consciousness can be treated as data just as experimental observations are treated as the data of empirical science. The trouble with this is that, although it may work for some moral questions on which nearly everyone in a given society agrees, it breaks down when we are discussing any at all disputed question. Try, for example, using this approach when two people are disagreeing about whether it is right to seek equality of wealth in society even at the expense of diminishing the total amount of wealth to be distributed. Let us call this problem the 'cake' problem: is it right to increase the size of the cake or to divide it equally, if you cannot do both? A right-winger will think it obvious that it is right to increase the size of the cake; a left-winger will think it obvious that it is right to distribute it equally even if it is not then so large. It is no use their appealing to their respective moral convictions, because these disagree.

When two whole societies, or the politically aware parts of them, disagree with each other in this way (the Chinese and the Americans for example), the moral facts are not going to be determined by their consulting their moral convictions, because these differ in the two societies. People have just been brought up with different attitudes to the distribution of wealth. The effect of this approach to the problem is, as I said earlier, relativism. When we examine one society, the approach tells us that it is right to divide the cake equally; when we examine the other, it tells us that it is right to increase its size. So the 'moral facts' differ from one society to another, and what make them differ are the different moral traditions, and thus the different education that is practised, in the two societies. So whatever the merits of this approach might be, it is not a way of securing objectivity.

The other alternative, within the descriptivist approach, which I will call *naturalism*, is to say that we tell which factual claims about the rightness or wrongness of actions are true by applying what we know about the *meaning of the words* 'right' and 'wrong'. In one sense this is quite right, as we shall see. But the descriptivists go about it in too simple a way. They think that if we know the meanings of these words we shall be able to *recognize* acts which are wrong, just as, if we know the meanings of 'red' and 'triangular', we can recognize objects which are red or triangular. We might even be able to give a verbal equivalent of 'wrong', as we can give the verbal equivalent of 'triangular' by saying that it means the same as 'having just three straight sides'. But the effect of this approach is not very different from the other one. The reason is that if we try to determine the meanings of moral words by seeing what people apply them to, or what they recognize as proper applications of them (as we do with 'red' and 'triangular'), we shall again get different answers, depending on the mores of the society in which we do the investigation. To revert to our example, the people in one society will instantly recognize as right, actions which increase the wealth of the society; the people in the other society will instantly recognize as right those which lead to its more equal distribution. On this approach, these reactions tell us about the meanings the people in the two societies attach to the word 'right'. But since they are different meanings in the two societies, they do not even have a common word for discussing with each other the rightness of different economic policies. They have merely a homonym with two alternative meanings. The result again is relativism.

Descriptivists are likely to object to this that I have chosen an unfair example. Increase in wealth and the more equal division of wealth, they may say, are only means to an end, the end of satisfying human needs. We can all of us, in all societies, recognize as right the policies that do most to satisfy these needs. It does not matter whether we can recognize this because we can tell a right act when we see one, or because we know that 'right' *means* 'maximally satisfying human needs'. In either case, if we want to know which policy is right, we have to ask which does most to satisfy human needs. But the word 'needs' is as bad as the word 'right'. This difficulty has notoriously arisen with the Marxian precept 'to each according to his needs'. To say that someone needs something is to say something incomplete, unless we say what he needs it for. He may need it in order to survive, or he may need it in order to have some fun in life. Many people are so unhappily placed that if they are to survive they have to work at their crops from dawn till dusk, and get no time for fun. Others, more happily placed, can get some fun, but not for long, because the first lot are soon going to rebel and hang them all from lamp-posts. If you try to solve the cake problem by reference to needs, how do you tell which of these has the greater need?

Someone might try to solve the problem by reducing all needs to a common goal. This goal has had various names. Aristotle called it *eudaimoniâ*, for which someone (I think it was Mrs Foot) has suggested the translation 'human flourishing'. But if we say that the peasants in the example need money in order to survive, will that count as human flourishing if their life is so miserable? Might it not be better to leave the money with the capitalists so that they can have their fun while it lasts? They at any rate are having a good time, and perhaps that is flourishing. We may suppose that after the revolution *nobody* will have any fun; those that survive at all will be as miserable as the peasants were initially. Aristotle himself, who took this approach over from Plato, says that people agree verbally that the end for man is human flourishing, but that people disagree about what this consists in (*Nicomachean Ethics*, 1095a 18). His own answer was not the same as either of the two I have contrasted; he thought, perhaps naturally, that human flourishing was living the life of a scholar just like Aristotle himself; but are we bound to agree with him? My former colleague Sir Geoffrey Warnock (1967, 1971) thinks Aristotle's views so alien to what we now call morality that he does not classify them as *moral* views at all.

Questions about what counts as human flourishing are as difficult to answer as the original questions about what acts count as right. There are ways of addressing both questions, which I shall come to later; but the descriptivists, who rely on our inbred moral convictions or our understanding of the meanings of words, have not provided them.

I have been trying to show that descriptivism in both its forms leads inevitably to relativism. This is because the so-called 'facts' to which it appeals are facts only because the mores of the societies have made them so; people recognize certain moral statements as true because they have been raised that way. So any rebel or reformer who disagrees with the way they have been raised will dispute the facts. But, it may be asked, is there any harm in being a relativist? It is true that the philosophers I have been speaking of have been trying to avoid relativism; but this cannot be said of all philosophers. Some philosophers (Alasdair MacIntyre (1985) for example), *like* to be known as relativists. And it is said that many American undergraduate students think the same (though I have had only *one* in my class in Florida in the last few years). So what harm would it be if we all became relativists?

The answer to this question is to be found by asking what purposes moral language serves. I can think of two main ones. The first and obvious one is education. We do need to bring up our children in consistent kinds of behaviour which will not be harmful to themselves and others. So we need at least a language in which we can express precepts or prescriptions. We could of course use various circumlocutions and euphemisms. Some psychologists and others who do not like the words 'right' and 'wrong' speak, or used to speak, of 'anti-social' actions and 'not fully integrated' people. But it comes to the same thing really. Others, mainly philosophers, suggest that we could do without words like 'right' and 'wrong' by giving the reasons for the prescriptions instead of the prescriptions themselves. In the London Underground railway the notices on the doors no longer say 'Stand clear of the doors'; they say 'Obstructing the doors causes delay and can be dangerous'. However, try using this technique on your children. Sometimes it works, and it is indeed a good thing for children to be given reasons for acting the way they ought to, as soon as they can understand them. But we do need a less long-winded way of saying what they, and we, ought or ought not to do; and so we have invented one, the moral language.

A more important reason, however, is to enable us to discuss with one another how we ought to behave. If we did not have the moral language or some equivalent language, we could not do this. If you and I disagree about some proposed behaviour, and want to discuss our disagreement in the hope of resolving it, we need to be able to express it. The disagreement is about what should be done. You are saying that some act should be done, and I am saying that it should not. We need words for saying this. And we need, if we can get it, words whose logical properties enable us not merely to contradict one another (one of us saying 'Do it' and the other saying 'Don't do it'), but to argue, in the sense of 'reason', with each other. As we shall see, the moral language meets this need.

Relativism makes both these purposes impossible of attainment. There are, of course, many different positions all called by the name 'relativism'. The one we are considering makes it the case that whatever answer people give to a moral question is, for them, the right answer. But 'people' might mean 'individuals' or it might mean 'societies'. That is, the relativity in question might be relativity to an individual or relativity to a society. Whichever way we take it, we are in trouble. Suppose first that morality were relative to individuals. If that were the sort of morality we taught our children, we should have to give up trying to teach them to behave one way rather than another, or even to think about how they *and others* ought to behave; for they would be free to think just what they felt like thinking; and so would the others, even if it were quite different. For want of a common moral language, the mores would just disintegrate. That would be the effect of a consistent individual relativism. Some people might say they welcomed this prospect; but not, I think , if they had to live in the society so affected. They would have to put up with a situation in which anybody who wanted to rape and murder somebody else could say that was what he ought to do.

This consequence might seem to be avoided by the two descriptivist positions that I considered earlier. But they avoid individual relativism only to fall into social or cultural relativism. They anchor our moral judgments to the already existing mores, so that to depart from these is to display either a kind of moral colour-blindness or ignorance of the meanings of words. This puts on us a strait-jacket, so that we cannot have any new thoughts about what is right or wrong. Morality thus becomes relative to the *society*, but not to the *individual*. The individual might think he had the worst of all worlds; he cannot think morally for himself, but has no universal objective morality to appeal to outside the mores of his society.

What, then, we may ask, is needed in order to escape from relativism in both its forms (both individual relativism, which says that individuals are free to think whatever suits them, and cultural relativism, which says that societies can impose their mores on individuals without any right of appeal)? What is needed is nothing else than an understanding of the moral words, words like 'right' and 'wrong'. It is misunderstanding of these words, their logic and their function in our discourse, that has got us into this impasse. In particular, it is misunderstanding of one of their features. Since nearly all philosophers misunderstand this, I do not hope easily to remove the misunderstanding. But I will try. The feature we need to understand is their prescriptivity. And misunderstandings about this are many, and almost universal among philosophers at the present time.

We make moral statements in order to guide conduct, our own

and other people's. They are not the only kind of statements that do this. As we have seen, ordinary statements of fact, like 'The door is locked', can guide conduct if conjoined with general prescriptive statements like 'do not try to open a door when it is locked'. There are also non-moral *prescriptive* utterances, such as plain imperatives, and statements about etiquette, technical prescriptions, and many others. One thing that gets in the way of understanding the prescriptivity of moral statements is the thought that prescriptions are irredeemably relative to a speaker. But actually they are no more so than any other kind of utterance. If I say 'Please shut the door', I am indeed making a request on my own part. Nobody else may want the door shut. But equally, if I say 'The door is open', I am making a statement on my own part, with which others might disagree. *I* am saying it, not somebody else. Nevertheless, people think that prescriptions lack a property which they call 'objectivity', and which factual statements possess. It is this property that we ought to look at more closely.

One common mistake, which often makes people look askance at the idea that moral judgments are prescriptions, is to think that if in saying something was wrong I were issuing a prescription, I could *make* acts wrong, or make them not wrong, just by issuing, or not issuing, a prescription prohibiting them. This would be so, if a prescription were equivalent to the *statement that* the prescription was issued. If it were, then by saying some act was wrong (that is issuing a prescription against it) I would make the statement that it was issued true, and so, on this mistaken view, make the act wrong. And then nobody would be able to deny that it was wrong; for to say that it was wrong would be saying no more than that the prescription was issued. This would be yet another route to relativism; I do hope that, when I say that moral statements are prescriptions, this absurd view will not be attributed to me. It is in fact a kind of descriptivism—a naturalist kind which equates the meaning of a moral judgment with a statement of non-moral fact, namely the statement that someone (myself) has said a certain thing.

If we could understand *why* the various sorts of descriptivism that I mentioned earlier are so attractive, then we might understand the whole issue better. People are attracted by descriptivism because they think it is the only way to achieve a kind of objectivity in moral statements that they want them to have. We may express this by saying that they want to be able to establish some moral principles that no rational person who knew the facts could disagree with. What they are after, then, is *rationality* in moral thinking. But can they have it? In particular, can they have it without the disadvantages incurred by descriptivism, which claims to provide objectivity? These disadvantages, as I said, are irrelevant to our decisions what to do, and the collapse into relativism. The idea that only some kind of descriptivism—some kind of factuality in moral judgments—can make objectivity possible rests on a very fundamental mistake which nearly everybody commits who studies this question. I think that there have been some great philosophers (Kant for example) who did not commit it; but nowadays moral philosophers fall for the most part into two camps, both of whom commit the mistake. One lot says that, because moral judgments do not state facts, any kind of moral reasoning is impossible. This view is sometimes attributed (though I think wrongly) to Hume. The other lot says that since moral reasoning must be possible, moral judgments must state facts. The mistake committed by both these kinds of philosopher is to think that reasoning can only be about matters of fact. Hume, however, said not this, but that it can only be about matters of fact *or relations of ideas* (1729: 3, 1, 1); and this is what made me say that the mistake I have been talking about was wrongly attributed to him. For by saying this he left open the possibility that there could be ideas which were not about matters of fact, and that reason could concern itself with the relations between these.

This way out for practical reason was not taken by Hume; but it was later taken by Kant. Kant seldom if at all speaks of moral statements as if they were statements of fact. He speaks instead of imperatives and of maxims, both of which are prescriptions not fact-claims—they are expressions of the *will*. But he thought, nevertheless, that moral reasoning was possible. It consisted in the establishing of relations between ideas—*prescriptive* ideas. Kant's programme was to find a way of so co-ordinating our prescriptions—our maxims and imperatives—that they did not contradict one another. He was not concerned with stopping them contradicting the moral facts; the idea of correspondence with moral reality is very far from Kant's thought. What he was trying to do was to find a kind of moral objectivity different from factuality—a kind which demands only that all who think rationally will agree in their prescriptions.

I am not going to have time to discuss whether Kant was successful in this enterprise, nor how similar his way of securing rational objective prescriptions was to that which I have myself advocated. I certainly owe a great deal to Kant; but my way of securing them has led me in a direction which is generally thought to be very *un*-Kantian, namely to a kind of utilitarianism. In other places I shall be defending the view that Kant's system, properly

11

understood, is not incompatible with a *sort* of utilitarianism, properly understood (Hare 1993). But this will seem a strange idea to those who have been reared on the common dogma that Kantianism and utilitarianism are opposites. So I will just try to tell you how *I* think objective prescriptions can be established.

The key to this approach to objectivity, which I shall be bold enough to call the Kantian approach, is this. It avoids appeal to anything (any feature of language) that is tied to a particular culture. If, that is to say, we appeal only to the meanings of the moral words, and do not write into this meaning any substantial moral claims as the naturalists do, then our moral language and its logic will be usable by all cultures, whatever their substantive moral opinions. The vice of descriptivism is that it cannot do this, and that is why it lands in relativism. We can have objectivity in our moral prescriptions if the language in which they are framed, and its logic, constrains all rational thinkers to come to the same moral opinions, *even if* they start from opposing moral viewpoints.

I am not saying that all cultures have identical, or even inter-translatable, moral languages. This is unlikely to be the case. I am claiming only that their languages, or most of them, share their main logical features, which I shall be giving in a moment, and which are enough to constrain them to reason according to the same rules even if their initial moral opinions are different. There may well be languages of which not even this is true; but even if it is not, their speakers can at least *learn* the moral language that is governed by this logic, and so enable themselves to talk to each other about their moral differences, reason about them, and thus, we hope, reach agreement. The crucial point is that in this language people who have different moral opinions, and therefore think that one ought to do different things, still mean the same by 'ought'; otherwise they would not even be able to *express* their differences, because 'one ought', said by a member of one culture would not contradict 'one ought not' said by a member of the other culture. We should be back again in the same kind of relativism as before.

The two features of the logic of this potentially culturally invariant moral language are prescriptivity, about which I have said all I have time for, and another feature of *moral* prescriptions which Kant also noticed, namely what is called their *universalizability*. This is not exclusive to moral prescriptions; it is shared by some other kinds of prescription. But it at least distinguishes moral prescriptions from simple imperatives like 'Shut the door', which may be no more than expressions of desires. If moral judgments lacked this feature, we could again, if we simply wanted something not to be done, say that it ought not to be done, that is, that it was wrong; and between us and anybody who said it was not wrong, or even that it ought to be done, there would be no way of deciding—no way we could argue with one another to determine which verdict on the act to accept. But moral judgments are different. It is, I think (though some people disagree) a fact of language that if I say that an act ought to be done, I am committed to saying that a similar act ought to be done in all circumstances resembling these, whoever is in whichever position in the situation. It is, on this view, logically inconsistent to say that, of two identically similar acts in identically similar circumstances, one is wrong and the other not. The circumstances are of course to be understood as including the desires of the people in them. Even those who disagree with me, and think that universalizability is not a *logical* truth, still, nearly all of them, think that it is true.

It is this feature of moral judgments which prevents us making just whatever moral judgments we please. For if we make a moral judgment, we are committed to prescribing the same thing for all similar situations. But we could imagine ourselves in just the same situation, but at the receiving end, in the position of the victim of the act. For example, suppose we are thinking of torturing somebody for fun. If we say that we ought to do this, we are committed to saying that he ought to do the same to us if the roles were reversed. And we are unlikely to be willing to say this. I have elaborated this style of argument in other places (Hare 1963: ch. 6; 1981: chs 5, 6), and there are complications and difficulties in it, which can however be overcome.

The structure of the argument now becomes clearer. What we have to do is to find a set of moral prescriptions (maxims in Kant's expression) which we are prepared to see followed whoever is at the receiving end, including ourselves. That is, we have to find maxims which we can will to be universal laws. And this will constrain us, because in the situations in which we find ourselves there are a lot of other people affected by our actions, and they all have likes and dislikes (for example dislike of being tortured). But we shall not be able to will a maxim that would allow us to be tortured if we were those people. Of course there are complications in the argument, as I said; but that is the general idea. The claim is that this constraint will make everybody who thinks rationally about the morality of acts in this situation say the same thing. So objectivity, which is what we were looking for, is achieved, without saying that moral judgements are purely descriptive and factual, and without abandoning their prescriptivity.

Now we can return to the matter of human flourishing. I said that people all have likes and dislikes. If these words are taken in a broad enough sense, we could say that someone flourishes to the extent that he gets what he likes in life, and avoids what he dislikes. Of course it is a mistake to say *human* flourishing, because there are other sentient creatures, and their likes and dislikes count too. But I shall ignore this for the present. Here again there are complications; I am only trying to give you the general idea. Perhaps it will appease some people if I put the matter in Kantian terms: if we are trying to universalize our maxims, we shall try to further the ends of other people on equal terms with ourselves, treating them as if they were our own ends. Kant says this in almost these words (*Gr.* BA69 = 430). But to have an end is to have a liking in this broad sense. In this sense, if we get what we like and avoid what we dislike, we are happy, and this is what Kant calls 'the supreme end' *(KrV.* A951 = B879). And although this may surprise some people, Kant frequently speaks as if it were a duty to do just this, that is, promote others' happiness (e.g. *Tgl.* A34 = 398). But I said I would not deviate into the exposition of Kant.

Perhaps, though, I have said enough to show how flourishing comes into the picture. A morality constructed on the lines I have sketched will give it a predominant place in our aims. Now I must say something about how such a morality would work out in practice. Earlier I mentioned the education of children. This, I said, is one important thing we have moral language for. But we ought not to confine it to children. We need, even as adults, to think about virtues and vices; that is, about our behaviour, attitudes and dispositions; we can be sure that they could be improved. What principles or maxims or habits of mind and action ought we to cultivate both in ourselves, and in our children? You might think from what I have been saying that all we need say to them and to ourselves is 'Promote people's happiness or flourishing'. But this might be disastrous.

The reason is that we and our children are not angels. Lacking information, clarity of thought and impartiality, we shall certainly, in trying to follow such a maxim, do the thinking wrong, and end up with precepts which may suit us personally very well, but not be morally acceptable. The situations in which we find ourselves are too complex and varied. As human beings we need simpler guidance in the form of general intuitive principles to which we can anchor our dispositions. And these are what we have in fact got for ourselves in the form of virtues like honesty, or principles like that which bids us keep our promises. In any even moderately stable society these virtues and principles and moral standards are entrenched and well understood. If someone errs against them we all immediately recognize this, and without hesitation call him a bad person. To put it more technically: the truth conditions of moral statements are well established, at this level of moral thinking. In this way it is perfectly in order to call moral statements true or false. And this explains the attractiveness of descriptivist ethical theories.

But what advocates of such theories have not realized is that all this is relative to a given society. *Different* standards, virtues and truth conditions for moral statements are entrenched in different societies. In the heyday of the British Raj, associating on too familiar terms with educated Indians made a British army officer a bad person (Hare 1952: ch. 9). And even in our own society, however stable (in fact, especially if it is stable) there is a need to examine our moral habits and see if they ought to be improved. This happens all the time in societies in which people *think* about moral questions. It happened in Britain when we abandoned imperialism and jingoism and with them most of the so-called patriotic virtues. If the accepted truth conditions were all that there were, there would be no basis for such an examination; we should simply have to go on with the entrenched virtues as before. And even in the stablest of societies, the world being so complex, the accepted principles will conflict in particular cases, and then appeal to them will yield no determinate answer as to what we should do in such cases.

For both these reasons (the need to examine the principles, and conflicts between them in particular cases) we have to have available a higher level of thinking to do the adjudication. This is not understood by descriptivists, who simply leave us in our dilemmas. The higher level is that at which we have to return to the question about flourishing. What we should be asking at this higher level is what principles, what dispositions, what virtues would, if adopted, conduce to the happiness, in the widest sense, of society. And at this level descriptivism, and with it our entrenched dispositions, have to be left behind; they cannot be the basis of the examination, for they themselves are under scrutiny. And here, if there is a question of the truth of moral statements, it cannot be a truth ascertained by comparison of the statements with a known standard. The standard is no longer secure.

To explain this I shall have to say a little more about the truth of moral statements. I have learnt a lot about this question from Crispin Wright's Waynflete Lectures on 'Truth and Objectivity' that he gave in Oxford in 1991, (Wright, 1992)— though I fear he will not agree entirely with what I say. There are at least three

15

meanings or functions or features that the word 'true' seems to have in language. The first is that highlighted by the formal features of the word noted by Tarski and others: for example, that for any statement that P, if it is true that P, then P, and vice versa. The second is the function of *endorsing* a statement, to which Strawson drew attention a long time ago (1950). The third is that in which 'is true' means 'satisfies the truth conditions, whatever those are'. Philosophers being (some of them) as clever as they are, it is not surprising that they have found cases in which these three features of 'true' cause trouble, or even come apart. I am going to draw attention to just one such case. In the great majority of cases they do not come apart, and that is why the concept remains serviceable.

Let us attend for a minute to truth conditions. I said just now that these vary from one society to another. That is to say, in one culture a moral statement will be universally acknowledged as true, whereas in another culture it will be called false. For example, in Saudi Arabia someone who says that a woman did wrong not to obey her husband will be acknowledged to have said something true; but in Australia his statement would probably be called false. The truth conditions are relative to the culture, which is why descriptivism, which finds the meaning in the truth conditions, collapses, as I said, into relativism. Another way of putting this is to say that the *descriptive meanings* of the moral words vary with the culture.

To say this is quite consistent with holding that the other two features of 'true' that I mentioned—its endorsing function and its formal Tarskian features—are culture-invariant. A non-descriptivist like myself can readily admit that moral statements can be true or false. He will then be agreeing that, when applied to moral statements, the word 'true' functions *in these respects* in just the same way as when applied to any other kind of statements. But this does not do enough to establish the objectivity of moral statements, because of the remaining feature (the feature that true statements have to satisfy their truth conditions). For if the truth conditions can vary with the culture, then the truth of the statements will be relative to the culture.

What is needed, in order to establish the objectivity of moral statements, is a way of establishing culture-invariant truth conditions. But to accept certain truth conditions for moral statements is nothing but to accept certain moral principles. These are substantial moral principles, not logically true or analytic statements. That, indeed, is why they can vary from one culture to another. What is needed, then, is a way of reasoning that will lead us from disagreement about these substantial moral principles to agreement. Such reasoning cannot be guided by truth conditions, because that would be circular. Different cultures will, following their different truth conditions, or different descriptive meanings for the words, arrive at different moral principles. To avoid this relativism, they have to have a way of reasoning with one another which appeals to the formal features of moral statements alone—to their logic. I am convinced that it was Kant's ambition to find such a way, and that has certainly been my endeavour.

It is mistaken, therefore, to think that for a moral statement to be true is *simply* for it to satisfy the truth conditions. We have also to be able rationally to endorse it, and it must also satisfy the Tarskian formal requirements. I spoke earlier about a higher level of moral thinking. If we call a moral statement at this higher level true, that will signify our endorsement of it after the most rational thought we can command. I repeat, in order to forestall the old misunderstanding, that it will not be a *statement that* we endorse it, but an *expression of* endorsement. So we cannot make standards acceptable simply by accepting them; rather, in saying that they are acceptable we are expressing our acceptance of them; and whether we should accept them is a matter for rational thought, on the lines I have been explaining. We have to do this thinking, and there are ways, determined by the logic of the moral concepts, of doing it well. If we do it well we shall attain *knowledge* of the *truth* of moral statements—knowledge of the only sort that is deserving of that name, i.e. rational certainty.

To help us do this thinking well is the task of moral philosophy. Many of the troubles of the world trace their origin in part to bad moral philosophy. Good moral philosophy (by which I mean clear and honest moral philosophy) could help to put them right. But whether there will be such good moral philosophy, either here or elsewhere, is a big question. I think that there will be, and are, some good moral philosophers; but the bad (that is the confused) ones make all the running; so I am not very hopeful.

Integrity and Self-Identity

STEWART R. SUTHERLAND

Introduction

The title of this paper proclaims its central interest—the relationship which holds between the concept of integrity and the concept of the identity of the self, or, for short, self-identity. Unreflective speech often suggests a close relationship between the two, but in the latter half of this century, notwithstanding one or two notable exceptions, they have been discussed with minimum cross-reference as if they belonged to two rather different philosophical menus which tended not to be available at the same restaurant on the same night. My intention is to argue that our account of the one carried implications for the other and that this relationship is reflexive. My argument will proceed by stating and criticizing a common account of the relationship between each of these concepts which tends to offer mutual support for the implied account of each. Thereafter an alternative account will be outlined.

I

The Concept of Integrity

Consider the following account of 'the character of the man of integrity' from Hugh Blair's Sermon, 'On Integrity as the Guide of Life':

> He is guided not merely by affections, which may sometimes give the colour of virtue to a loose and unstable character. The upright man is guided by a fixed principle of mind, which determines him to esteem nothing but what is honourable and to abhor whatever is base and unworthy in moral conduct. Hence you find him *ever* the same; at all times, the trusty friend, the affectionate relation, the conscientious man of business, the pious worshipper, the public-spirited citizen. . . . (Blair,1801)

This is a veritable eulogy to integrity which we all naturally endorse with a 'Hear! Hear!', or 'Amen', to taste. And yet, is it quite like that? Equally, how can the question be raised without the appearance of being totally cynical? I shall try.

19

Stewart R. Sutherland

First however, consider the language used by Blair: the reference to unity as ('fixed') principle, to the man of integrity being 'ever the same', and to what is to be found 'at all times' to be true of such an individual. Ethical theories which give primacy to consistency of principles, to consistency of action and thought, to forms of universalizability all draw strength from such language. The search for integrity becomes the search for what gives a human life such unity. (In passing, though, I shall return to this point at greater length in section II: there is a point worth making simply because it is so obvious that we, or Blair, might overlook its importance. This ethical picture implies a corresponding picture of the individual or self of comparable and substantial unity. Quite what Blair made of the scepticism of his friend David Hume about the idea of the self, will give us reason to pause in due course.)

In the Sermon, Blair lists and analyses various virtues which are to be found in the man of integrity—trustworthiness, conscientiousness, piety, public-spiritedness and so on. We might choose to expand or amend the list, but we would not find it difficult to agree that the rather abstract term 'integrity' must be given greater specification in one form or another. Bernard Williams is, I believe, right to point out that integrity is not logically on all fours with the virtues of the sort listed above. Indeed, he goes as far as to claim that integrity is not a *virtue* at all ('Utilitarianism and moral self-indulgence', 1981, 49). His argument is that 'it is not related to motivation as the virtues are' for if it were, 'integrity, regarded as a virtue, can seem to smack of moral self-indulgence'. Whether or not we accept Williams' reasoning here, he does give grounds for arguing that the relationship between integrity and (? other) virtues requires careful examination.

A picture, implied by Blair, and lying behind many other popular accounts of integrity is that integrity has to do with unity and consistency. A very good example of such a perception is to be found in some of the essays of Vaclav Havel (e.g. 'Summer Meditations', 1992). Havel does not declare himself as the sort of man who would fall victim of Williams' warning about the self-indulgence of integrity as a motivating principle, but he does write with both conviction and experience of the need for the same kind of unity to which Blair points. His metaphors are different:

'I must do my utmost to act in harmony with my conscience and my better self'; and 'I wish to remain faithful to myself' ('Politics, morality and civility', 1992, 7). I thoroughly endorse all that Havel writes about decency, honesty and the importance of 'living in truth', and we cannot have anything other than the deepest respect for what Havel's own life teaches about these things, but once again he raises implicitly the question of the nature of the integrity which we do see in that life, and of the kind of unity which seems to be demanded.

One of the standard responses to this question is give an account of integrity in terms of consistency. In so doing we are offering consistency as a formal condition of integrity and the next step in the argument is to consider whether it is not simply a necessary condition of integrity, but also a sufficient condition. In fact it is clearly not a sufficient condition as one or two examples make plain. A serial killer may in comparable circumstances act with horrifying consistency but the gap between that and moral integrity is only too apparent. More philosophically and by analogy, the inadmissability of Thrasymachus' account of the nature of justice is certainly not simply that the formal characteristic of consistency is absent.

However, the issue of whether consistency is a necessary condition of integrity is a rather tougher question which lies at the heart of this part of the paper. Blair's implied perception that it is, has much support in the historical writings which bear on this point. For example, it is not only Bentham and Mill who offer accounts of the nature of ethical judgement which place a high premium on consistency, so also do Kant and Rawls. In each case, their respective accounts of the moral life are based upon the identification and application of a hierarchically consistent set of moral principles.

Consistency and Counter-Examples

Sartre poses the question very well for us in his famous example of the waiter. It comes from the section of *Being and Nothingness* (1969) in which he is discussing the phenomenon which he calls 'Bad Faith'. In the end he is discussing the metaphysical question of what it is to be, and in appropriating his example for rather different purposes, the issue with which Sartre is concerned has been somewhat but not wholly displaced. It remains in the wings rather than strides centre stage:

> Let us consider this waiter in the café. His movement is quick and forward, a little too precise, a little too rapid. He comes towards the patrons with a step a little too quick. He bends forward a little too eagerly; his voice, his eyes express an interest a little too solicitous for the order of the customer. Finally there he returns, trying to imitate in his walk the inflexible stiffness of some kind of automaton while carrying his tray with the reck-

lessness of a tight-rope walker by putting it in a perpetually unstable, perpetually broken equilibrium which he perpetually re-establishes by a light movement of the arm and hand. All his behaviour seems to us a game. (Sartre, 1969)

The most obvious, but perhaps irrelevant, comment to be made about this is that Sartre clearly had more luck with waiters than I do. More significantly we experience Sartre's concern about a game being played, but perhaps we also have sneaking sympathy with the waiter.

The important questions morally arise because the man in question is taking on a role. He is, in Sartre's terms, representing himself as the waiter. *Ipse facto* he is *not* the waiter. The dangers, morally, are of the gap created which leaves room for hypocrisy and evasion. Thus, as Sartre points out, there is created fertile ground for excuses of the sort used in the Nazi War Crimes Trials—'I was simply a soldier doing the duty which my role gave me'.

These possibilities show the moral complexity of the idea that someone might be playing a role or representing himself as other than he might be. (Recall Havel's insistence on being 'faithful to myself' and acting 'in harmony with . . . my better self'). But there remains a sympathy for the waiter. It could simply be the sympathy of a shared weakness—'We all have to compromise sometimes' – but I suggest that a consideration of some further examples might mitigate this rather severe view of the matter. The relationship between these issues and the theme of the lecture is this: Is it conceivable that we could think of the waiter as a man of integrity? Of course, there are waiters who show consistency, for example of disdain for friend, foe and client alike just as there are some who seem to be apprentice members of a Triad gang and who will doubtless show to future 'clients' the same ruthlessness as that which greets an order for one number twelve, two thirty-twos and a seventy-eight.

Sartre replies negatively to our question in the second place because of dangers of hypocrisy (as would Blair), but in the first because it runs counter to his answer to the question of what it is for the individual to *be*.

The example of the waiter is no longer sufficiently robust to carry the weight of the discussion and we must consider some further examples, initially from areas rather closer to Havel's experience. For example, rather than ask whether in certain areas of society it is possible to be both a waiter and a man of integrity, we might ask whether in Stalin's Russia it was possible to be a prisoner and to live with integrity? Solzhenitsyn forced us to ask this question as we read 'One day in the Life of Ivan Denisovitch'. Or again, what did it mean to be an artist of integrity in Stalin's Russia. What about Shostakovich?

As a recent study of Shostakovich (MacDonald, 1991) shows, the issue of Shostakovich's artistic, as well as moral, integrity is indeed complex. The pressures which he was under directly to take the official line on the nature of artistic realism, to compose accordingly and to shun those artists who strayed, were applied with the uncompromising pressure of a rack. Anna Akhmatova's account of this in her writings raises central questions about the adequacy of Blair's characterization of the man of integrity. Their mutual friends the Mandelstans were subject to direct versions of all these inroads into normal life as Stalin created a version of a Hobbesian state of nature in 1930s Russia[1].

In Shostakovich's case, the question of what we may understand of the nature of integrity comes to be focused upon the technicalities of the interpretation of music. For example, is it the case that in his Fifth Symphony, which was heard by the regime as a recantation of previous deviant tendencies (artistic and social) he risked the equivalent of the hostage's sympathetic 'raising' of two fingers on the television shot?

> Are these configurations musical ways of saying 'Stalin'? If they aren't, something coming soon almost certainly is. With the thrumming accompaniment tossed from trumpets to high strings and back again, the 'menace' theme drives to an agitated climax—whereupon a startling cinematic cut sends us tumbling out of the world of abstraction and into representation of the most coarsely literal kind. We are at a political rally, the leader making his entrance through the audience like a boxer flanked by a phalanx of thugs. This passage (the menace then dissonantly harmonized on grotesquely smirking low brass to the two-note goosestep of timpani and basses) is a shocking intrusion of cartoon satire. Given the time and place in which it was written, the target can only be Stalin—an amazingly bold stroke (MacDonald, 1991, 74)

This is from comment on the symphony which to some extent rehabilitated Shostakovich in 1937. The primary issue for us is not in fact whether this is the correct interpretation of that detail of composition (let alone whether in performance there is irony rather than crude 'literalism'), but that the question of Shostakovich's artistic and moral integrity could in part be weighed in this particular balance.

[1] See N. Mandelstam's *Hope against Hope*, e.g. pp. 7ff, for a description of arrest.

Stewart R. Sutherland

The point I am making is that this is a long way indeed from Blair's eulogy to integrity. The music here has to be weighed against the rest of the music (just as the two-fingers on the elbow have to be weighed against the rest of the body-posture) for there was enough in that for the party hacks to judge that Shostakovich had learned the error of his ways. Equally it must be weighed against what Shostakovich was prepared to sign from time to time, that he was in due course allowed to represent the USSR musically by visiting and conducting in the West, and so on.

Far be it from me to even try to answer the question of whether in all the to and fro of government artistic policy, Shostakovich could have presented a picture like that sketched in Blair's sermon. In fact that picture is clearly not there. If he challenged the system, the signs that he did so are as much in what he did not say and do as in what he did; the signs are the inclusion of patterns of composition in his music which allowed the total piece the degree of ambiguity which in this case produced the official view, but also the ironical (and not perceived as such) allusions to what he thought of the regime.

(There is a general point about irony here. It only has place where there is the possibility of ambiguity. This is the real difference between le bon David and open uncomplicated honest Hugh Blair. Is Hume's integrity in question because his drafts of the *Dialogues Concerning Natural Religion* gave the literal final word to the supporters of solid Cleanthes (Blair) rather than allusive sceptical Philo (Hume)?)

My tentative conclusions here are as follows:

(i) Blair's picture of integrity has, at best, limited applicability in the context of life in which Shostakovich found himself

(ii) One specific consequence is that the type of irony to be found in Shostakovich's music (if MacDonald is correct!) presupposes an ambiguity of context; irony has no place in the life of honest fresh-faced innocence.

(iii) The ambiguities have to do with the pressure of external circumstances defining what is possible.

(iv) These pressures put under strain neat and clear hierarchical value systems in which in the end there is a single 'right' answer to the question 'What must/shall I do?'

(v) Would it have been better for Shostakovich not to have written the Fifth Symphony (and by implication perhaps anything else) than to have written a symphony which is at least sufficiently ambiguous to pass the Party test?

(vi) What sort of question is that?

The movement of my argument is to raise in one form the question of whether consistency is a necessary condition of integrity.

On the one hand we could argue that it is. The consequence would be either tough judgments about Shostakovich which amount to saying: For 'ambiguity' read 'compromise' or an elaborate attempt to show that there really was a consistent thread of judgment according to which Shostakovich measures up or, the equivalent of a moral gold standard, the necessary minimum of irony compatible with the judgment that he was acting with integrity.

On the other we could, and I shall, argue that the model of integrity which serves us well in many contexts offered by Blair, is simply not adequate to all situations. Its weakness is the attachment to a moral theory which cracks under the strain. Elaborate 'gold standard' defences of it begin to look like the type of religious apologetic which will stretch the theory to accommodate any counter-example as long as the theory remains in place.

The problem is that the theory in essence pre-supposes that there is in principle a means of settling every question about what we should do without ambiguity if only we can discover the correct hierarchical decision-making procedure. This lies at the heart of the demand that consistency is a necessary condition of integrity, which in its turn lies at the centre of both Blair's account of integrity and surprisingly Sartre's criticism of the waiter. The difference between the two is that Sartre would, for quite other reasons, shun the talk of 'consistency' in terms of a metaphysical account of what it is to be.

In focusing on the example of Shostakovich, I have tried to raise questions about the quite plausible account of integrity offered by Blair without reworking the ground of 'conflict of values' and 'conflicts of duties' discussed for example by Berlin, Williams and Winch, but all that they argue has clear purchase power here also.

II

The Conflict of Self-Identity

I shall start here, perhaps perversely, with the counter-argument to which I have already referred. Blair's friend Hume, in a famous passage, teases us as follows:

> For my part, when I enter most intimately into what I call myself, I always stumble on some particular perception or other, if heat or cold, light or shade, love or hatred, pain or pleasure. I never can catch *myself* at any time without a perception and never can observe anything but the perception. (*Treatise* I.iv.vi)

Of course, Hume is here also savouring his discourse with a pinch of irony. But the question stands: 'What constitutes the self, and by implication the identify of the self?' In the context of this paper, I must also ask whether, for example, Blair's account of integrity presupposes a specific account of the self and of self-identity as a necessary condition of that account.

Certainly Blair's description fits well with the picture of a substantial self of whose identity a clear account can be given.

Accounts of the nature of the self can be based on a number of different possibilities which cannot all be reviewed in detail in the latter part of a single lecture. However, by way of a perhaps rather cavalier philosophical memorandum, we can recall that each has substantial problems attached to it. Thus an account of the self as the source of action (normally in terms of will) has the difficulty of accounting for weakness of will. Equally an account of the self in terms of the seat of knowledge and intellect must confront the realities of self-deception, and the view of self as the subject of experience has Hume's question to contend with as well as Parfit's more recent probing of these issues.

As philosophers have moved from the question of the nature of the self to the related issues of the criteria for self-identity and time, one set of criteria of uniqueness has emerged to a status which is virtually unchallenged—spatio-temporal continuity. The difficulty here is that though this may well give us a unique way of correctly identifying human beings over time, it cannot give us an account of what the nature of the self or person is, for what it gives is a set of criteria for identity over time which we share with trees and shoe-boxes. And one of the obvious differences is that we do not worry about the integrity of either!

My proposal, which within the limitations of this paper I can only state rather than argue in detail, is that these philosophical concerns about the nature of self and self-identity have two consequences. On the one hand they show an incompleteness in what I shall summarize as the 'standard' account of integrity in so far as that account presupposes the existence of a 'substantial' self in whose actions are to be discerned all those characteristics so well identified by Blair.

To quote and apply Parfit,

Because this belief is false, we cannot explain the unity of a person's life by claiming that the experiences in this life are all had by this person. We can explain this unity only by describing the various relations that hold between these different experiences and their relations to a particular brain.

The second consequence is that there is a need to re examine not only *either* our account of self-identity *or* our account of integrity, but to re examine both in relationship. I am not advocating that we jettison either, but it may well be, and indeed I should argue that it is the case, that we have been over-influenced in our wish to solve the philosophical problems arising in the one context, by what is unexamined from what we have presupposed in the other.

The Better Part

STEPHEN R. L. CLARK

1. Aristotle's Picture of the Worthwhile Life

According to Aristotle, the goal of anyone who is not simply stupid or slavish is to live a worthwhile life.[1] There are, no doubt, people who have no goal at all beyond the moment's pleasure or release from pain. There may be people incapable of reaching any reasoned decision about what to do, and acting on it.[2] But anyone who asks how she should live implicitly agrees that her goal is to live well, to live a life that she can think worth living. That goal, *eudaimonia*, is something that is sought for its own sake, and for nothing else. Anyone who asks herself how she should live can answer that she should live well. The answer, admittedly, needs further comment. Aristotle went on to suggest that 'living well' amounted to living in accordance with virtue, or if there is more than one virtue, in accordance with the best and most complete. *Eudaimonia,* happiness, is virtuous activity over a whole life. To live a worthwhile life we must acquire and practice habits of doing the right thing, for the right reason. Equivalently, we must do what a virtuous person would, and in the way she would, for the sake of *to kalon,* or beauty.

My remarks so far have been uncontentious, at least as an account of what Aristotle said. We may see reason ourselves to doubt that every worthwhile life is one devoted to living for the sake of beauty, but I shall argue that those doubts can be assuaged. For the moment, let me keep to the uncontentious. Has anything, so far, been said except that those of us who wonder how to live are almost bound to agree that we should so live as to have lived a worthwhile life, a life endowed with its own 'moral' beauty, when we come to die? This need not, so far, specify any particular life-path, nor any particular account of 'moral' beauty. A sensual or slavish life could not, itself, be chosen (since to *choose* such a life would, exactly, be to surpass mere sensuality or slavishness), yet

[1] Aristotle: *Eudemian Ethics,* 1.1214b7ff.
[2] See Clark, 1985

29

someone might choose, as worthwhile, a life that no outsider could distinguish from the life of a mere slave to appetite, or fear, or ignorance. Aristotle would himself consider such a choice mistaken, a willed surrender of what makes us human, but there may be those who think surrender is worthwhile. As long as it is their choice, we may agree that they chose it with a view to living well, and observe that the choice dictates what habits they should form.

But of course the decision to surrender ourselves to appetite or to another's will is itself a decision that might be well-made or ill. If we are seriously asking how to live, it is because it is up to us how we shall answer. If we are to have any chance of living well at all, we had better start by *deciding* well. Even if we eventually decide to make no more decisions, that decision (that above all, perhaps) had better be well-made. Even those who decide to sell themselves to slavery had better begin by cultivating habits of decision-making that will help to ensure the sale is one that they could think worthwhile. Someone who thinks so ill of her own capacity to choose sensibly as to wish to surrender it can hardly think her choice of a particular despot is likely to be very sensible. So the primary virtues needed for a life well-lived are practical wisdom, the capacity to take sensible decisions in the light of what seems good, and 'ethical virtue', the habit of feeling as a sensible person would about the various goods of human life. Better begin (whatever happens later) by trying to cure oneself of over-passionate attachments, childhood fears and too strong or weak a sense of one's own importance.

It may be that the close examination of the character and intellectual capacities we need even if we intend to end as slaves will gradually identify for us what the virtues of a free person are. Those who live well are those who can govern their own lives, in company with other free people, for the sake of living well. Maybe such a life, in the end, forbids any permanent submission to another's will, or to the demands of appetite. Just because free people need to make their own decisions, and to stick to them despite temptation, they will not follow appetite or fear even at their will. If they were the sort of people who imagined that sensual pleasure or release from pain was what made life worth living, they could not resist enslavement nor stick by their own perception of what they should do. 'He who has located the absolute in pleasure cannot help being dominated by it'.[3] Even if the 'necessitating pleasures' of food, drink and (to a lesser extent) sex, whose very absence are themselves a pain, were all that mattered to us, we

[3] Weil, 1959, 128

30

should have to work quite hard to obtain them, and to endure the depression that followed in their wake. Cultivating the virtues necessary even to a life of pleasure we would begin to find that other things than those necessitating pleasures mattered. Free people, accordingly, do not even imitate the sensual or slavish types who never ask themselves how they should live.

Eudaimonia, in brief, is the exercise of practical wisdom and ethical virtue, over a whole life. Even this, although I have now begun to draw a more particular picture of the Aristotelian saint, is probably uncontentious, at least as an account of Aristotle. It is here that most recent commentators halt. The good life for human beings must consist in a life that human beings can live, of their own will. It must be complete, and therefore be lacking nothing of the goods that human beings can virtuously desire. The majority of commentators seem to conclude that 'the good life' includes anything that makes a life worth living: moderate pleasures, civil honours, great achievements, friends. It does not include, but still requires, material advantages, health, stature, and good birth. These latter are no part of *eudaimonia,* because they are not things that we can secure by any choice of ours. 'That is why good fortune is not the same as a good life'[4]. The good life for human beings is doing what human beings do, and doing it well: 'what human beings do' includes many forms of craftsmanship and pleasurable association. For that very reason, it must include, and must above all consist in, the exercise of practical and political virtue. If we are to live well we must sort out our own priorities, and learn how to deal with other people on whom we depend and who have their own policies. Those who live well are those who live politically, and do it well. Anyone who really wishes to live entirely by herself is either a wild beast or a god:[5] the rest of us, requiring to live well, must organize our lives so as to live with others.

To have much hope of living well we must discover how to live with others well, and how to reach good decisions. We need to have some insight into the needs of our particular situation, and characters that can cope with threats and with temptations. All this is, commonsensically, correct. No-one would seriously recommend that character and insight do not count.

Nobody would call someone ideally happy *(makarios)* that has not got a particle of courage nor of temperance nor justice nor of

---

[4] Aristotle, *Politics,* 7.1323b26f.
[5] Ibid., 1.1243a27ff.

wisdom but is afraid of the flies that flutter by him, cannot refrain from any of the most outrageous actions in order to gratify a desire to eat or drink, ruins his dearest friends for the sake of sixpence and similarly in matters of the intellect is as senseless and mistaken as any child or lunatic.[6]

No-one would seriously recommend a life blown by the wind of fortune, both because it would be very risky and because 'be lucky' makes no sense as any sort of recommendation. Even to recognize good luck we need to have some idea of what we would prefer to happen, and to have. All this is truism, though not entirely trivial. But the question still remains: what is it, exactly, that we should do? Exercise good sense, having first ensured that we suffer from no obvious, debilitating weakness of character, no doubt. But what is it that such people actually do, and why?

The first answer, and the one that most modern commentators wish Aristotle had insisted on, is that there is no single thing at all that such good people do (except, of course, that they always do what's right). To stand and fight is not always the courageous thing to do, or else the courageous thing is not always the right thing. Certainly the right thing is not always the courageous thing (since courage may not be at issue). Setting ourselves to live well we find that there is no one thing that we must always do, except of course live well. Translating that near-truism into other terms: the good life must consist of many different goods or goals; whatever is personally worth doing must be included in the worthwhile life. There is nothing so worthwhile for anyone as to be worth her giving up all other goods; there is nothing that everyone must find it worthwhile to do. What we deliberately do we do because we see it to be worth doing; we do it so as to be doing what's worthwhile. But 'doing what is worthwhile' is not a separate act from doing the worthwhile thing in question. There are some things that we do, or seek to get, only for the sake of something else, but there are many things that are worth having for their own sake, by themselves, and we would still wish to have or do them even if they led to nothing else, even if we did not succeed in doing well, over all, by doing them. Amongst such goods are health, pleasure, honours, noble actions, wisdom, good friends and happy children. To do right is to choose the right thing in the circumstances, because it is right, or beautiful. Anything at all (almost) could be that right, though Aristotle is careful to add that there is no 'right amount' of adultery, theft or murder.[7]

[6] Ibid., 7.1323a27ff
[7] Aristotle, *Nicomachean Ethics*, 2.1107a8ff.

So the first and easiest interpretation of Aristotle's remarks is that the worthwhile life is one consisting of a sufficiency of worthwhile activities, chosen because they are seen to be worthwhile in themselves. It requires the exercise of practical virtue, both ethical and intellectual, by someone who lives with others, and must collaborate with them in the management of their joint life. It is what Aristotle calls the practical or, sometimes, the political life, well-lived, and will include a sufficiency of all the goods available to human beings. Some commentators have added that *eudaimonia* must be something that cannot be counted alongside any other goods, since there would then be something preferable than it, namely the conjunction of *eudaimonia* and that other good.[8] This seems to me to be an obvious misinterpretation. There are good things that are no part of *eudaimonia,* since they are not subject to any choice of ours, and one who has them has a luckier life, even if not more worthwhile. Moreover the claim that the worthwhile life must include *all* worthwhile activities, everything worth doing, everything worth having, is a recipe for disappointment, or disaster. 'The root of all evil, so the Buddha taught, is the wish to live all one's possible lives'.[9] The point of Aristotle's argument is rather that a worthwhile life must be one that remains worthwhile even without such extra goods as human beings cannot choose (they not being in our power), and even without such things, worth having in the abstract, as we cannot have compatibly with what we actually choose. Justice, so Plato argued in *The Republic*, is enough by itself to make a life supremely worth living, even if we miss out on the other goods often associated with being just, but which we cannot guarantee. It might be absurd not to allow that one who is *eudaimon* has 'all the good things there are',[10] but that very passage (which is in any case not necessarily *in propria persona*) makes it clear that the contemplative does have all the goods there are, merely in virtue of his exercise of that virtue. He has, that is, all the pleasure, honour and riches that he needs. The point is emphatically not that one needs all the little goods there are to be happy: how could there be an end to such an accumulation?

If a worthwhile life were constituted by doing everything worth doing, then everyone must have the same, concrete goal: namely to do all the things worth doing, have all the things worth having. If we accept instead that different people will do different things, and

[8] Ibid., 1.1097b16ff.
[9] Dunne, 1965, 113,122.
[10] Aristotle, Ibid., 9.1169b8f.

have good reason still to think that their lives were worth living, then a worthwhile life need not consist (fortunately) in doing *everything* worth doing. It need not even consist in doing everything that the particular agent thinks it worth her while to do. I may wish that I could excel in any number of professions, and sincerely think that if I had chosen differently my life would have been worth living, without in the least suggesting that my life isn't worth living as it is. So a worthwhile life requires me to make choices among many worthwhile activities, that I can honour other people for pursuing and that I can agree I would myself think worth doing—if I weren't doing what I am.

So my problem still remains. I can agree, I must agree, that 'a good human life' requires the exercise of practical virtue, choosing between goods of differing weight, so as to live a worthwhile life. But what does this tell me about what choices I should make? In the real, human world we often have to give up the chance of one worthwhile career in order to pursue another. That is the problem which requires us to be 'choosing animals', that we have many possibilities. That is why the exercise of practical, or political virtue is 'architectonic'.[11] But what is to count as a good choice? Is it enough to know that someone 'chose' her life to agree that she is living a worthwhile life? Do I choose my path merely in order to have chosen? In so far as I have indeed *chosen*, I must conceive that my path is worthwhile: to *choose*, in Aristotle's stronger sense, just is to select as being worthwhile (which is why non-human animals, and children, though they show preferences, don't really *choose*).[12] But it can be no part of Aristotle's theory that just any choice would do: there is room for diversity in human life, and there may at times be nothing to say between one life choice and another, but not all choices can be equal. Living a good life can't just consist in choosing to live, no matter what the choice.

> The real difference between the test of happiness and the test of will is simply that the test of happiness is a test and the other isn't. You can discuss whether a man's act in jumping over a cliff was directed towards happiness; you cannot discuss whether it was derived from will. Of course it was. You can praise an action by saying that it is calculated to bring pleasure or pain, to discover truth or save the soul. But you cannot praise an action because it shows will; for to say that is merely to say that it is an action. By this praise of will you cannot really choose one course as better than another. And yet choosing one

[11] Ibid., 1.1094a6ff.; see 1.1102a7ff.
[12] And so can't ever be *eudaimones*: Ibid. 1099b32f, 10.1177a8ff.

course as better than another is the very definition of the will you are praising. The worship of will is the negation of will. To admire mere choice is to refuse to choose. If Mr. Bernard Shaw comes up to me and says 'Will something', that is tantamount to saying, 'I do not mind what you will', and that is tantamount to saying 'I have no will in the matter'. You cannot admire will in general because it is the essence of will that it is particular. (Chesterton, 1961, 39)

Some choices are ruled out from the start. 'No-one chooses to go to war for the sake of going to war: it would seem altogether murderous to make enemies of one's friends for the sake of battle and slaughter'.[13] The phrase *'no-one chooses'* is of course persuasive: actually, that is a possible, though murderous, choice, and we cannot discount the possibility that there are those who find the life of war congenial, who really would—if they had to—start a war merely so as to fight it. The facts of human history are such that they probably don't need to: there is always a war to join. To those who say that their lives are likely to be short ones, they can reasonably retort that length of life may be a good, but it is not enough to make a life worthwhile. None the less, it may be enough to agree, here—now, that 'war is for the sake of peace', and that there are many things that are worth doing in their context, and even things in which the agents involved take pleasure, that should not be preferred. We should not abandon friendship for the sake of war; we should abandon war for the sake of friendship (speaking generally). Human life being what it is we had better prepare ourselves, no doubt, for both, but we should not reckon it an absolute loss if we never had to fight a war again.

Consider other, more civilian virtues: the exercise, perhaps, of civic pity. Part of what we should do to live a life well-lived is to care for the lives and livelihood of our fellow citizens. We will be able to choose better, to live better lives, if we are not condemned to solitude outside the city, nor condemned to live among the impoverished and desperate relics of a broken world. Better, if people are in need, to help them where we can. By doing so we live more worthwhile lives than ones devoted merely to our own economies: the virtue particularly of a free person, *eleutheria, is* shown in knowing when to give and take. But *eudaimonia* cannot consist in being generous, in exercising civic compassion, any more than it could consist in going to war, and exercising military virtue.

---

[13] Ibid., 10.1177b9ff.

Pity would be no more
If we did not make somebody poor;
And Mercy no more could be
If all were as happy as we'.[14]

It would be altogether murderous to make paupers of our friends for the sake of charity raffles and the sly pleasures of patronage.

The 'efficient cause' of a worthwhile life is the exercise of practical, and political virtue, but we are hardly closer to discovering its 'formal cause', its essence. What would the virtuous person choose, for herself and for her country? What would she be willing to give up, for what? None of us can achieve everything that is worth having, nor do everything worth doing. Often we are faced by choices between goods, any of which we would be glad to have. Some things that we think are goods turn out to be so only derivatively: wealth, and honour, for example. No sensible person would give up all other possibilities simply to make money, because 'money' is only worth having if it can be exchanged for real, immediate goods. No virtuous person would pursue honour, which is public admiration, at all costs, because such admiration is only worth having if it is a real acknowledgement of real achievements. Pleasure, as a goal of life, is either slavish (if it is the tactile or 'necessitating pleasures' that is meant), or vacuous (since every sort of achievement carries its own pleasure with it). Pursuing pleasure is like pursuing 'success': we need to decide what it's worth succeeding in, and what counts in that case as success. So of the four main goals of life that moralists sometimes identify (which are: wealth, pleasure, honour, wisdom), only wisdom is left. And it is wisdom, or the activity of wisdom, that Aristotle says is the formal cause of *eudaimonia*.[15] The really worthwhile life, for which all other activities might be surrendered, is the life of wisdom.

Perhaps with a little irony Aristotle elsewhere poses this question by way of a comparison of the life of citizen and resident alien (of whom he, of course, was one).[16] The citizen chooses what to do, in company with other citizens, and exercises virtues both civil and military to try to live a life as beautiful, as noble, as they can. The alien who is relieved of civil and military responsibility may instead live the 'theoretic' life. Both lives may be worthwhile, but the questions still remain: first, what is it that the citizen, the city aims at; second, what could we give up, or lose, and still live worthwhile lives?

[14] W. Blake, 'The Human Abstract', in Blake (1966). See also 'America' 11.10ff., Ibid. p. 200: 'pity is become a trade, and generosity a science / that men get rich by'.
[15] Aristotle, Ibid., 6.1144a3F
[16] Aristotle, *Politics*, 7.1324al3ff.

A citizen, or city, that aims only at the continued exercise of powers of choice (whatever it is that is chosen) is embarked upon world-
conquest. If the power to decide things is what makes life worth living then we must seek new worlds to conquer and administer. To
make this life sound sensible we probably have to persuade ourselves
that the well-administered individual, city, tribe or empire will then
live worthwhile lives doing something else than simply being admin-
istrators or overseers. Ruling free peoples is different from ruling
slaves, precisely because rulers and subjects in a free society can
change places, and have other goals than those of administration.
The point of any decent statesmanship is to make it a little easier for
people to live worthwhile lives. So the statesman must have some
other goal than merely to be a statesman. According to
Theophrastus, 'practical wisdom orders what must be done so that
theoretical wisdom may have leisure for the contemplation of what is
most worthy'.[17] The justification of active politics is to enable someone to be relieved of political duties and to live a life that much more
worthwhile.

In brief: if it comes to a choice between the exercise of practical
and theoretical virtue (both of which are worthwhile in their way) we
must prefer the latter. The 'theoretician' lives the happiest life of all,
and one that is least at the mercy of changing circumstance. The
'politician', to live a worthwhile life, must have it in mind that there
is more to life than politics. In both cases, the individual exercises
practical virtue (though the alien theoretician is relieved of many
time- consuming chores) in order to facilitate the exercise of theoretical virtue (more easily by those who have been thus relieved). The
citizens of Athens were justified by their support of Aristotle and his
peers. The mediaeval philosopher John Buridan makes exactly this
point: that there are workmen who look after others 'and thus without achieving happiness bring others closer to it. Thus on his view
there is only one happiness to which the activity of all men has to be
orientated; active happiness can only be regarded as preparatory to
contemplative happiness' (Wieland, 1982, 685).

2. Ascetic versus Bourgeois Virtue

Nothing that I have said so far should really be contentious. It is
simply true that Aristotle identifies the life of theoretic virtue as the
superior life, the exercise of what is most godlike in us. He recog-

[17] Fragment cited in Burnet, 1900, 287n (see also ps-Aristotle, *Magna
Moralia*, 1198b9ff.), from a scholiast.

nizes that even the wise require the self-same goods that others do, material and civil, and that even the exercise of theoretical virtue may grow too tedious for us to carry on.[18] Human beings are changeable: we cannot sustain ourselves in one activity for ever, even the one we think most worthwhile. It follows that even the wise must exercise some other virtues than mere wisdom. It does not follow that we should be content to 'think and act as mortals'. We should, he says, as far as possible 'immortalize ourselves',[19] and give up whatever we can give up to sustain our 'theoretical' activity. If we are lucky we may not have to choose too harshly: maybe we can achieve an ordinarily pleasant life, some public admiration, even some success in civil action and still 'theorize'. But if we are required to choose, it is the superior virtue we should exercise.

Yet modern commentators are convinced that Aristotle couldn't, or shouldn't, really have meant it. He must have meant that the good life was simply one that ordinarily decent people lived together, with enough worldly goods to do their various duties, and with an eye to ordinary, bourgeois successes. He must have agreed that there is no one right way of life for all; and that the one right way of life for all must consist in some expedient selection from the goods available.[20] If he seems to say otherwise it is by mistake, or else the offending passages were by another.

Why do we find it so difficult to think that Aristotle meant exactly what he said? Partly, I suspect, we are uncomfortably aware that 'philosophers' were once supposed (even the most hedonistic of them) to be immune to local circumstance. 'Being once asked what advantages philosophers have, [Aristippus of Cyrene, the hedonist] replied, "Should all laws be repealed, we shall go on living as we do now"' (Diogenes Laertius, 1925, 2.68). It was as important for philosophers 'not to shave their beards' as for pious Hebrews not to eat a pig, or Christians not to drop a pinch of incense in the fire. By doing so they would have signalled their apostasy, and nothing at all was worth that price. The philosopher is one who glimpses 'as through a narrow crack' the divine reality (Boethius, 1973, 3.9.8). Till we have done so, and so

[18] 'According to Aristotle (*Nicomachean Ethics*, 10.1177a21f.) even the absolute Good can be a "bore"' (Zaehner, 1974, 163)! This is admittedly a slightly dubious interpretation of the text. Aristotle elsewhere insists that we can 'theorize' with fewer breaks than we can do anything else (*Nicomachean Ethics*) 10.1177a21f.).

[19] Aristotle, *Nicomachean Ethics*, 10.1177b31ff., after Plato, *Timeaus* 89e.

[20] The two claims are rarely put as bluntly, and as contradictorily, as that, but what else can be meant?

shaken free of the false glamour and fake terrors of this world, we shall not even be freemen: we are slaves until we are ready to die by torture if it is our job (Epictetus, 1926, 4.1.173). It seems an alarming prospect. Epictetus himself confessed that he and his disciples were, as it were, Jews in word but not in deed: 'not dyed-in-the-wool Jews', very far from applying the principles they teach: 'so although we are unable even to fulfil the profession of man, we take on the additional profession of the philosopher' (ibid. *Discourses*, 2.9.21). Most of us had probably better be content as sophists or as state-kept schoolmen. Epictetus' challenge remains: 'even if you are not yet Socrates, you ought to live as one who wishes to be Socrates' (Ibid. *Encheiridion, 51.3)*.[21] If we shrink from that challenge it is very much easier to believe that, really, Aristotle meant us to.

But there are other reasons to be wary. There have been people who declared that 'science' was their only goal, and that they need not be troubled by the laws that govern lesser peoples. 'It may be wrong (at least it shows a vulgar taste) to torment animals for "fun" or even to improve their flavour: it cannot be wrong to do such things for "science"'. No doubt some people only mean that knowledge of the world has brought such great advantages that we are bound to advance our knowledge at whatever cost. The calculation is far less secure than propagandists say, and the morality of such calculations far more suspect, but those who use them have only bourgeois goals. The professed aim is to secure a pleasurable, and more pain-free life for our descendants by inflicting pains here—now on those who cannot defend themselves. The radical alternative, that we might instead renounce some pleasures, or endure some pains, rather than act as if the world was made for us alone, is now considered crankish. Some moralists take it for granted that whatever minor disagreements there may be, 'all men of good will agree that it is their duty to improve the world, to make things better than they otherwise would be'. That illusion is one I shall address below.

But some of those who say that things are allowed 'for science' that would otherwise be banned mean something slightly different from the progressive's dream. Their professed aim is not the bourgeois one, of helping to secure our earthly pleasures, but simply to increase knowledge.

From this disease of curiosity it is that some dive towards the discovery of secrets in Nature, whereof the knowledge—though not beyond our ken—doth profit nothing, yet men desire to

[21] See Clark (1992).

know it for the sake of knowing. From this perverse desire of knowledge also it groweth that men inquire into things by magical arts. (Augustine, 1923, 10.35, pp.3f.)

Consider a conversation in James Blish's *Black Easter*: an arms-dealer has hired a black magician, and set his own tame scientist to work with him. The scientist, Hess, at first inclined to think the magician a mere sham, has come to recognize him as 'a dedicated man working at something he thinks important', and asks why, by his own lights, he has damned himself to make himself an expert in this peculiar craft. The magician answers:

'I think what I'm after is worth the risk, and what I'm after is something you understand perfectly, and for which you've sold your own soul, or if you prefer an only slightly loaded word, your integrity, to [the arms dealer]—knowledge. . . . In other words—just as you suspected—I'm a fanatic.' To his own dawning astonishment, Hess said slowly: 'Yes. Yes, of course . . . so am I.' (Blish, 1968, 78f.)[22]

Blish's fable, of Armageddon, concerns the price of knowledge, and identifies those who are greedy for such knowledge at whatever cost as black magicians. It is some such fear that makes us doubt that any decent, serious moralist could ever suggest that knowledge, of itself, is enough for decency. Forced to choose between an ordinary, unheroic, civil virtue and that kind of fanaticism, most of us will choose to be bourgeois. Why should any increase in human knowledge matter more than maintaining decent, human, humane life? Blish's magician, though he thought that he would carry knowledge with him to the pit, and that it would be worth the price, is compelled to see at last that selling his soul for 'unlimited knowledge is . . . nothing more than an instance of gluttony', and that it has done him no good at all (Blish, 1972, 108).[23]

The kind of ascetic virtue, or feigned virtue, that gladly neglects the exercise of ordinary civil virtue, cannot constitute a life well-lived. Even if there were some human being able to live without the friends she has betrayed, and without any need to control her appetites, her life would not be one that decent folk could choose. If there were no wars, we should not wish to fight them; if there were no necessitating impulses, we might be glad enough—like Sophocles[24]—that we were free of them. But as it happens, none of

[22] Blish was well aware of the background to this debate.
[23] See Clark, 1990, 100ff.
[24] Plato, *Republic,* 1.329.

us can manage without friends, and bodily needs demanding courage and temperance. Even if we could we would not easily wish to. The ideal of an Epicurean god, wholly indifferent to the passing chances of the world, was not even an Epicurean ideal. Such beings are less, not more, than human, even if they are invulnerable and at peace: maybe, *because* they are at peace. Epicureans believed that tranquil friendships were the key to worthwhile life, and even tranquil friendships carry the threat, or promise, of distress.

From this it must seem to follow that *eudaimonia* must include more risks, more 'lesser' virtues than Aristotle thinks. A mere theoretician, even if she were possible, would not have a worthwhile life. Think of a glutton, crouched over a bowl of fruit to the neglect of anything beyond it. Faced by the forced choice between such theoretical knowledge and an ignorant love of equally ignorant creatures, between knowledge and noble deeds, we surely should prefer the latter. But is that really the choice, and have we understood what 'theory' is?

3. The Love of Beauty

The pleasures of curiosity are no better excuse for wrong than the pleasures of bed and board. Investigation is not something that is always right, and virtuous people will investigate things that it is not wrong to know, in ways it is not wrong to attempt. That there are things that it is wrong to know may seem implausible even to those who can agree that not all ways of finding out must be alright. Actually, the idea is obvious. There are many things it is not worth burdening our minds to know: every fifth page of the Merseyside telephone directory, or misprinted words in Anglophone newspapers published on 30 October 1945. There are many things it would sully our minds to know: the taste of broiled baby, or how to cause exquisite agony to a tethered goat. There are many things that are simply not our business to find out: the familiar aphorism that 'I am a man, and everything human is my business' is the pompous pretext of an interfering gossip. Knowledge is not of itself a good—and Aristotle does not say it is. It does not follow that knowledge is good merely as a means, say to bourgeois comforts. On that account the knowledge of the directory might be of use, if only as a stage demonstration of memory techniques or as a tool for cryptograms. The point about the triviality of such knowledge is that such things are not, in themselves, worth knowing. The point about the evil involved in knowing other things is that only the depraved would wish to. 'There are hundreds of paths to scientific knowledge. The cruel ones can teach us only what we ought not to know'.[25] The knowledge that is worth having is the knowledge of what is worth knowing.

Yet there are forms of knowledge which have more than instrumental value. Augustine himself insisted, only a few pages earlier, that 'to joy in the truth is the desire of all men' (Augustine, 1923, 10.23, p.293), and applauded that desire. In fact, he identifies the love of truth with the love of God Himself. 'I had promised to show you, if you recall, that there is something higher than our mind and reason. There you have it—truth itself! Embrace it if you can and enjoy it' (Augustine, 1968, 144). Or as Malebranche put it: 'the truth is uncreated, immutable, immense, eternal and above all things. It is true by itself. It draws its perfection from no other thing. It renders creatures more perfect and all minds naturally seek to know it. Only God can have all these perfections. Therefore, truth is God' (Malebranche, 1980, 234). Aristotle declared that everyone desires to know, and identified a certain sort of knowing with God Himself. The knowledge that is best has the best of all possible objects, which is to say the very thing that knows it.[26] 'We ought to practise virtue for the sake of wisdom, for wisdom is the supreme end.'[27]

Moderns have so far lost the sense that truth is always someone's truth, and that the Truth Itself is God's Truth, that they usually miss this association of truth and conscious being. Descartes' rediscovery was that the mere possibility of his being mistaken not only showed that he existed, but that there was indeed a truth about which he might be mistaken. That transcendent truth could only be conceived as the mind and will of God: a merely impersonal, external truth could neither be known nor even conceived. But that is another story.[28] The point to acknowledge here is that even Augustine, who recognized that curiosity could be a sin, and was certainly no excuse for wrong-doing, also saw that a certain sort of knowledge was supremely important, that there was a truth, the whole truth, that it was our business to discover. Aristotle makes no explicit reference to the perils of curiosity, but we should admit the possibility that he would—if chal-

[25] G. B. Shaw, 22 May 1900 (Wynne-Tyson, 1985, 327). Strictly they might *also* teach us things that, in the abstract, are legitimate, but Shaw was right to believe that means condition ends.

[26] Aristotle, *Metaphysics* 12.1072a31ff.

[27] Aristotle, *Protrepticus,* fr. 11: see Chroust, 1964, 9. The convenient idea that this is a piece of juvenile Platonism seems to me to be unwarranted.

[28] See Clark 1992.

lenged—have agreed that there were things not worth knowing, and methods not worth pursuing even if we could thereby uncover some important truths. What seems clear is that he thought there was a form of knowledge that we should pursue, as the one true goal of human life. That is to say, there is an activity that we should never give up in order to pursue some other goal, which makes a life supremely worth living and without which, in the last resort, we live merely slavishly: the life of the theorizer.

One thing that this does not mean is the life of the petty calculator, as though it were worth spending one's life thinking how to find things out. It is not 'coming to know' but 'knowing' that is an activity worth doing in itself: the value of coming to know is dependent on actually knowing, and it is certainly not better to travel hopefully than to arrive (what then could we hope for?). Nor is 'theorizing' a matter of inventing speculative hypotheses which must then be checked by lesser handymen. The 'theorizer' contemplates a truth, and—specifically—a truth that is worth contemplating, because it is beautiful. The theorizer, in brief, sees beauty, and may do so, Aristotle assured us, on the word of Heracleitos, in the most trivial-seeming circumstances. The relevant passage, from his Parts of Animals is regularly quoted by working scientists (almost, indeed, the only passage of Aristotle that some scientists seem to have read, though this does not stop them abusing him), and can stand another citation:

> We must avoid a childish distaste for examining the less valued animals. For in all natural things there is something wonderful. And just as Heraclitus is said to have spoken to the visitors, who were wanting to meet him but stopped as they were approaching when they saw him warming himself at the oven—he kept telling them to come in and not worry 'for there are gods here too!'—so we should approach the inquiry about each animal without aversion, knowing that in all of them there is something natural and beautiful.[29]

There is an echo, doubtless deliberate, in Claude Bernard's more sinister observation, about 'the science of life [as] a superb and dazzlingly lighted hall which may be reached only by passing through a long and ghastly kitchen' (Bernard, 1949, 15).[30] Bernard missed Aristotle's point, that there was a real, discoverable beauty

---

[29] Aristotle (1972), *De Partibus Animalium*, p. 118 (see p. 123: 'possibly a polite euphemism for "visiting the lavatory"' which is also a euphemism).

[30] Bernard was the father of modern physiology, and an unrepentant vivisector who conducted many of his brutal experiments on dogs immobilized with curare.

in the most trivial or even immediately disgusting things: a beauty to be acknowledged, even worshipped, and not torn apart to add a little detailed 'knowledge' to the library. Not every philosopher, despite Keats' rebuke, works to unweave rainbows or clip an angel's wings.[31] What matters to the kind of philosopher that Aristotle, and many others, praised is to fill her soul with the sight of beauty. There is another kind, whose aim is to master beauty, to remove its challenge by getting it in our power, by showing or pretending to show that it is nothing very special. Reductionist science of the kind that explains medium-sized objects and events by showing them to be the mathematical results of microscopic objects and events, need not have the reductionist effect of eliminating beauty. In fact, the reduction usually depends for its plausibility on the amazing beauty of the microscopic universe revealed as underpinning the universe of our immediate experience. But it may be that some such scientists really believe what is often said, that there is no 'real beauty' out there in the world, that it is only a projection of our aesthetic appetite upon a literally unmeaning realm of matter in directionless motion. What value there is in discovering such a 'truth' is more than I have ever seen, unless it is the familiar effort of the tailless fox to persuade his fellows that they would be better off de-tailed.

If there were no beauty to be discerned in nature it would not be worth discovering this. 'The scientist does not study nature because it is useful; he studies it because he delights in it, and he delights in it because it is beautiful. If nature were not beautiful, it would not be worth knowing, and if nature were not worth knowing, life would not be worth living' (H. Poincaré, cited by Weber (1986, xix)). If nature were not beautiful, it would not even be possible to know it: as I remarked above, scientific theories about the unseen structure or forgotten past depend on our recognition of the subtle beauty of the mechanism involved. If there is no real beauty it is absurd to think one theory is more veridical because it is more beautiful. But the truth to which great scientists have testified is that Beauty is their firmest guide to truth: 'it is indeed an incredible fact that what the human mind, at its best and most profound, perceives as beautiful finds its realization in external nature' (Chandrasekhar, 1987, 66). This may also serve to explain Hermann Weyl's apparently shocking claim that he had 'always tried to unite the true with the beautiful; but when [he] had to choose one or the other, [he] usually chose the beautiful'.[32] A great scientist's educated sensibility is sometimes more

[31] J. Keats, 'Lamia', II, 229ff (Keats, 1956, 176f.).
[32] Chandrasekhar (1987, 52) quoting Freeman Dyson's quotation of Weyl. Compare Dostoyevsky's preference for Christ over the true, or the probably true, in *Letter to Family and Friends* (Dostoyevsky, 1962, 71).

reliable than what can—at the time—be demonstrated to less subtle wits. We can rely on that sense of beauty to lead us to the truth, because the truth is fixed by the demands of beauty. 'The plant is not in love with the Fibonacci series [which describe its stalk-production]; it does not seek beauty through the use of the golden section; it does not even count its stalks; it just puts out stalks where they will have the most room' (Stevens, 1976, 166).[33] But the order it unfolds or reveals is undoubtedly a real and powerful one, that is made known to us as beauty.

No-one in this century has put the issue more eloquently than Simone Weil. 'The beauty of the world is the co-operation of divine wisdom in creation. . . . The object of science is the presence of Wisdom in the universe' (Weil, 1959, 122, 124). She was also well aware of the temptation that beauty creates:

> It may be that vice, depravity and crime are nearly always, or even perhaps always, in their essence, attempts to eat beauty, to eat what we should only look at. . . . If [Eve] caused humanity to be lost by eating the fruit, the opposite attitude, looking at the fruit without eating it, should be what is required to save it. Weil, 1959, 121)

Does that seem absurd? If it does, it can only be because you see the only value of the fruit as instrumental, or wish to eliminate what might confront you with a more absolute demand. The impulse to use, to destroy, to humble what should be sacred to us has its effects elsewhere. Those who pride themselves on being 'practical' (in a lesser sense than Aristotle's) in effect deny the challenge that the beautiful presents. Nothing is worth admiring—except the products of their own determined efforts, and these not because they are beautiful but because they are their own. That is an understandable emotion—that is often how we love our children, after all—and one that should not be entirely dismissed. But admiring what we have done or made merely because we have done or made it is no recipe for a worthwhile life—because it isn't a recipe at all.[34] More probably such practical people really see one form of beauty but neglect another: they may suggest that the conservationist's desire to maintain the beauty of a wood, or a cathedral, is only 'aesthetic preference' while themselves seeing the beauty (it may be the real beauty) implicit in the human endeavour to survive in spite of 'nature'. William James, walking through the woods, sees a forest made ulcerous by a squatter's hut 'without a

[33] M. Mothersill (1984, 125ff.) discusses Fibonacci and the Golden Section, unsympathetically.

[34] See Chesterton, 1961, p. 39.

single element of artificial grace to make up for the loss of Nature's beauty'. But the squatters see a personal victory, a living torn from the wilderness.[35] Noble deeds are beautiful as well, and human beings themselves, though they are not the most important entities, display the beauty that the theorizer loves. Someone living a worthwhile life has friends—precisely because such friends are beautiful, and do beautiful things (for noble deeds are 'noble' only because we are too shy to say they are beautiful, *kalai praxeis*).[36] Socrates was right to say that the sight of a beautiful boy could open our eyes, and right to say that physical consummation was a wrong response precisely because the lover would no longer think the boy was something still worth wondering at, nor would the boy benefit. Beauty is to be worshipped, and cannot be possessed.[37]

Practical virtue is exercised in doing what is beautiful, but it is the contemplatable beauty of the act that makes the exercise worthwhile. The beauty of ordinarily moral action is not the only beauty (and it is indeed a beauty possible only in a fallen world), but it is a manifestation of the quality the theorizer sees. That moral approbation comes under the same heading as aesthetic is a thought that has been out of fashion for many years,[38] partly—no doubt—because we have come to think that 'beauty' is only a projection, and fear to think the same of moral goodness. We have so far forgotten our past as to imagine that calling a character beautiful is only a strained metaphor. But Plotinus meant what he said:

> As it is not for those to speak of the graceful forms of the material world who have never seen them or known their grace—men born blind, let us suppose—in the same way those must be silent upon the beauty of noble conduct and of learning and all that order who have never cared for such things, nor may those tell of the splendour of virtue who have never known the face of Justice and of Moral Wisdom beautiful beyond the beauty of Evening and Dawn. Such vision is for those only who see with the Soul's sight—and at the vision they will rejoice, and awe will fall upon them and a trouble deeper than all the rest could ever stir, for now they are moving in the realm of Truth. This is the spirit that Beauty must ever induce, wonderment and a delicious trouble, longing and love and a trembling that is all delight. (Plotinus, 1956, I.6.4, p. 59)

[35] See Roth, 1969, 215f: James realizes the conflict, and attempts some resolution.

[36] Aristotle, *Nicomachean Ethics,* 9.1170a2ff.

[37] See McGhee (1993).

[38] See Sircello, 1985, 81ff.

Beauty, in brief, has in the past been reckoned not merely analogous to Moral Worth: it is what Moral Worth consists in, the beauty of action and the virtuous soul, the sight of which induces 'wonderment and a delicious trouble'. 'The equivalence of moral beauty and the good was a conception inherited from the Stoics, from Cicero and from Augustine, very likely from Aristotle's *Rhetoric* (1366a33) as well' (Eco, 1986, 22). If that is not how most of us feel about morality, so much the worse for us. Why should we mind about beauty? 'That is a blind man's question', said Aristotle (Diogenes Laertius, 1925, 5.20).

Perfect virtue is complete virtue, with every disposition well-proportioned, and the goal of action Beauty. Truly virtuous people, according to tradition, do not merely recognize natural goods as being good-for-them, and act accordingly. They act for the sake of the beautiful—not, that is, to benefit the beautiful, but to exemplify it, to give it an entry to the changing world. They act so as to be performing beautifully, whether their act must be to deal with ill-health and poverty, or with the natural goods.[39] Perfectly virtuous people act so as to embody in their character and conduct the ideal of sound, and lively, proportion that our evolution has constrained us to intuit, the beauty that Plotinus praised so largely.[40] This, traditionally, has been the ethical ideal: not simply to secure what is good-for-oneself as a healthy and harmonious human being, things like honour and friendship and a quiet life, but to do what is fine and noble, what is objectively required not simply for the good of the agent, but by the beauty of the act itself.

A truth is worth knowing, a city worth preserving, a friend worth loving, a moral act worth doing, because they are all beautiful. The casual hedonism that has afflicted so many of this century's moralists draws part of its strength from the conviction that a certain sort of 'enjoyment' is what makes life worthwhile. That is not unreasonable: beauty exists as the objective correlate of an appreciation, an enjoyment of that beauty. But it is all too easy to be sucked down into a merely subjective pleasure. The pursuit of merely tactile pleasures is at once a hopeless and a deeply slavish pastime, because such pleasure-seekers are indefinitely manipulable by those with the will to do so. They can be bribed or threatened to do anything at all, and are paid in fairy gold which, notoriously, turns to ashes on the morning after. But careful hedonists may think that they have some conception of an earthly paradise for which they must make efforts and endure sacrifices: *there* people will live restful,

[39] Aristotle, *Politics*, 7.1332a20f.
[40] See Clark (1993).

friendly lives, spared all the major sicknesses and disappointments, and free to soothe themselves with whatever tactile pleasures, hobbies and excitements that they please. Action, as Aristotle said, is for the sake of leisure, and *there* there will be no longer any need for moral effort or nobility. It must be a vision that has some appeal to all of us. The trouble is that even if, especially if, we believe it practically possible, the vision actually subverts our present moral endeavour, while gradually leaving us without any real idea of why the 'earthly paradise' should be desired.

If the only point of moral action is to bring about that leisure-park, then any sacrifice of present honour can be defended. Such 'idealists', even more than hedonists, are indefinitely manipulable, and because they put all value far away in an unrealized future they lack any sense of what that value is. They will never know if their life has been worthwhile, because they will never know if they have succeeded (as seems to me to be unlikely). They can be fairly confident that even if, especially if, they do succeed their beneficiaries will not think of their lives as worthwhile ones, except as instruments for the creation of the leisure park they themselves inhabit. The people whom their imagined beneficiaries will admire and imitate will instead be those whom they now most despise. The idealistic hedonist is working to create a bourgeois society whose value rests entirely in the sensual thrills that non-idealistic hedonists oppress the present to ensure.

Both idealistic and non-idealistic hedonists, by putting the value of moral action in the imagined consequences of those acts, specifically the pleasures they perhaps engender, licence oppression, and the alienation of value. Aristotle's conviction, shared by other ancient moralists, was that the value of moral action lay in its beauty, the self-same beauty that is displayed in the world's order, in well-built friendships and in well-built cities. The only final end is beauty, and the best life for human beings is to see and serve that beauty. Tactile pleasures and future achievements (valued for increasing tactile pleasures) are no sure basis for a worthwhile life. One question remains: is it better to build beauty or to worship its presence in the world (the world, that is, of stars, trees, flowers, beetles, horses, birds and people)? Is it better, in short, to be a citizen or a resident alien? Unless God keeps the house their labour is but lost that built it: unless, that is, the love of present beauty is alive there, the citizen works in vain (however many temples, courts and palaces she builds). But even if the citizen's labour is not vain it struggles against fearful odds. No-one can ensure that someone else experiences the love of God, or lives by it, and even if the labouring citizen is confident that she lives with beauty her failure or possible failure to preserve the city must weigh on her. Because her hope is placed outside herself she must so act as to preserve some few who live in beauty more securely than she does.

I conclude with another, longer quote from Weil:

> We live in a world of unreality and dreams. To give up our imaginary position as the centre, to renounce it, not only intellectually but in the imaginative part of our soul, that means to awaken to what is real and eternal, to see the true light and hear the true silence. A transformation then takes place at the very roots of our sensibility, in our immediate reception of sense impressions and psychological impressions. It is a transformation analogous to that which takes place in the dusk of evening on a road, where we suddenly discern as a tree what we had at first seen as a stooping man; or where we suddenly recognize as a rustling of leaves what we thought at first was whispering voices. We see the same colours, we hear the same sounds, but not in the same way. To empty ourselves of our false divinity, to deny ourselves, to give up being the centre of the world in imagination, to discern that all points in the world are equally centres and that the true centre is outside the world, this is to consent to the rule of mechanical necessity in matter and of free choice at the centre of each soul. Such consent is love. The face of this love which is turned towards thinking persons is the love of our neighbour: the face turned towards matter is love of the order of the world, or love of the beauty of the world which is the same thing. (Weil, 1959, 115)

Those who make no attempt to live 'in the presence of God' or (equivalently) 'in beauty' are not living worthwhile lives. Those who do will also seek to do their duty in the world, but will not imagine that their job is to 'improve' the world. Nor will they imagine, like so many modern moralists, that the better life is one most filled with sensual entanglements or free-est of sensual pains. The good life, the life well-lived, is the one lived for the sake of beauty, and, therefore, for *theoria*. If this were truly impossible (because beauty, after all, is no real object of intelligent apprehension) then we could neither rely upon our scientific intuitions to show us truth nor have any duty to submit to truth. In that extremity the life of slaves or beasts would be all that we had to live, and the question 'how shall we live well' would have no meaning.

Invincible Knowledge

RENFORD BAMBROUGH

As there is a condition of mind which is characterized by invincible ignorance, so there is another which may be said to be possessed of invincible knowledge; and it would be paradoxical in me to deny to such a mental state the highest quality of religious faith,—I mean *certitude*. (J. H. Newman, *Grammar of Assent*, 138–139)

'She's an artist. She keeps saying the same thing without repeating herself'. (Iris Murdoch, *The Good Apprentice*, 66)

In being initiated into our life as human beings we are subject to causal influences; guiding, teaching, restraint, compulsion, incentives, rewards, warnings, penalties. Until such influences have achieved their most important work we do not share the human understanding within which there can be ratiocination, evidence, argument. So there is and must be a causal story of how we come to acquire a human understanding; a causal story for the species as a whole and a causal story for each of us; and there is not and could not be any acceptable account, either for the species or for the individual, of how we reasoned or argued our way into our initial and fundamental understanding. I say the same thing without repeating myself if I call such knowledge and understanding *invincible*. It is not possible to overthrow it by reasoning any more than it is possible to establish it by reasoning.

One of the most striking causal properties of human beings, and especially of young human beings, is their *credulity*. We tell children that the surface of the earth is curved, that the sun is more distant than the moon, that there was a historic battle in 1066, and the result is that they believe it or know it.

The causal story for you will not be the same in detail as the causal story for me because in our childhood, and later, we have been told different things by those who have had the greatest influence over us. As Wittgenstein says, some children are told that there is a God, and some are brought up as atheists, and each group will learn to *argue* for their opposed beliefs (OC, 107).[1] This reinforces the tendency to relativism or scepticism that the

[1] References in this form are to Wittgenstein, 1969.

thought of the *causal* origins of our knowledge and understanding easily encourages; if infantile credulity leads to opposed beliefs in different children, or different adults, how can such *telling*, and such credulity, amount to a ground or justification for our believings?

Wittgenstein tells a story of a king who has been told that the whole history and frame of things began with his own beginning (OC, 92). The elder Gosse believed that the earth was created in 4004 BC complete with a geological structure and fossil record that suggested a much longer history; and most of us do not believe this. Many of us believe that every human being has two human parents, but some or all Christians do not believe this. Some believe in transubstantiation and some do not.

Yet the causal story for you must be very similar to the causal story for me if we are to be said to share a general common understanding. One of our great difficulties in philosophy is to reconcile justice to individual differences with justice to the unity and community of the human understanding.

The difficulties are greater, but still not insurmountable, when the question is about the unity of all understanding and not merely about the unity of human understanding.

Does a parent or teacher give a child *reasons* for accepting the most fundamental beliefs instilled by authority and received with beneficent credulity? (The credulity is beneficent because the child—and the species—would not long survive without it). The process is *causal*. Does the child have reason to accept because the parent or teacher says thus and so? The child believes, accepts, because the parent says so; is that a causal or a logical 'because'? That reasons are *not* given, that the process *is* causal, is often regarded as scandalous, or made the basis of a relativistic argument.

Newman (1985) speaks of *credence* where I have spoken of credulity:

These informations, thus received with a spontaneous assent, constitute the furniture of the mind, and make the difference between its civilized condition and a state of nature. They are its education, as far as general knowledge can so be called; and, though education is discipline as well as learning, still, unless the mind implicitly welcomes the truths, real or ostensible, which these informations supply, it will gain neither formation nor a stimulus for its activity and progress. Besides, to believe frankly what it is told, is in the young an exercise of teachableness and humility. (41)

He too makes clear that such credence is not confined to children, but is

> the sort of assent which we give to those opinions and professed facts which are ever presenting themselves to us without any effort of ours, and which we commonly take for granted, thereby obtaining a broad foundation of thought for ourselves, and a medium of intercourse between ourselves and others. (41)

Hence 'these remarks hold good in secular subjects as well as religious', and apply, for example, to my belief that I live on an island, that Julius Caesar once invaded it, that it has held imperial dominion over other territories.

In the causal story that we tell about the origin of our corporate understanding, about our origin as a species, we need to remember our relation to non-human animals. We are *rational* animals, but we are rational *animals*. Wittgenstein says that at the root of our understanding is 'something animal'; that we see what intention is if we watch a cat stalking a bird. Newman reminds us that our belief in the existence of things external to ourselves is founded on an instinct that we share with the brutes, and is not dependent on the use of reason.

Newman's *Grammar of Assent* and Wittgenstein's *On Certainty* chime together across the century in many other particulars, but accordingly neither of them is joined in harmony with many other philosophers, and certainly with few in our day. Even many 'Wittgensteinians' are less faithful to their master than they think they are. But I will from now on try to show this by direct attention to the issues, without further invocation of Newman and Wittgenstein and their beneficent credibility.

To speak as I do of *credulity* is already to appear vulnerable to sceptical or relativist suspicion. For we ordinarily use the word 'credulity' to refer to over-hasty or insufficiently grounded acceptance of a belief. And my fuller story will at first merely extend the target area: for I am saying that we are right to accept so much of what we are told or otherwise caused to believe, and to accept it without giving or receiving any justification. At best, it would appear, I am accounting for our having our basic beliefs, explaining what brings it about that we have them, and not providing even a hint of what might amount to adequate grounds for our confidence in them. When we note and approve Wittgenstein's injunction to go 'back to the teaching' are we not also endorsing his notorious dogmatism? He himself volunteers only to describe the nature and content of our human understanding, and not to offer any validation of its claim to *be* an *understanding*. He does not defend his view against rival views, or give the arguments that might support his theory or doctrine against possible alternatives.

We shall cope better with his objection if we first attend to Wittgenstein's remark at *Zettel* (1967, 455) that the philosopher is not a citizen of any community of ideas, and that that is what makes him a philosopher. This remark needs watching at least as closely as most of his remarks. If we do not watch it closely enough we may respond like this: surely, we may say, Wittgenstein acknowledges and insists that the human community, to which we all belong, is a community of ideas. The philosopher, as much as any other human being, is a member of this human community. Even one who did not regard the human community as being united by a single initial common understanding, but who wished to associate himself and perhaps Wittgenstein with some relativistic scheme of thought, might think that each of us is initiated by early training into one or other of the alternative communities of ideas into which the human species is divided.

This way of reading the remark is appealing but misguided. We can resolve the difficulty by noticing that Wittgenstein is using the expression 'community of ideas' in a narrower way. I take him to be using it in a way that makes it akin to *ideology*, or *body of doctrine*, or a set of views or opinions. The remark would thus most naturally be associated with his view that the philosopher does not advance theories or views or opinions. The common understanding is to be contrasted with anything specialized or sectarian or doctrinaire. It is accordingly to be described—articulated—rather than argued for or justified.

Communities of ideas are therefore analogous to ideologies, doctrines, theses, languages. And the ordinary understanding is accordingly not to be regarded as an alternative to others in the way that one ideology or doctrine is an alternative (and a rival) to another.

At least two kinds of rivalry need to be distinguished: rivalry between hypotheses or views between which a rational resolution is envisaged; and rivalry between systems of ideas, frameworks, ultimate principles etc. The second kind is not in one clear sense a kind of rivalry at all. There may be no winning and losing where there is no conflict. London Welsh and London Irish are rivals. The Oxford University Boat Club and the Cambridge University Boat Club are rivals. Rugby football and rowing are not rivals in the same way.

This is not however to be taken to mean that questions of the truth or falsehood of the content of the ordinary understanding do not arise. It is amply confirmed by passages in *On Certainty* (83,

403) that the 'inherited background' consists at least largely of what stands fast, is secure against dismissal from our understanding because it is *so*, so much so that anything that conflicts with it thereby discredits itself. Wittgenstein may wish to discourage Moore from claiming *knowledge* that he has two hands, but when he speaks of the 'peculiar logical role' that such a proposition may fulfil he is translating into another idiom Moore's main point: that such a proposition is usable as a means of *refuting* whatever conflicts with it.

So truth and falsehood are not excluded, as knowledge is, from Wittgenstein's description of our form of life, our natural history; and *certainty* is so prominent that it has to be honoured in the title. Even if we wish to guard against too *propositionalist* a conception of what is fundamental to our understanding, and hence share Wittgenstein's suspicions of the use of some of these other epistemic terms in this context, we should still remember that the use of the word 'understanding' itself imports notions of *correctness* and (again) certainty: getting things right that we are capable of getting wrong. I cannot know what is false, and by analogy I cannot be said to understand what I *mis*understand.

Yet as long as Wittgenstein is content with description, with natural history, and dispenses with all attempts at justification or explanation, he will be subject to a persuasive challenge to his whole approach. The question that arises, his critics will insist, is not a question about *what we do*, but about whether we are *right* to do it. Nothing historical or causal can amount to a *ground* for adopting our actual language and our actual network of concepts; our choice between one network or system and another remains *arbitrary* for all that Wittgenstein's description and articulation can show to the contrary. We must attend, the critics will insist, to the importance of the distinction between reasons and causes, the logical and the causal, the logical and the psychological. After nearly a century of conscientious purgation of idealism or psychologism from our logical and epistemological thinking, we must not lapse into a mere articulation of the structure of our thought that gives us no grounds for adopting or retaining the network of concepts that exhibits the structure.

Wittgenstein is prepared to call the network, the inherited understanding, a *system* of understanding. It forms a unity, in spite of the need for so much emphasis on its internal complexity and intricacy. Such a notion of system or network is needed as soon as we begin to describe the nature and mode of acquisition of understanding or knowledge of any kind. It is illustrated in any plausible description even of the more formal modes of reasoning and enquiry that Wittgenstein accuses philosophers of employing as tyrannical paradigms. It emerges in a simple and abstract account of the notion of a proposition or conclusion and its relation to evidence or reason. What is offered as reason is meant to be logically related to what is defended as conclusion. An allegation that the conclusion is unacceptable may be supported by eliciting consequences from the conclusion. Here intricate questions may arise about the individuation and identification of propositions. A simple consequence of p, or something of which p is a simple consequence, may need to be regarded as a component or ingredient or reiteration of p rather than as a proposition q in such and such a logical or evidential relation to p. The picture given in *On Certainty* of a system or network is soon built up from these simple beginnings.

My knowledge or understanding is from the start systematic, complicated, pluralistic. 'To understand a sentence is to understand a language.' The initiation of a child into understanding and knowledge, even when it may be expressed propositionally, is not an initiation into the understanding or acceptance of isolated propositions. Much scene-setting is needed before the point at which it is possible to tell the child that it is five o'clock or ask the child where the red-headed doll is now. To ignore this is to be guilty of one of the worst instances of the philosopher's besetting unrealism. The isolated proposition, like the notion of a *rule* of reasoning, is taken as a starting point when it is nearer to being a remote abstraction, the *result* of a tendentious characterization of what should be described by the type of description that 'leaves everything as it is'.

Socrates can ask me a difficult question only because he and I are individually and jointly orientated in a space in which that question is in perceptible relations with other questions and assertions, relations that constitute the intelligibility of all the mutually related items. It is a part of the same truth that Aristotle recognizes when he remarks that deliberation is of means not ends, and that Descartes tries to conceal from himself when he asserts or enacts the *cogito* and tries to embark on a 'project of pure enquiry'.

The use or misuse of the 'Archimedean point' will not save the project of 'pure enquiry'. When we present the supposed parallel accurately it defeats its ostensible purpose. Archimedes is himself a solid body located in the space in which he exercises his leverage. He would be unable to exercise it if he were out of contact with other solid bodies. The Archimedean analogy, when accurately drawn, also helps us to see the scope and limits of ideas of relativity and perspective in epistemology. Where I stand now to exercise

my leverage may be the fulcrum of my next exercise, and the position of the far end of my lever in the one after that.

Aristotle's remark about deliberation indicates that there is
invincible practical and ethical knowledge as well as invincible
knowledge of matters of fact and matters of logic. I do not understand the question I am deliberating about—and hence am not
deliberating about any question—unless I am aware of the considerations relevant to the determination of the question, and of the
nature and direction of the bearing of each of them upon the resolution of the disagreement (even when it is a disagreement only
with myself). The point here is a special case of a wider observation of Wittgenstein's: that I cannot even make a mistake unless I
reason in conformity with mankind. (OC, 156)

It is a related point that a person or a community may be said to
lack a certain concept or distinction or item of knowledge only by
virtue of being possessed of other knowledge and concepts and distinctions. The lack is one that might have been filled, and may con-
ceivably yet be filled. For example, a particular society may lack the
distinction between the raw and the cooked. This is a contrast—a
part of a possible network of concepts—that a particular actual network may lack. The space that it would occupy in the network
remains vacant. The space and the vacancy enter into the description or specification of the network. It could come to be filled later,
either by reflective development or new experience within the society whose network it is, or by encounter with another society. The
vacancy has a shape, like the shape of ignorance (see 'The Shape of
Ignorance', Lewis, 1976). Lack of acquaintance, lack of understanding, lack of knowledge: these are three parallel structures. But
some concepts are inescapable—elements of the understanding of
one who has a human understanding.

This small scale example illustrates the wider view. Every actual
society has concepts and institutions related to food: meals, hunger,
hospitality, hunting, growing, gathering. Some of the more specific
ones may be absent from particular societies; others are inescapable
—invincible understandings that are elements in the structure of
any life that can be called human. Another such cluster is of concepts concerned with the mutual support that the human condition
requires of us: help, care, collaboration, co-operation.

Against this wide background—which could bear much more
detailed characterization—I now wish to raise some issues of epistemology into which it has not sufficiently been drawn.

One is a disagreement about how *systematic* philosophy can be.
One way of showing that there can be *logic* without such *machinery*
is to look at the Socratic procedure of *elenchus*. Coherence and

contradiction and other logical notions are more than indispensable to this purpose: they *constitute* the *method*. In being called *dialectic* it is being recognized as logic without losing its recognition as the articulation of the structure of human *conversation*, a *central* activity of a creature that is *logikon*. To attend to this is to attend to conflict, to the clash between your understanding and mine and to the clash between some elements of my understanding and other elements of it. Callicles is in conflict with Socrates and in conflict with himself. Socrates is in conflict with himself when he is in *aporia*.

At this or some other early stage there arises the difficulty of being realistic about what *we* can do, while at the same time doing justice to the prospect of unifying my understanding both with itself and with your understanding.

The confusion between what is indefinite and what is indeterminate is clarified out of sight by attention to the ends and means of conversation. We enter the necessary qualifications and refinements to each other's incomplete or misleading descriptions and thus allow the relativists what can be allowed to them. We also recognize the *necessity* of such qualifications and that is close to recognizing the source of the engine power that drives a conversation. We might wish to say that we are pushed from behind towards the truth that is ahead of us, especially if we are troubled as Williams and Wiggins and Rorty are by the failure of fit between ethics and philosophy and criticism on the one hand, and on the other the blueprint of *convergence* and Nozick's notion of 'tracking the truth'. This way of putting it is acceptable if it is recognized to be compatible with—and indeed to *involve*—an objectivity as objective as that of physics.

'Back to the teaching': Wittgenstein's slogan recognizes that we may be constrained (pushed) by what is behind us as well as constrained (pulled) by what is ahead of us.

The comparisons and contrasts with mathematics and logic and philosophy are as important as the contrasts and comparisons with physics and history and cartography.

The cry is always for a new theory, but often for an old song and an old story. The child asks for the same story again and again and is again excited and surprised by the expected outcome. We want our favourite hymns, and are especially irritated if the tune or the words are familiar but the words or the tune are strange, or, still worse, are familiar but in unfamiliar association with other words or notes.

Yet we enjoyed learning the tunes and words when they were new and we are happy to add the new hymns or songs or stories to our repertoire when they too have become familiar.

The link with our epistemological or metaphysical theme is this: we need a familiar framework—as the sceptics and dogmatists in their opposing tall stories have always said—against which we can adjust to what is new or strange. The rehearsing and rehearing of what is familiar is accordingly a familiar and central element in religion and ethics and criticism and philosophy. The contrast between the two things is this: that we desire and delight in the familiar song or story, whereas we *need* (even if we also delight in) the familiar background in which we are oriented and must be oriented if we are to possess human understanding.

So how is originality possible in any of these fields? This question deserves to be dealt with only in a way that leaves room for the question '*Is* originality possible here?' and 'Is originality, *if* it is possible, also desirable here?'

Originality is as often as not a matter of style or idiom rather than purpose or content. Clothes are in nearly all respects a paradigm of fashion. The objectives remain the same—warmth and comfort, coolness and comfort, allure and modesty and decency, conformity and individuality—while the shapes and colours and lengths and patterns come and go.

The manners and idioms of philosophers change like that, but not their aims or even their methods. Their purpose remains the articulation and resolution of perplexity and conflict—i.e. of conflict and of inner conflict; and articulation of what is prior to all conflict because it belongs invincibly to the common understanding.

I am not saying that there is no such thing as a great and original philosophical mind. Finding new ways—in philosophy as in literature—is originality. Though great qualities of mind—coming together in the guise of realism—of being *realistic*—are needed for purposes that have nothing to do with the *newness* of the thoughts conveyed—except perhaps sometimes their newness to the person or people to whom they are now being conveyed. I may know that *I* have made progress in philosophical understanding even if I do not know whether there is such a thing as progress in *philosophy*, as there is progress in mathematics and physics. (I ought of course to ask myself the question: Could there be progress by and for individuals without there being any possibility of progress by or on behalf of all of us?)

We need also to ask why progress in philosophy should be assumed to be more like progress in physics than it is, and why it is assumed that unless progress in philosophy is very like progress in physics then there is no progress in philosophy.

The difficulty of setting all this down without obscurity or confusion or inexactness illustrates several things about philosophical and quasi-philosophical enquiries generally.

(a) The qualifications one wants to make tumble over each other as each sentence is said or written.

(b) For related reasons conflict or conversation will serve as a mode of description or representation in which descriptions or representations that are partial (in two senses) are corrected or supplemented or mutually reconciled. Philosophy is the conflict of the obvious with the obvious, so it often involves the denial of what seems obvious, as well as the assertion of what is obvious: both forms are offensive to many tastes, including the tastes of many philosophers, and not many philosophers are wise enough to object to both and also to employ both.

(c) The concepts we are concerned with come in clusters, yet we still like to try to pick them off singly. Here we may think of the 'implicit logic' involved in resolutions of perplexity and of conflict; of the folly of isolating *knowledge* for departmentalized treatment; and of Dummett's isolation of *meaning* from the cluster of epistemological concepts to which it belongs: knowledge, truth, proof, evidence, assertion, implication, understanding, justification . . . Dummett's ascription of primacy to the philosophy of language over epistemology involves giving too much independence to knowledge as well as to meaning.

One response to the difficulties we have considered is to try to treat philosophy as if it were a branch of science or logic, and hence as something that has the mode of progress appropriate to science or logic. A variant is the treatment of philosophy as a purely or largely historical enquiry; and a variant of the variant is what has been called therapeutic philosophy: the philosopher treats a question—like an illness. (Does the philosopher deal with a question like an illness or with a *questioner* like a patient—a *sufferer* from perplexity or confusion?)

Then there are the *institutional* distortions, the difficulties which arise from making philosophy into an academic *subject* and a profession and the concern of *departments* which need (a) to defend their professional and specialist scope, (b) to compete with other departments for buildings, funds, staff and students, and hence (c) to cramp and crumple themselves and their 'field' into a parody of the shape that a science or an art must have in order to engage in such competition. The troublesome questions are many and of various kinds: What do you philosophers contribute to the economy, the war effort, the happiness of mankind? What contribution to *research* have you and your staff made during the last quinquennium? What are your graduates fit to do—other than philosophy—when the philosophy has to stop?

That those who are not philosophers should ask such questions is not surprising, since many philosophers ask the same questions of themselves and others, and act in ways that reinforce the impression that such questions are straightforwardly in place. They ask 'What is your field?'; they 'keep up with the latest work' in whatever field they think it is; they advise their research students to begin by entangling themselves in the woods and thickets of the *Philosopher's Index*. Above all they ignore what is *not* their 'field'.

This soon leads to thinking of all *amateur* philosophers as incompetent philosophers. And some plausibility is given to the assumption by some of the effects of professionalism in fulfilling its own implicit prophecies. For philosophers take to writing in ways that are unreadable to those who are 'not philosophers'. The isolation is made more nearly complete by the mutual suspicions of the amateurs and the professionals. The impression given and received on one side is that all non-professional writers are 'mere' journalists or preachers or poets; on the other side that all the specialists are barbarian logic-choppers or youth-corrupting sophists.

Some of these very terms of abuse point towards a partial correction of the misunderstanding. For many if not most of those who in this context speak so demeaningly of literature and religion and of newspapers and magazines do not renounce their use for all purposes or condemn all those who use them for any purpose. They recognize in their practice the continuities between their supposedly 'professional' products and the common terms of ordinary discourse, including imagery and hyperbole, caricature and parody.

And while they retain this recognition hope is not lost of bringing them to see that the very roots of their or any other specialist activity are to be found deep down in the soil of the common understanding.

This is not however to be taken to mean that questions of the truth or falsehood of the contents of the ordinary understanding do not arise. To repeat: it is amply confirmed by passages in *On Certainty* (83, 403) that the 'inherited background' consists at least largely of what *'stands fast'*, is secure against dismissal from our understanding, because it is *so*, so much *so* that anything that conflicts with it thereby discredits itself.

When we add the *logikon* and the *politikon* to the *zōon* the scale and scope are increased, and the degree of unity displayed.

Note the implications of the concept of *description* whether used by Wittgenstein or another: 'telling it as it is'. This applies even to oblique modes of representation.

Wittgenstein's description of 'the workings of our language', in being a contribution to the 'natural history' of human beings, will be faithful or unfaithful to how 'our language' *does* work. We must 'reject false accounts of the matter *as* false'.

The hardest part is to understand and describe the relation between this description and *logic* (a particular case of the hard task of relating and separating the logical and the causal). An important part of the story is the same as for Logic (with a capital L): e.g. the link between Aristotelian syllogistic logic and the pre-existing practice that it codifies. Comparisons and contrasts between logic and grammar may be helpful. In grammar, too, the descriptive has intricate relationships with the normative.

Compare the rules of games. They too may be formulated only after the practice is ancient and established.

The rules 'govern' only in a Pickwickian sense. They do not *direct*, or in any relevant sense *determine* the practice.

The epigraph from Iris Murdoch, about the artist saying the same thing without repeating herself, is on the same page as a reference to a character who wants somebody to look at azaleas or *an* azalea. It is parallel to Iris Murdoch's example of the kestrel seen through the window, and in general to the themes of contemplation, celebration, remembering or recalling the familiar, recollecting in tranquillity. (Old song, old story.)

The artist says the same thing without repeating herself by saying the same thing *differently*. (Every different saying of the same thing is the saying of a different thing. This remark applies also to itself.)

Notice also the intimacy between this theme and that of dialectic. Tom Stoppard speaks of using dialogue in order to contradict himself with impunity. The same thought could be expressed—without repeating oneself—by saying something so much tamer that it appears *not* to be the same thing: that intricacy and many-sidedness of description require the qualifications and reservations and complications that are facilitated by dialogue or by the dialectical structure that is found in the work of Plato and Aristotle, Hume and Wittgenstein, and in the work of most of those whose philosophical work deserves to be remembered.

Emmanuel Levinas: Responsibility and Election

CATHERINE CHALIER

Although some people argue Emmanuel Levinas is a Jewish thinker because he introduces in his philosophical work ideas which come from the Jewish tradition, I want to present him as a *philosopher*. A philosopher who tries to widen the philosophical horizon which is traditionally a Greek one but, at the same time, a philosopher who does not want to abandon it. In one of his main books *Totality and Infinity* (1969), he describes western civilization as an hypocritical one because it is attached both to the True and to the Good, but he adds:

> It is perhaps time to see in hypocrisy not only a base contingent defect of man, but the underlying rending of a world attached to both the philosophers and the prophets. (p. 24)

When reading Levinas we may realize that such an 'hypocrisy' might well be a blessing from a philosophical point of view. One of Levinas's philosophical aims is to refer to the Greek language of philosophy—a language he asserts to be of universal significance—in order to elucidate ideas that come from the Hebrew world view, from the prophets and from the sages. He wants to give a new insight into Greek categories and concepts but he refuses to abnegate the philosophical requirements for accuracy. That is why when he refers to biblical verses or to Talmudic apologues, he does not want *to prove* anything. His philosophical writings are indeed philosophical because he does not yield to the temptation of substituting the authority of a certain verse or of a certain name to the philosophical requirement of argumentation.

In this paper I should like to explain why one main idea in the Jewish tradition—the idea of *election*—is a key word in Levinas's philosophical endeavour to understand in a new way the idea of *responsibility*.

1. The Jewish election as an infinite responsibility in Levinas's thought

And they shall fall one upon another (*Leviticus* 26.37)

One upon another, one as his brother's keeper, one in charge of his neighbour (Levinas, 1972, 14)

Catherine Chalier

When the rabbis in the Talmud quote the Bible, they do not intend to prove something but to give evidence in favour of a tradition and a spirituality, since without these quotations 'treasures of significance' would be lost. In the same way, when Levinas quotes the Bible or the Talmud, he does not try to prove anything—this is not the way a philosopher writes an essay—but to introduce in the heart of his philosophical work a 'strangeness' that is also the source of 'a new thinking', if I may take this expression from F. Rosenzweig (1925).

When he deals with the question of responsibility, Levinas often quotes this maxim from *The Sayings of the Fathers* (*Pirqé Avot*) (1962): 'R. Hillel used to say: If I am not for myself who is for me? And when I am for myself, what am I? And if not now, when?'. He thinks he is entitled to quote the Talmud and the Bible as well as Heidegger, for instance, is entitled to quote Hölderlin and Trakl. But the present quotation also aims at a new idea as regards responsibility. I should like to explain how.

What about responsibility?

Generally speaking to be responsible means to answer for one's acts and words before one's judges and before other men. Such is indeed the definition of responsibility in a dictionary. Yet, according to Levinas, we have to dig much deeper into the matter of responsibility. And if we have to do this, it is perhaps because the Judaic tradition prevents us from being content with such a definition. He teaches us a new way of understanding responsibility: responsibility is *the* key word in his analysis of the life of the subject and it is linked to the idea of election as will be explained later on.

What is a *human* subject according to Levinas? In *Otherwise than Being* (1981) he writes:

> Responsibility for another is not an accident that happens to a subject, but precedes essence in it, it has not awaited freedom, in which a commitment to another would have been made (. . .). The word 'I' means 'Here I am', answering for everything and for everyone. Responsibility for the others has not been a return to oneself, but an exasperated contracting, which the limits of identity cannot retain. (p. 114)

Levinas here analyses the life of the human subject in a new and difficult way. He describes it as *an answer* to a calling: a calling that is both singular and disquieting. Man becomes a human subject on the condition that it answers for everything and everyone.

64

Man does not *choose* to answer for everything and everyone, he *has* to if he wants to become a human subject, which of course is not always the case. But Levinas argues that this responsibility is at the basis of man's life as a human subject: caring for the other is not an act of free choice but the very structure of his definition of subjectivity.

In *Humanisme de l'autre homme* (1972) he writes that it is even more difficult to ignore responsibility than 'to ignore one's skin'. It means that it is impossible for a subject to be quiet and peaceful since man as a human subject is infinitely exposed to the other, he has to answer for him. Yet he often prefers to remain an *ego* pleased with itself and full of pride and contempt. According to the quotation I have mentioned, we understand also that Levinas thinks responsibility *precedes* freedom. He does not speak of a man who decides to be responsible for the other and who refuses to be responsible beyond his freedom. If responsibility is the structure of subjectivity, it is indeed beyond freedom, it has nothing to do with man's free will.

Responsibility is an answer to a calling which has chosen man from birth. It is even an *obsession*, a reality one cannot forget in the same way as it is impossible to forget election. Man is under this obligation to care for the other as the Jew is under the obligation to be concerned with election. Levinas even says responsibility is a *trauma*, that is to say a wound that is perhaps a blessing. What is the· significance of this wound? It means man cannot forget the other man's fate: that is why the 'I' is indeed a 'Here I am' (*Hinneni* in the Hebrew Bible).

Let us turn to the philosophical tradition for a while in order to understand better what is new in Levinas's analyses. When philosophers are worried about the problem of responsibility, when they try to think about it and to conceptualise it, they usually refer to the idea of a free subject, a free choice, a free will and a free decision, as if responsibility remained impossible and unthinkable without freedom. Responsibility means man is not bound to a tragic fate decided by the gods as is the case in the Greek tragedy. According to Aristotle for instance, man is 'the principle and the generating force of his own acts as he is the parent of his children'. Which means that virtue and vices rest upon him, upon his free choice.

Kant introduces the idea of 'an intelligible character' in order to exclude man from the jurisdiction of determinism and to prove man is a responsible being. Thus, even if the liar has received a very bad education and has been living in bad conditions too, he is responsible: 'His act rests upon him, upon his intelligible character: he is utterly guilty when he lies; therefore, despite all the empirical conditions of his act, his reason was fully free and this act rests upon his negligence.' For Kant, man is thus fully responsible: the freedom of his reason justifies this responsibility to himself and to society for everything he is and does. This kind of responsibility is linked to a solitary subject, a subject who has to take on his acts and life provided that he is also a free subject thanks to his reason. Since, according to Kant, man is not responsible if he is not a free subject, I do not intend to explain in detail Kant's position on responsibility, I only wish to examine this question in some of its classical bearings in order to underline Levinas's novelty. For this most classical figure of philosophy, responsibility is closely connected to the 'metaphysics of presence': a free subject is set free from the enigmatic weight of the past and from all passivity, he is the initiator of his acts. But it also means that this subject's commitment is limited since man is not held responsible for his neighbour's fate, for his suffering and death.

In a similar way, Sartre underlines how responsibility is impossible without freedom. It is true that he often speaks of man's responsibility for all men but on a basis of freedom which, according to him, is inescapable since 'man is condemned to be free'. From this viewpoint, man's commitment to other men is also inescapable, Sartre argues that: 'When I choose for myself I also choose for all other men' (1965, 27). One is unable to choose something that will be good only for oneself: if I choose such and such a value, this value is also good for my neighbour. Yet Sartre thinks it is impossible to speak of responsibility beyond freedom. Since without freedom, without this foundation—'freedom is indeed the foundation' responsibility would become an absurdity. On the other hand, Sartre underlines the responsibility for oneself, 'When I choose for myself', and he explains how this responsibility is also a responsibility for the other as a consequence.

Levinas's thought is very different indeed. He does not agree to the precedence of freedom over responsibility and to the precedence of the self over the other. He wants to explain how it is possible 'to be responsible over and beyond one's freedom' (1981, 22). He gives a philosophical meaning to some strange ideas such as the idea of a calling, of an election and of a persecution and he analyses responsibility as 'a malady of identity' and as 'a possession and a psychosis', he even describes the soul as 'a seed of folly' (1981, 69, 191). He uses words such as anarchy, hostage, passivity, traumatism and persecution in order to describe the life of subjectivity. Let us try to understand what he means.

His philosophical writing is not a classical kind of writing. He uses words that do not belong to a classical list of concepts in order to explain how the idea of *responsibility beyond freedom* is a significant idea: more significant indeed than the classical idea of a responsibility that relies on freedom.

A man is *invested* with responsibility. Responsibility is an obsession that comes from a past that a man does not remember, it describes the situation of a man facing another man:

> Responsibility in obsession is a responsibility of the ego for what the ego has not wished, that is for the others. This anarchy in the recurrence to oneself is beyond the normal play of action and passion in which the identity of a being is maintained, in which it *is*. (1981, 114)

Man is not only responsible for himself and for his acts in front of others, he is responsible for others and for their fate. Even when he denies this truth. He is responsible for others in such a way that he loses his innocence when he looks at them. He becomes really human when he is ready to answer 'Here I am', '*Hinneni*', to the call of another.

Now let us try to explain how the Judaic tradition on election leads us to a better understanding of Levinas's thought on responsibility.

I do not intend to find in an etymological investigation the secret of a strange idea, but it is worth mentioning that in Hebrew, responsibility, *ahariout*, and other, *aher*, are closely linked. Both words share the same root. It does not prove anything but in Hebrew words that share the same root also share a certain kind of meaning. Responsibility in Hebrew is also linked to time and faithfulness since the word 'after', *aharei*, shares the same root as well.

Now what does the Torah say about responsibility? When we read the story of Cain and Abel we understand that responsibility does not mean freedom. God asks Cain: 'Where is Abel thy brother?' (*Genesis* 4.8). If God thinks this question is a relevant one, it means that according to Him Cain is responsible for his brother's fate even if he does not want to be. Levinas quotes this verse and he writes: 'one is his brother's keeper, one is in charge of his neighbour'. It is true that the story of Cain and Abel is a story of a real and terrible guilt but the Torah emphasizes man's responsibility for the other and the question: 'Where is Abel thy brother?' is asked to everyone as if everyone were responsible for all the Abels who are suffering and dying in the world even if one has not really killed them or made them suffer.

In the Talmud the Sages also argue in favour of a responsibility beyond freedom. In their commentary on the Biblical verse—'And they shall fall one upon another' (*Leviticus* 26.37)—they explain 'It means they shall fall because of their brother's guilt, it teaches us that we all are responsible for one another'. (*T. B. Sanhedrin* 27b).[1] If a man is not opposed to his brother's guilt, he is responsible for this guilt. He will have to answer to this charge. According to R. Papa, 'The Princes of the world have to answer to all charges' (*T. B. Chabbat* 55a). And it is also worth quoting the famous sentence: 'All Jews are responsible one for the other' (*T. B. Chevovoth* 39b). This sentence means no one in the Jewish people may care only for himself. The Jews have an essential solidarity among them and this solidarity is so deep as to include the *Chekhina*, the invisible presence of God among them, since, according to the Sages, the *Chekhina* does not hesitate to go with them in exile. And it is worth remembering here that, again according to the Sages, hatred and a lack of responsibility brought about this exile.

The Sages teach that it is impossible to manage on one's own without taking care of the other. On the contrary they think the fate of the just relies on the iniquity among the people: 'The just man perishes and no one cares: good men die and no one realizes that it is because of the surrounding perversity that they die'. It is as if the weight of evil was so heavy on man's shoulders that he could not remain alive and even less take refuge in an easy conscience. No one may thus try to save one's life when humanity is in distress and unable to find those true values which would help it to recover. It is impossible for some one who is part of 'the Covenant of responsibility', '*Brit Hahariout*', to desert and to choose the easy way of a proud and selfish freedom.

Even the non-Jews are bound to a Covenant of responsibility since, according to the Tradition, they all belong to the Covenant of Noah. In a beautiful comment upon the verse—'And they went in unto Noah into the ark . . . and the Lord shut him in' (*Genesis* 7.16)—Levinas explains it was impossible for Noah to shut the door and be safe with his family and the animals while all the other peoples were doomed to die.

> A human soul does not retreat into itself. . . How would it be able to retreat when humanity is perishing? Here lies the impossibility of interiority. . . No one may remain in one's self: man's humanity, subjectivity, is a responsibility for the other, an extreme vulnerability. (1972, 97)

[1] I quote from the Talmud of Babylon, name of the tractate and page (number and letter).

The Jewish tradition constantly underlines the importance of this responsibility for the other and the feeling that one has to be liable for what one does or does not, it stresses the impossibility of forsaking one's neighbour. Even Moses had to suffer with his people. According to the Talmud (*T. B. Taanith* 11a), he used to say— 'Seeing that the people of Israel suffer, I suffer with them'—and we know he did not enter the promised land.

But this responsibility and this feeling are *not* born from free choice. Man *does not want* to be responsible instead of selfish. He *is called* to this responsibility because he belongs to the Covenant of Noah or to the Covenant of Abraham. Responsibility does not result from a free choice but from the conscience of this Covenant that has elected man before he could utter a word. And of course it does not mean man is happy to be responsible for the other, he will most likely try to forget it.

In the Torah, election does not give man special rights of superiority or priority. On the contrary it stresses man's duties and man's responsibility. A responsibility that is incumbent upon him and him alone. Man may not be released from it. He may not pass over his responsibilities to someone else. Election is also linked to the feeling of strangeness in the world and to the necessity of a 'teaching' which is not a 'natural' one—'I am a stranger in the earth: hide not thy commandments from me' (*Psalms* 119.19). These commandments must help man to live according to values that are different from what we find in nature. Election means obedience to them. Instead of being proud and eager to dominate, instead of thinking one's own conscience is the true measure of all values and meanings, a man who obeys election knows he has to submit to a teaching that requires a lot from him, most of all humility, *anava*.

Humility is indeed a high value in the Bible; Abraham in his prayer for Sodom says: 'Behold now, I have taken upon me to speak unto the Lord, which am but dust and ashes' (*Genesis* 18.27). And Moses is said to have been the humblest man of his generation, yet the best example of humility lies in Abraham's answer to God when He calls him and orders him to leave his country: 'Here I am'. It is indeed not an easy answer when this calling prevents one from remaining serene in one's own country and forces one to go into exile. But this answer 'Here I am' is also the beginning of humanity, since humanity begins in this alertness of mind that helps man understand that the calling is indeed for the benefit of humanity. Thus when one hears the calling, one has to leave one's native country if one wants to be human.

Consequently we may argue that the significance of responsibility in the Torah is linked to a very special idea of a truly human man. For this man, election prevails over freedom, solidarity prevails over peace of mind and humility and alertness of mind prevail over concern for oneself. Yet in the Judaic tradition such ideas are not explained in a philosophical way. The rabbis were not concerned with philosophy, they even were suspicious of it, except some great philosophers in the Middle Ages such as Maïmonides. Now when Levinas writes:

> The responsibility for another is precisely a saying prior to anything said. The surprising saying which is a responsibility for another is against 'the winds and tides' of being, is an interruption of essence, a disinterestedness imposed with a good violence. (1981, 43)

or when he explains how one must:

> show in saying, qua approach, the very deposing or desituating of the subject, which nonetheless remains an irreplaceable uniqueness, and is thus the subjectivity of the subject (*ibid.* 48)

he argues, in a philosophical way, the significance of the idea of election. He gives a new insight into the philosophical ideas about responsibility, freedom and subjectivity thanks to the faithfulness to his Jewish heritage.

After the dedication 'to the memory of those who were closest among the six million assassinated by the National Socialists and the millions on millions of all confessions and all nations, victims of the same hatred of the other man, the same antisemitism', *Otherwise than Being* (1981) bears in its first epigraph a quotation from *Ezechiel* (3.20):

> Or if a righteous man turn from his righteousness and do what is wrong, and I make that the occasion for bringing about his downfall, he shall die; because you did not want him, he shall die for his sin, and the righteous deeds which he has done shall not be remembered, but *his blood will I require at your hand*.

This epigraph is significant, it is linked to Levinas's main idea of election as an infinite responsibility. The calling is indeed a calling to a responsibility for the other, without explanation and without justification. 'The surprising saying' is inscribed in man's subjectivity even if he is not well aware of it.

When Levinas explains how responsibility is indeed infinite and prior to freedom, when he analyses how this responsibility is above all explanation and justification, and how man's subjectivity is structured as a ('*for the other*'), he does not only try to philosophize otherwise: I think he is trying to use the philosophical medium, the *logos*, in order to help us understand the significance of ideas that come from the Torah, and above all the significance of election. The 'break' in man's desire to be, the interruption of being because God is calling and man's answer—'Here I am'—are the source of his new way of understanding responsibility. Levinas uses a philosophical language that in spite of all its greatness was compromised by the terrible calamities of this century. We may think that if such was the case, it is because many philosophers were faithful to the idea that responsibility must be limited by freedom. These philosophers also thought that what happens to the neighbour is indeed less important that the fate of being (Heidegger, 1927). But for Levinas, the ontological question is not the first question in philosophy. According to him the main question is indeed the question of the Good beyond being.

2. Jewish election and substitution

> Surely he hath borne our griefs and carried our sorrows; yet we did esteem him stricken, smitten of God and afflicted. (*Isaiah* 54.4)

> A substitution of me for the others. It is, however, not an alienation, because the other in the same is my substitution for the other through respponsibility, for which I am summoned as someone irreplaceable. (Levinas 1981, 114)

We have now to understand the significance of a strange idea: the idea of substitution. Levinas describes it as 'an inspiration by the other for the other', as an existence through the other and for the other 'but without alienation'. It is 'an inspiration' and this inspiration is the true life of the psyche.

> I exist through the other and for the other, but without this being alienation: I am inspired. This inspiration is the psyche. The psyche can signify this alterity in the same without alienation in the form of incarnation, as being in one's skin, having the other in one's skin. (1981, 115)

It is an 'expiation' and 'the passion of the self':

> The *ego* is not just a being endowed with certain qualities called moral which it would bear as a substance bears attributes, or which would take on as accidents in its becoming. Its exceptional uniqueness in the passivity or the passion of the self is the incessant event of subjection to everything, or substitution. (*ibid.* 117)

And Levinas characterizes it as 'the religiosity of the self' (*ibid.* 117) beyond egoism and altruism. It is also beyond the classical categories of action and passivity. Substitution is 'a being divesting itself, emptying itself of its being, turning itself inside out, and if it can be put thus, the fact of "otherwise than being"'. (*ibid.*, 117)

Now when a being divests itself and bears the weight of the world, it is not a question of freedom. Such a being has nothing to do with the freedom of a subject who decides to behave morally or to live a holy life. It has nothing to do with the naive wish we sometimes have 'to take somebody's place', with the wishful thinking of the *ego* that thinks it is able to take the place of a suffering man for instance. It is not at all a choice but *the very structure of the psyche*. This structure comes from a past we remain unable to remember, from an anarchical past. This goodness of substitution is not the opposite of evil but 'otherwise than being'.

Substitution is described in very concrete terms by Levinas: 'This inwardness without secrets is a pure witness to the inordinateness which already commands me, to the other taking the bread out of my mouth, and making a gift of my own skin' (*ibid.* 138). It is also an exposure to suffering and insult. But this idea also leads towards 'beyond essence', it is indeed the beginning of the 'one for the other', the beginning of humanity and the beginning of the meaning of all meanings. This 'proximity is fraternity before essence and before death, having a meaning despite being and nothingness, despite concepts' (*ibid.* 139). And it gives us the orientation we need in a world that would be otherwise lacking an absolute orientation. The ethical orientation is prior to all cultures which despite their greatness remain unable to give us the meaning of all meanings.

In his most recent books, Levinas expresses this idea in a new way. He explains that *the question of my right to be* has priority over the ontological question. 'The question of my right to be is inseparable from the "for the other" in me, it is as ancient as this "for the other"' (1982, 257). Substitution is linked to 'the fear that by simply being I may be violent and murderous, in spite of my wish and my consciousness' (*ibid.* 262). A subject is overcome by this fear when he faces his neighbour, and this fear does not mean this subject is neurotic but that he begins to understand what is the meaning of all meanings.

We now have to understand what in the Jewish tradition could lead Levinas to this strange idea of substitution. Can we find some similar ideas in this tradition? What does it mean to be bound by the weight of the world and to fear what happens to the neighbour more than what happens to the 'I'? What does 'election' mean for the rabbis?

It is a well known idea in the Jewish tradition that the world would perish if it were not sustained by the Just. The world, in spite of all its iniquity, its immorality and its violence, is forgiven for its wickedness thanks to the just who intercede on its behalf. We already have a famous example in the Torah, when Abraham tries to intercede on behalf of Sodom. That is also why the Jewish tradition thinks he was a more just man than Noah. 'Abraham stood yet before the Lord. And Abraham drew near and said, wilt thou also destroy the righteous with the wicked.' (*Genesis* 18.23). The same idea appears in the Talmud (*Chabbat* 33b): 'When just people do exist, they are responsible for their generation; when they do not exist then children who attend school are the ones who are responsible for their generation'. The Talmud also mentions (*Soucca* 45b) the thirty-six pious men who celebrate the Presence of God among men. It is said that the world is supported by these humble and unknown people.

In the Bible God introduces Himself to the people as the One who supports it and carries it, even in old age. He suffers with the people, goes with it in exile and cries for it. 'Even to your old age I am he; an even to hoar hairs will I carry you: I have made and I will bear, even I will carry, and will deliver you.' (*Isaiah* 46,4).

For his part Levinas quotes the famous passage on the suffering servant: 'He is despised and rejected of men; a man of sorrows and acquainted with grief . . . Surely he hath borne our griefs, and carried our sorrows: yet we did esteem him stricken, smitten of God and afflicted. But he was wounded for our transgressions, he was bruised for our iniquities.' (*Isaiah* 53. 3–5). According to him we have to understand what Isaiah says about the suffering servant as a true description of the suffering subjectivity of a man who atones for the other man's guilt, without being able to hide himself or to protect himself. It fits with his description of the just who gives his life for the other and it also fits with the traditional idea of a God who wants mercy to prevail over harshness. If He was not ready to do so, how could the world survive? In the Talmud the rabbis say: 'Three times a day, God judges the world, when He sees that the world deserves punishment, He leaves His throne of Justice and sits on His throne of Mercy' (*Avoda Zara* 3b). While the *Zohar* does not hesitate to link the verses of Isaiah I have just quoted to the sufferings of the Messiah, of the celestial David:

In heaven, there is a palace which is called the palace of the sick people. The Messiah enters this palace and he calls all sicknesses, all pains, all distresses and all sorrows, and he asks them to come on to him; and they do so. If he had not been ready to undergo Israel's punishment, no man would have been able to put up with the suffering due to man because of his sin . . . Now the Messiah is the one to bear the pains and sorrows of everyone.

According to the Sages, one of the Messiah's names is *Menahem*, which means 'the comforter'. Who is 'the comforter'? He is the one who takes on the suffering of men. Levinas analyses the meaning of this name and stresses its ethical significance, the significance of an 'I' ready to substitute himself for the other, an 'I' ready to take on the distresses of man. Levinas concludes that it means everyone has to act as if he was indeed the Messiah. He adds:

Messianism does not mean we are convinced a man will come and put an end to history. Messianism lies in my ability to take on the suffering of men. It starts when I recognize this responsibility in myself and when I acknowledge my universal responsibility. (1976, 120)

We understand here that, according to him, there is *a connection between the idea of messianism and the concept of substitution* which is a very demanding one since it means the watchfulness of a conscience that is called to suffer for the other, to take on his distresses, to feel guilty if he dies. Levinas wants to give meaning to *our* suffering for the suffering of the other but he never searches for the meaning of the other's suffering.

Philosophers usually do not appreciate such ideas. They do not agree to this meaning of a suffering subjectivity, they are reluctant to abandon the idea that being is the only source of meaning and they oppose the idea that freedom may be immoral. Such ideas may indeed seem very strange and perhaps very devout—which means not philosophical—to thinkers who are accustomed to the absolute priority of ontology. It is true that these ideas are connected to another tradition than the Greek one—the only one which is worth learning according to most philosophers. But it does not mean these ideas are irrational and in Levinas's books they are very rigorous and well argued.

The Sages also speak of suffering out of love—*yessourine chel Ahava*—and they even think these sufferings may bring salvation to the world: 'The one who rejoices when he suffers, brings salvation to the world' (*Taanith* 8a). Such ideas do not only help the Sages find meaning to the just man's misfortune—'The Lord trieth the righteous' (*Psalms* 11.5)—they are connected to the idea of messianism as the advent of a humanity fully for the other. Levinas would say, a humanity called to answer for the other's life; an unselfish humanity, a humanity ready for substitution.

In the *Song of Solomon* (5.8), we can read: 'I charge you, O daughters of Jerusalem, if ye find my beloved, that ye tell him, that I am sick of love'. This verse expresses not only the distress of someone who is lonely and desperate because her love is looked down upon, but also the hope of a salvation and of peace which will occur through love and only through love.

According to the Sages, the need for messianism comes from the exposure to suffering, to its radical evil, the face to face with the invisibility of a death that may occur any time and with an inconsolable despair, a despair that cannot be compensated by anything else. God Himself cannot take on all this despair, but only the 'I' who agrees to his messianic calling. Only man's willingness to take on the other man's despair and his humility will 'relieve the soul'. Only this willingness prevents evil from winning and makes salvation possible. However, for the time being, 'the comforter that should relieve my soul is far from me' (*Lamentations* 1.16).

In the Talmud, Rav Nahman used to say: if the Messiah 'is among the living people, then it is "I"' (*Sanhedrin* 98b.99a). Such is also Levinas's thought: an 'I' which would be really human would indeed be the Messiah. Messianism and Levinas's thought about subjectivity are very similar: *substitution is a messianic idea*. We have here a very good example of Levinas's attempt to explain in philosophical terms an idea—messianism—of which the Greeks were unaware. This messianic idea means it is worth understanding what the Hebrew heritage can teach us when we start listening to its call. A call which is 'beyond being'.

> Substitution, at the limit of being (. . .) is a sacrifice without reserve, without holding back, and in this nonvoluntary—the sacrifice of a hostage designated who has not chosen himself to be hostage, but possibly elected by the Good, in an involuntary election not assumed by the elected one. (1981, 15)

We may of course argue that this messianism or this substitution does not occur in everyday life. Every day we face egoism and evil and not saintliness. Levinas knows substitution is not a mere fact but he explains that it is the prerequisite of humanity. It is the prerequisite of 'otherwise than being', of otherwise than being violent and unconcerned about what happens to our fellow man.

> It is through the condition of being hostage that there can be in the world pity, compassion, pardon and proximity—even the

little there is, even the simple 'after you, sir'. The unconditionality of being hostage is not the limit case of solidarity, but the condition of all solidarity. (1981, 117)

And when the Sages say the world—while waiting for its salvation—relies on the just, on some humble and hidden just people whose goodness and purity counterbalance men's savage egoism, they know as well that the messianic utopia is not a fact but is *the condition* of a little humanity among men. They know that a single good act may comfort men, may sustain the world. 'The one who sustains but a single soul in Israel it is as if he had sustained the whole world' (*Baba Bathra* 11a).

Messianism, substitution, man's feeling that he is responsible facing his neighbour's suffering, 'the scruple to live' when the other man dies, when confronted with his demanding face, do not make man guilty but are signs of his ethical awareness. This awareness comes from a very ancient past, from a very ancient election for which a people had to suffer greatly. As regards Levinas, I think it is also connected with the terrible feeling of surviving while so many others had to die during the Choa. Levinas does not only want to explain the Hebrew idea of messianism and of election in philosophical terms, he wants to give an answer to the terrible anxiety of the survivors, an anxiety which is indeed his own. And his answer is: to survive means to be more and more demanding of oneself. As if the other man's death, that event six million times reproduced in such terrible conditions and with not a single word of comfort, was ordering us to be faithful to a holy command—'You shall therefore be holy, for I am holy' (*Leviticus* 11.45).

Ethical Absolutism and Education*

PETER GARDNER

At a conference I attended not so long ago I suggested to someone who had just read a paper that beneath his apparent commitment to a kind of ethical relativism he was in fact an ethical absolutist. The person I was addressing seemed quite upset by my suggestion and proceeded to argue that my understanding of his paper was somewhat awry. This experience was not new to me. Having taught ethics and philosophy of education courses for many years, courses which have been taken by undergraduates and by members of the teaching profession, I know that if I ever say to those I teach that they are adopting or favouring an absolutist position, then, more than likely, they will regard my remark as something to be opposed and they will often suggest that there must be some misunderstanding on my part. Judging by my experiences, 'absolutist' is a label most undergraduates and teachers wish to disown, particularly at the outset of ethics and philosophy courses, even though many of these disowners seem to subscribe to absolutist positions on such issues as racism, rape and child abuse. In his book *Ethics; Discovering Right and Wrong* Louis P. Pojman, talking about his own findings in this area, makes it clear that my teaching experiences are not unique. Over a period of several years and in several universities Pojman found that most of the students who took his ethics or philosophy courses explicitly rejected absolutism and affirmed support for some kind of relativism even though several of these aspiring relativists subscribed to absolutist positions on various ethical matters (Pojman, 1990, 19).

All of this supports the view that while people might not be too sure what an ethical absolutist is (and for the remainder of this paper I will use 'ethical absolutist' and 'absolutist' interchangeably), many are quite sure that they aren't and don't want to be thought of as absolutists. Indeed, even at the end of my courses, when some students say they are absolutists, this is more of an

*I am most grateful to Mr Steve Johnson, Dr Michael Luntley, Professor Terry Penner, Mr Glynn Phillips and Professor A. Phillips Griffiths for detailed discussion of several of the issues raised in this paper. I am also grateful to all who discussed a shortened version of this paper at the Royal Institute of Philosophy Conference for Teachers of Sixth Forms and at F. E. Colleges, University of Warwick, March, 1993.

admission than a guilt-free declaration, like a revelation about themselves that they wish to be treated confidentially.

But what is it that leads to these states of affairs? For a start we may note that there is often a tendency to associate absolutism with a commitment to simple rigid principles which admit of no exceptions. In fact those who are familiar with some writings in ethics may associate absolutism with some kind of Kantian inflexibility, and, in opposition to such inflexibility, they may argue that situations alter cases, and, as situations change, so we should qualify and amend our principles. Amongst those who are familiar with some writings in ethics there is also a tendency to associate absolutism with the kind of ontology favoured by ethical intuitionists, or to think that, since absolutists are certain of their moral views, they must surely believe that such views can be readily 'seen' by intuition or arrived at by some route which might lead to such certainty. In this connection some people may think that absolutists believe that moral views are readily deducible from facts. But given that many people reject intuitionism and its ontology and endorse the idea of there being a fact-value distinction, absolutism again attracts opponents. In addition, absolutists might be thought of as accepting a kind of ethical fundamentalism and believing that there is a single criterion for determining all rights and wrongs, as well as believing that they know what that criterion is.

More generally, it may be suggested that we live at a time when both prevailing values and prevailing propositional attitudes in the realm of ethics are out of step with absolutism. If, as some suggest, our predominant values as well as much of what is recommended by many contemporary educationists reveal a concern for personal autonomy, freedom, tolerance and respect for different cultures and life-styles, then this may seem difficult to reconcile with the prescriptive nature of moral absolutes, especially as in the past many absolutists in education have been concerned to impose and cultivate particular conceptions of what they have regarded as the good life. There again, in recent times haven't many people, including many teachers, become less sure about what is right and wrong, less certain that they know the answers, in contrast with the supposed moral assuredness of the absolutist? There is, too, a kind of pretentious arrogance associated with absolutism. Not the indifferentism of 'I'm alright Jack', but the presumptive haughtiness of 'I am right Jack', and such an attitude, while it may have characterized the confident inflexibility of Victorian moralizing, may seem hardly suitable for an education for a pluralistic, multicultural society. In a world of many views, the promulgation of one and the berating of opponents may seem at best a matter of crass insensitivity.

These observations may go some way towards explaining absolutism's lack of popularity and attraction, not least in education. They may also go some way to show what people think absolutism is and involves. This in turn helps reveal that absolutism may be thought of as having various strands and facets. But is there something central to absolutism? And must absolutists be committed to questionable meta-ethical and normative positions? Need absolutists be haughty and pushy? Can absolutism be reconciled with educational recommendations that endorse the importance of autonomy, freedom, tolerance and respect for different cultures? These are some of the questions that this paper is concerned to tackle, and I want to begin by considering what we may regard as the logic of absolutism, this being an attempt to identify what is central to the absolutist's position, and to indicate in what ways such a position differs from some other meta-ethical stances. After this I will consider some positions which are often associated with absolutism, then how absolutists may determine right and wrong, and, finally, in my fourth section, I will turn to absolutism and education.

1. The Logic of Absolutism

It is customary for writers on ethics to contrast absolutism with relativism. But this needs to be done with care, for some relativist claims, such as the claim that different people hold different moral views, may be perfectly compatible with absolutism. Where an illuminating incompatibility occurs is when the relativist advances ideas about truth or correctness. For instance, if a relativist supports the conventionalist theory that the truth of a moral view is dependent on whether or not that view is in accord with the conventions and values of some society or culture, then since different societies or cultures may have different conventions and values, the way is open for there to be two conflicting views both of which are true or correct. Similarly, if a relativist favours a kind of subjectivism and maintains that the truth of a moral view depends on whether or not that view is held by someone, then, since different people may have different moral beliefs and attitudes, the way is also open for two conflicting views to be true. In addition, if a relativist subscribes to the normative theory that whether or not an action is right or wrong depends on the values or conventions of the society or culture within which that action is performed, then again it is easy to see how this conventionalist position could lead to the conclusion that there can be conflicting moral views both of which are true or correct. Now it is when relativistic theories lead to conclusions of just this kind that a contrast can readily be drawn and is often drawn between such theories and absolutism, for absolutism has at its centre the idea that if there are conflicting moral views, they cannot both be true; one might be, but at least one is false (see Brandt, 1959, 154).

Seen in this way, two aspects of absolutism may seem particularly worthy of attention, especially at this stage in our inquiry. First, the absolutist accepts that moral views can be true or false. I am aware that some philosophers may prefer to describe this particular matter in different terms to those I have chosen. Some may prefer the claim that moral views are propositional, and some that moral views are assertoric. But rather than become embroiled in arguments about the nature of the bearers of truth, I will content myself with the simple claim that absolutists accept that moral views can be true or false, though I am confident that alternative formulations of the point I am making need not affect what stems from this as far as this paper is concerned. The second matter I want raise here is that the absolutist accepts that the law of the excluded middle applies in ethics, although the absolutist may well add that in ethics, as elsewhere, we need to be careful in identifying contradictories (see Hare, 1989, 25; and Hare, 1967, 318–322). Following on from the warning just given, absolutism can allow for two conflicting views both to be false. It may be argued, for example, that the contradictory of 'X is good' is not 'X is bad' but 'It is not the case that X is good', and if X is morally indifferent, then both 'X is good' and 'X is bad' are mistaken (see Hare, 1967, 318–320).

As for the relativist positions we have mentioned, even though it takes me beyond my brief, it would be remiss of me not point out that supporters of some of the positions we have outlined face difficulties in identifying what are to count as societies or societal or cultural groups, in accounting for the possibility of moral reformers (see Feldman, 1978, 166–167), and in accepting what for many will be seen as an important strand of absolutism, that is, that some things are morally important irrespective of what certain people or societies think of them. This does not mean that absolutists must turn their backs on public opinion, although some may do so; rather, it is to point out that absolutists will recognize there is more to morality than public opinion, and more to determining right and wrong than market research.

While what has been said so far is at best minimal, it is sufficient

to indicate that absolutists will be opposed to various ethical positions, not least to several meta-ethical stances. In this connection,
the absolutists' acceptance of the idea that moral views can be the
bearers of truth values has various implications. It is because of
their acceptance of this idea that absolutists stand opposed to emo-
tivism, which would have us believe that moral views can be no
more true or false than boos and cheers, and to prescriptivism,
which maintains that while moral views may be based on what is
true or false, moral views themselves are prescriptions and, like
imperatives with which they share certain similarities, cannot be
the bearers of truth values (see Hare, 1989, 26; and Hare, 1952,
Chs. 1, 2, 11 and 12). We can add that insofar as absolutists accept
that moral views can be true or false, accounting for the formal
validity of moral argument, as well as accounting for the nature of
moral belief and assertion and the logic of moral disagreement
hold no terrors for absolutists, though those who see moral views
in a different light have often worked long and tortuously attempting to explicate these matters.

Some might also claim that the absolutist will oppose J. L.
Mackie (1946, 1977) and those who subscribe to his and similar
error theories, but this may not be clear cut. If error theorists
claim that all moral views are false, then they endorse the idea that
moral views can be the bearers of truth values and they also support the thesis that if there are two conflicting ethical views they
cannot both be true. Yet it might be claimed that there is a clear
point of difference here because, unlike the error theorist, the
absolutist accepts that some ethical views can be true. But, then, it
might be argued that, when pressed, even an error theorist would
accept that the statements 'Nothing is good' and 'Nothing is bad'
are true. If so, then, perhaps, to draw a contrast here we may have
to insist that absolutists accept that some non-negative moral judgments are true.

So far we have tried to say something about the logic of absolutism and the ways in which the absolutist stands opposed to
some influential ethical theories. What I turn to next are attempts
to attribute to absolutism or to associate it with positions which, as
we saw in our introduction, might serve as grounds for criticism
and which may encourage people to deny that they are absolutists.

2. Attributions and Associations

Two attributions of particular importance are to be found in the
work of two influential writers on ethics, Bernard Mayo and R. M.

Peter Gardner

Hare. In *The Philosophy of Right and Wrong* Mayo raises the question: 'Do the facts of moral progress and decline, properly understood, support absolutism or relativism?' (1986, 86). Later, after examining how absolutists may account for such progress and decline, he concludes: 'So, on the realist view of morality, moral progress and decline do make good sense' (1986, 90).The assumption here is that absolutists are realists. Now realism in ethics is usually understood as a theory which supports a particular ontology and which endorses the assertion that there are moral properties which, borrowing from Mackie, are 'part of the fabric of the world' (Mackie, 1977, 15). Moreover, realists often seem to embrace a particular kind of moral epistemology which likens our coming to know in morals with our perceptions of or our ways of knowing about the 'natural' world.

What can be pointed out here is that even if all moral realists have been or need be absolutists, this does not mean that all absolutists need be realists. A commitment to moral truth is not *ipso facto* a commitment to the ontology and epistemology of moral realism. Precisely why Mayo moves from talk about absolutism to talk of realism is not something I feel I can explain. But it is a move we should be mindful of and, in so far as 'realism' is understood in its customary way, be ready to correct. As I remarked earlier, those with some familiarity with moral philosophy may also think that absolutists need be realists, so it is not just moral philosophers who need correcting on this matter.

Turning to R. M. Hare, he sees a commitment to moral truth leading to what he calls *descriptivism*. This is borne out not just by the fact that Hare sees a commitment to moral truth challenging what he describes as 'non-descriptivism' (Hare, 1989, 25), but also by the way he responds to this 'challenge'. For he does so by saying that a moral statement has descriptive meaning, this being our reason or ground for holding that statement, and then he adds: 'it may be this element (its descriptive meaning) to which we are adverting when we call a moral statement true or false; (but) . . . this does not prevent there being other, non-descriptive elements in its meaning, which are sufficient to make it altogether misleading to call it a descriptive statement *tout court*' (Hare, 1989, 26). Given the start of this line of reasoning, we might have expected Hare to have concluded: to make it altogether misleading to call it a true or false statement *tout court*. But in place of 'true or false' we have 'descriptive'. For Hare, then, if one accepts that moral views themselves, and not just their grounds, can be the bearers of truth values, one is a descriptivist. This means that to be an absolutist is to be a descriptivist.

Those familiar with his earlier works may think that for Hare 'naturalism' and 'descriptivism' are synonyms, but it is clear from his later writings, from which the previous remarks are taken, that for Hare descriptivism covers both naturalism, including what Moore called metaphysical ethics, and intuitionism (see Hare, 1981, 76). So, for Hare to accept that moral views themselves can be true or false is to accept that factual statements, where a metaphysical statement counts as factual, entail moral views or it is to accept the kind of ontology one associates with ethical intuitionism and with it what Hare describes as the view that moral truths are 'known to be true by the special faculty of moral intuition, by which we . . . discern . . . moral properties. . .' (Hare, 1981, 77–78). With Hare's approach, unlike Mayo's, the absolutist has a choice, though the two options Hare proffers have both come in for much criticism. But why should Hare be concerned to restrict those committed to moral truth in this way? The answer, I believe, lies in Hare's views on the truth criteria of what he regards as non-analytic truths (see *ibid.*). For Hare, it seems, these criteria either entail, without being explicitly described by, or they are explicitly described by the statement for which they are the truth criteria such that moral terms in moral statements refer to and identify moral properties. Those who wish to argue that whether or not something is true in morals depends on what exists in the world but that this relationship of dependency is neither a matter of entailment nor a simple matter of mapping the elements of a moral statement on to reality will wish to contest Hare's restrictive approach to truth criteria, and those who would wish to argue this way seem to have an approach to truth criteria not considered by Hare. This is why one may argue that one can be an absolutist without having to accept either of the options offered by Hare. Of course, some absolutists are naturalists and some are intuitionists; but there is no necessary connection here. And this needs to be pointed out not just to philosophers but also to those whose contact with ethics has led them to form this conclusion as well.

In response to what has been said, some may counter: but since absolutists are certain of what is morally correct, then surely they must accept either that there are moral properties whose presence they grasp with some kind of certainty or that their moral views are entailed by facts about the world of which they are certain. For how else can they be so sure of their moral views? The error here, of course, is that of accepting that absolutists need be sure or certain of their moral views. Admittedly some absolutists may be exemplars of moral confidence and assuredness, but, as will be stressed later, some absolutists may not feel at all confident that they know what is right or wrong or even of how to achieve such knowledge. Absolutism, as I have been trying to show, is rooted in a commitment to truth and consistency; it is not an epistemological position about being sure or certain.

Turning to associations, the one I want to consider concerns simple rigid principles. Maybe it is a consequence of the association of Kantianism with absolutism that many people associate absolutism with simple rigid principles, and the following remarks from Pojman reinforce this very association: 'The absolutist believes that there are nonoverridable moral principles that ought never to be violated. Kant's system . . . is a good example of this: One ought never break a promise, no matter what' (Pojman, 1990, 30). There again, when absolutists are criticized for encountering problems over conflicting principles, those principles are frequently presented as simple and general, and not allowing for qualification (see Mackie, 1977, 161).

Because of his rejection of absolutism's supposed commitment to the general and the unqualified, Pojman distinguishes between what he calls objectivism and absolutism, for the objectivist, he insists, can have principles which are qualified, principles like, 'It is morally wrong to torture people for the fun of it' (Pojman, 1990, 31), where the words 'for the fun of it' provide a significant qualification. As far as Pojman is concerned, then, correct moral principles may well be qualified; they need not be simple and rigid.

I am reminded here of Hare's observation, an observation made when he was distinguishing between universal and general principles, that 'the principles which are adhered to in making moral judgments are seldom very simple or general, at any rate when the judgments are made by intelligent people who have had any wide experience of life' (Hare, 1963, 38). Now I see no reason why commitment to the logic of absolutism prevents absolutists from having principles which are universal with regard to quantification, but which might be qualified in all sorts of ways and, so, be far from general. In brief, I see no reason why absolutists cannot be intelligent people with a wide experience of life. Looked at in this light, Pojman appears just as much an absolutist as a Kantian; it is just that Pojman's principles are qualified in various ways. And if they are to avoid the impasse that can occur when simple principles conflict, absolutists with more than one basic principle may have to qualify their principles. That they can do this and that they need not be stuck with simple and rigid beliefs, is well worth emphasizing, for, as we noted at the outset, it is something of a popular view that all absolutists are committed to Kantian-like principles.

Concerning the title 'objectivist', favoured by Pojman, this is most frequently used in ethics to describe someone opposed to subjectivism, and, unfortunately, the term 'subjectivism' is used somewhat loosely (see Mackie, 1977, 17; and 'Some Confusions about Subjectivity' in Hare, 1989). Yet, if we stick with our earlier account according to which subjectivism is a particular species of relativism, we can agree that Pojman is opposed to subjectivism and can be called an objectivist. But since under our account subjectivism is only one species of relativism and Pojman is not a relativist, we may seek a more precise description of his position. Furthermore, if one of the differences between the objectivist and the subjectivist is that the former rejects the idea that the determinants of truth in morals are personal matters, like a person's beliefs or attitudes, then conventionalists may also oppose subjectivism for this very reason, since they believe that the determinants of moral truths are objective, not subjective, matters. Bearing this in mind, it would surely be best to call Pojman an absolutist.

Our inquiries in this section have been undertaken with a view to showing that absolutists are not necessarily committed to the ontologies and/or epistemologies of realists or intuitionists or naturalists or to simplistic views about moral principles. What is central to absolutism is a commitment to truth and consistency. Those who have this commitment may endorse various meta-ethical and normative positions, but those positions that we have just considered, though they have been embraced by some absolutists, do not have to be embraced by absolutists. Absolutism is not the first theory, and no doubt will not be the last, to suffer from its associations or because of the additional preferences of some of its adherents.

3. Determining Right and Wrong

In our earlier consideration of relativism we identified some of the grounds that absolutists will dismiss as determinants of what is right and wrong, but we have not considered what else absolutists may have to say about this kind of determination. In this section I hope to shed some light on this matter.

As we saw at the outset absolutists are often thought of as believing that there is a single criterion or some single means for determining all rights and wrongs and, perhaps, of believing that they have discovered that very criterion. Fred Feldman had at least the first part of this view in mind when he claimed 'that absolutism is the view that there is one criterion of morality valid for all people at all times' (Feldman, 1978, 162). He went on to say that absolutists accept two schemata:

A: An act is morally right if and only if ....

and

B: There is a way of filling the blank in *A* that is nontrivial and results in *A* becoming a universally valid criterion of morality (*Ibid.*)

While various attempts to fill in the blank in *A* have been made by a variety of moralists who were absolutists, and various Kantians, utilitarians and theological moralists would be amongst those who could be mentioned here, what I want to consider is whether all absolutists can be accommodated within Feldman's account of absolutism.

If, for example, we were to understand Feldman as claiming that to be an absolutist one has to be able to outline what one takes as satsifying the demands of his schemata, then this would rule out those who believe there is a universally valid criterion, but who confess to not having found it and who admit that *they* may never do so, as well as some who may believe that no one ever will. Amongst these some may believe that they have arrived at sufficient conditions for determining some rights and wrongs, but they may also believe that they, and maybe others, are still a long way short of the all-powerful criterion that is needed to complete Feldman's schemata.

I would argue that all those just described are absolutists providing, that is, they accept the logic of absolutism and, thereby, oppose those relativistic ways of trying to complete schema *A* that would lead to those conflicts which are incompatible with the logic of absolutism. This helps explain why absolutists need not appear pretentious or arrogant or haughty. They need not appear as if they have discovered the Holy Grail of morality; they can be those who, though committed to its existence, have doubts about their or anyone's chances of discovering it. Absolutists can be sceptical.

Furthermore, there are those who, though committed to the logic of absolutism and convinced that some conditions that they can describe are sufficient to make some things right or wrong, may not wish to go much further than this. Take, for example, Pojman's claim, to which we referred at the outset, that many of his students, who profess to being relativists, are in fact absolutists. Pojman defends his claim by pointing out that many of his students accept such principles as 'abortion except to save the mother's life is always wrong' and 'capital punishment is always morally wrong' (Pojman, 1990, 19). Interestingly, the principle mentioned here which proscribes abortion except in certain cases looks like a paradigm case of a *qualified* principle, which casts doubt on the extent to which even Pojman is clear about his own distinction between objectivism and absolutism. Still, my point in quoting these remarks from Pojman is to draw attention to the fact that he is saying that someone is an absolutist in the event that they accept that there is a non-trivial way of providing sufficient conditions for some things being wrong and, we may presume, for some things being right. Bearing in mind what was said earlier, we may add that whatever sufficient conditions are provided should exclude those relativistic criteria, such as those concerned with conventionality, which yield conflicts.

Yet, it is difficult to see how one could argue that those who subscribe to this weaker position must be committed to the idea that there is a way of meeting the demands of Feldman's schemata, and even if some supporters of this weaker position accept that there is some ultimate criterion, they might admit, as we noted earlier, that they cannot say what that criterion is.

As for attitudes, some supporters of the weaker position we have been considering may feel confident and sure that they have identified what is sufficient to make some deeds right and some wrong. But some who support this weaker position may merely *think* they have identified what is sufficient in some cases, and feel neither certain nor sure. And, though it may seem obvious, in view of the unnecessary associations and misunderstandings that abound in this area, we could add that those who support this weaker position need not be assertive or be committed to the unbridled promulgation of their views or be ready to condemn those with whom they disagree. As absolutists they are committed to believing that those who hold conflicting moral opinions to theirs are mistaken, but one can believe others are mistaken without feeling certain that they are and without being abrasive or aggressive. You may believe others are mistaken without ever letting this be known. This is one of the important social arts.

In assessing the satisfactoriness of Feldman's account of absolutism, we also need to concern ourselves with those who hold that certain things are *prima facie* right and wrong. I am aware that in considering the principle about abortion above we may have touched on this matter already, but what I want to do here is to consider in general terms the position of those who hold that fundamental moral principles are of the *prima facie* variety. Those who subscribe to this position may have non-trivial ways of providing sufficient conditions for some things being actually right.

If, for instance, promise keeping is seen as *prima facie* right, then they could say: if it is true of an act that it is a case of promise keeping, then, all things being equal, that act is right, that is, actually right, and here the *ceteris paribus* clause could be unpacked in terms of there being no competing or overriding *prima facie* right deeds and of the act having no overriding *prima facie* wrong consequences, etc.

Now what I want to stress is that those who support this position, need not have available a non-trivial way of providing the ultimate criterion that Feldman's schemata demand. In fact within this group there might be those who might doubt whether it is possible to advance such a criterion. As for the attitudes of those who support this type of stance, it is worth recalling that W. D. Ross, arguably the most famous supporter of the position we are considering, insisted: 'There is therefore much truth in the description of the right act (meaning the actually right act) as a fortunate act' because, 'If we cannot be certain that it is right, it is our own good fortune if the act we do is the right act' (Ross, 1930, 31). There is no haughtiness or arrogance here. Ross may have felt certain about his *prima facie* principles, but the confidence of *a priori* insight did not extend to particular decisions.

The final position I want to consider in this part of my paper involves the idea that a variety of things are good, that these things can be in competition with each other and that when this happens we are faced with a conflict between incommensurable values (see Berlin, 1980, 198). Some who have written about such values seem to suggest that there is some way of deciding rationally between some incommensurables (see Williams, 1981, 77), which may call into call into question what some writers mean by incommensurability. Suppose, however, someone accepted that faced with a conflict between certain values, there could be no rational way of deciding between them, not because there are no right answers, but because there cannot be a criterion, calculus or standard to resolve such conflicts. Such a person could, it seems, be an absolutist, even though he or she would oppose Feldman's thesis that absolutists are committed to some single universal moral determinant. This again suggests that Feldman's account of absolutism is too restrictive.

Yet suppose someone went further than the position just mapped out and insisted that when incommensurable values conflict, it is not just that there is no means or criterion for reaching solutions; it is that there are no solutions. It is not that the claim that we are right to pursue one such value, say freedom, at the expense of another, say equality, in a particular conflict situation is true while the converse claim is false; it is that neither claim is false. Given this stance, and the law of the excluded middle, then we would have a challenge to the thesis that there is a single universal moral determinant for all that is right. More significantly, it is the law of the excluded middle that this stance challenges, just at it challenges the view that there cannot be conflicting moral views without one being mistaken. In short, this stance on incommensurables is incompatible with absolutism.

Now I would contend that with the exception of this last position, all of the other stances we have explored in this section are absolutist, even though in their various ways they may not satisfy Feldman's demands. Some absolutists accept there is and may be prepared to advance what they regard as *the* single ultimate moral standard, but this is by no means true of all absolutists. Absolutism, we can say, is much wider than Feldman suggests. In fact, given that I would hold back from any claim about completeness, absolutism could well embrace more normative stances than those I have adumbrated.

At the same time as developing my case against Feldman, I have also tried to indicate that the various absolutist positions I have outlined need not give rise to the attitudes and behaviour that many people associate with absolutism. The picture of the absolutist as the person who is arrogant, totally convinced of the certainty of a set of rigid principles, bent on promulgation and never refraining from condemning and castigating those who do not share his or her stance and values is a caricature and as wrong in its own way as the picture of the liberal as fence-sitting, uncommitted, wishy-washy and neurotically indecisive. Absolutists need not be convinced that they know all the answers, they might be unsure about many of the answers they have reached, they might reject the idea that they have a right to promulgate their answers, and they might in no way feel that it is right to object to or condemn those who have reached different answers. And this is something I will also pursue in my next section which deals with education.

4. Absolutism and Education

Education has frequently involved attempts by absolutists to impose their conceptions of the ideal society and the good life. From Plato to recent Prime Ministers absolutists have had their visions, their ideals, and have used the educational process as a vehicle for promoting their view of what is good and for cultivating those attitudes they have seen as desirable. Opposition to such strategies has often come from those who have stressed the importance of personal autonomy, of freedom and of individuals working out their lives for themselves. These same opponents, at least implicitly, have urged the need for more tolerance, for less concern to impose one set of ideals and for less antagonism towards pluralism. Indeed, as was noted earlier, the more multicultural and pluralistic societies become, the more an education rooted in some kind of absolutism will be seen as anachronisitic.

Those committed to absolutism cannot respond to such criticisms by denying that certain absolutist conceptions of the ideal society and the good life have been very influential in educational thought and planning. But what those committed to absolutism can do is to point out that not all absolutists need share the ideals or support the educational recommendations of those who are coming under attack here. As I trust our arguments have shown, absolutism is a broad church, and while it can list among its faithful some who may be criticized by those educationists who value autonomy, tolerance and pluralism, what must be emphasized is that those who would mount such criticisms may themselves be absolutists. Take, for instance, those who value the autonomy of the individual and whose educational recommendations reflect their position. Given their stance, then, I take it, they regard some moral views about the value or *prima facie* value of autonomy as correct, they may well regard the contradictories of these views as false, they may well believe that those individuals or cultures which support those contradictories are mistaken, and they may well believe that their stance on autonomy is true irrespective of what the conventions of different cultures might support. Indeed, if they were not prepared to adopt these positions, we would surely wonder what their commitment to autonomy amounted to. In brief, it is not too difficult to see how one may start to argue that those who are committed to personal autonomy, including those educationists who believe that it is one of the ideals that education should aim to develop, are themselves absolutists.

As for freedom and tolerance, we could repeat similar arguments to those just outlined about autonomy and claim that those who are committed to freedom and tolerance as important social and educational principles are likely to be absolutists as well. It might also be worth stressing that while people often assume there is some firm and unproblematic linkage between conventionalism and tolerance, the opposite is in fact the case. After all, there may well be societies or cultures where to be intolerant is to be conventional (see Feldman, 1978, 171–172). Possibly those who think there is a firm and unproblematic linkage between conventionalism and tolerance reason this way: when people act in accordance with the norms and conventions of their own societies, they are doing what is right, therefore, even though you may belong to a society with different values and conventions to some other society, you should not try to stop or change or condemn what those in that other society do when they are acting in accordance with their norms and standards; you should be tolerant towards their conventional deeds. But what is the status of the claims that you should not try to stop or change or condemn, but should be tolerant? And what if your society has the (imperialistic?) convention of condemning and being intolerant to anyone who acts in ways which differ from those your society regards as right, no matter who they are or where they live?

What, then, of pluralism? Is it incompatible with absolutism? Well, for a start we can repeat what was said at the outset that acceptance of the fact of pluralism, that is, that different people, cultures and societies subscribe to different values and standards, may be perfectly compatible with absolutism. Some absolutists may even welcome the fact that people have different life-styles. A hedonistic utilitarian, for instance, who accepts that different things make different people happy, will see it as morally important that life's rich tapestry does not give way to uniformity. There again, a utilitarian who is convinced that attempting to change cultural traditions can be painful and disruptive and that for long-term happiness people need firm cultural roots, may also support some kind of cultural pluralism.

However, in my experience, when people suggest that there is an incompatibility between absolutism and pluralism or multiculturalism, what they seem to have in mind is not that there is a conflict between absolutism and the fact of cultural or societal differences; instead, what they have in mind is a belief in the autonomy of cultures, a belief that each culture has its own moral truths and its own criteria for determining what ought to be done, and should only be assessed in its own terms. It is just this stance which is encouraged by the type of view advanced by Mal Leicester (1986) in her defence of multicultural education. According to Leicester: 'A multicultural education reflects a diversity of equally valid modes of thought and ways of life' (1986, 4).

Understood in these terms, a commitment to pluralism may well be incompatlble with absolutism, and I will have more to say about this presently, but even in this area absolutists need to guard against objections which may involve misunderstandings. Consider, for example, the following attack on absolutism from Leicester which is also part of her defence of what she regards as a

91

multicultural education: 'An absolutist assumes that her own cultural laws of thought and value judgments are *THE* only valid laws of thought and *THE* only valid value judgments and thus judges cultural alternatives from a perspective external to them. . .' (1986, 4–5; Leicester's emphases.) Against this we can point out that an absolutist need in no way endorse the kind of chauvinism or ethnocentrism that Lelcester seems to have in mind. In fact there is no reason why an absolutist may not criticize the values of his or her own culture, just as Leicester may criticize her and my culture for being racist and sexist. But the fact that one criticizes one's own culture in no way means that one is, *ipso facto*, engaging in some kind of self-criticism or that such criticism need detract from one's absolutism.

Of course, throughout this area there is the problem of whether a culture's values are as readily identifiable or as homogeneous as some might assume. But, leaving this matter aside, where I believe Leicester is right is that absolutists could accept that the value judgments of one culture, which might be their own culture, are correct. Yet there need be nothing sinister in this. Suppose, for instance, absolutists, who believe that what is in accordance with their culture's values is correct, were to offer as a defence of their stance the arguments that their culture's values were most likely to promote happiness or were best suited to allow people to determine their lives for themselves or respected human rights, or some similar line of reasoning. Then those who present such defences may be seen as stressing that it is a matter of coincidence that what they regard as morally important is in tune with their society's values. If sincere, such defences, though open to accusations about factual error, surely make the charge of being ethnocentric or some similar moral condemnation out of place.

Returning to the conflict between absolutism and pluralism, if support for pluralism is to be seen as endorsing Leicester's claim that each culture has its own valid modes of thought, then this, I take it, is something the absolutist could not subscribe to. For presumably one of the things Leicester would allow is that there can be two conflicting moral views which are both correct, and, as we have seen from the outset of this paper, this is something the absolutist would oppose. One consequence of this is that while an absolutist could readily take a stand on the evils of racism or sexism or slavery, and do so despite what his or her or any other society did, conventionalists, like Leicester, may well find this impossible to do. Equally absolutists could think that the norms and values of some cultures are wrong and be prepared to criticise those same cultures. Conventionalists, on the other hand, may wish to oppose these thoughts and activities on the grounds that such absolutists would be doing something mistaken, even something morally reprehensible, though given their own thesis it is difficult to see how conventionalists could consistently advance such criticisms. As when they recommend tolerance, conventionalists may often be inclined to challenge their own thesis.

It should be noted, however, that being prepared to regard the norms and conventions of some cultures as wrong does not mean that absolutists need advance naive, unreflective or uninformed criticisms or proceed to condemn or berate those whose values they regard as mistaken. To repeat what was said earlier: they might not even make their views known. In fact the principle that one inquire deeply into the underlying reasons of practices and norms before evaluating them, like a principle proscribing vituperation except under very special circumstances, is one that absolutists could support, though conventionalists, it seems, could again challenge their own thesis by trying to embrace these values.

It should also be noted that a preparedness to evaluate does not mean that absolutists cannot respect different cultures or that in some way absolutism need threaten respect. What we should guard against here is the idea that to be prepared to accept that some of the moral beliefs of a culture are mistaken is in itself to fail to show that culture the respect it deserves or even to be disrespectful towards it (see Gardner, 1992). What we ought to remember is that respect's quality is grossly constrained if it is only for those with whom we may not disagree. Were it not so, respect could start to look like a species of narcissism.

So it seems that many of the criticisms of absolutism which might be advanced by contemporary educationists are ones that can be met. Absolutists do not *have* to accept what some see as restrictive conceptions of the good life or the ideal state; and they need not turn their backs on autonomy or freedom or tolerance. In fact many of the stances taken on these matters, like many of the prescriptions advanced by those with a concern for pluralism and respect, seem themselves to be absolutist. Still, some might say that while I have defended absolutism against the reservations of various educationists, my defence could have been much more vigorous. The same people might argue that there is a strong connection, they might even speak of a conceptual connection, between education and truth, and, hence, between education and absolutism. That I have not pursued this line of reasoning reveals a desire to avoid being accused of using what might be seen as a persuasive definition of education. Fearful of founding my case on what may seem mere stipulation, I have argued along different lines. Those who think I could have been more vigorous are free to rehearse their own responses.

Conclusion

At the heart of absolutism, as I have tried to explain, lies a commitment to truth and consistency. This in turn has its implications for meta-ethics and normative ethics and for education as well, but these implications are by no means as numerous, as profound or as worriesome as many critics take them to be. Absolutists need not be committed to simple truths, to exotic ontologies, to some fundamental all powerful criterion or be ethnocentric. Equally, they need not be haughty promulgators; far from being pushy and assured moralists, absolutists could well be uncertain, diffident and restrained. And many of the values that in recent times have been espoused by educationists and which may challenge more traditional and prescriptive educational philosophies, do not involve a rejection of absolutism or show that absolutism is incompatible with liberal educational values.

Moreover, to abandon what is central to absolutism is to find oneself having to rethink and redefine moral argument, moral belief, moral inquiry and moral education. These are not problems the absolutist faces. But this does not mean that absolutism is free from problems. At the meta-ethical level absolutists face the difficulty of explaining how, if moral views can be the bearers of truth values, they can also move and guide us in the way they do. At the normative level absolutists face the problem of having to support their moral beliefs and defend their truth. The former problem is one that I believe can be tackled without sacrificing the logical status of moral views as bearers of truth values, though clearly this is not the place to pursue this matter. The latter problem will, perhaps, always be with us as long as we take morals seriously.

'Absolutist', therefore, is not a label we need shun or fight shy of. It is not a description that teachers should disavow or educationists disclaim or students disown. If in future you are called an absolutist, don't immediately insist you have been misunderstood, and if you recognize that you are an absolutist, don't admit to being one. Admitting is the wrong kind of illocutionary act altogether. Just say that you are. After all, most of us are. Aren't we?

Morals and Politics

ANTHONY QUINTON

I

My title, as it stands, is not very informative. The two terms that occur in it are so commonly conjoined, in the philosophical world, at any rate, that it can be no surprise to find them together. My aim, however, is to go some way, at least, towards disconnecting them. My thesis is, to put it briefly, that it is a mistake to see political philosophy as a subordinate part of moral philosophy and thus to suppose that the characteristic problems of the former are of the same kind as those of the latter. More concretely, the problems of politics itself are not generally or primarily, let alone exclusively, moral in nature. We all know that political problems are not, to any great extent, approached by those involved with them, from a moral point of view. I shall argue that it is not reasonable that they should be. But the philosophical habit of running the two things together encourages a kind of moral absolutism in political thinking, and from time to time in political practice, which has bad results, not necessarily morally bad, just bad.

The most obvious symptom of the unreflective institutional jumbling of moral and politics is the common exposure of students to courses, and subsequent examination papers, on 'moral and political philosophy'. This compound is correspondingly present in textbooks. It may be explicit as in Windelband's *Introduction to Philosophy* (1921) (where they stand cheek by jowl under the general heading 'practical philosophy'). in E. F. Carritt's *Morals and Politics* of 1935 and his *Ethical and Political Thinking* of 1947 and in C. E. M. Joad's *Guide to the Philosophy of Morals and Politics* of 1938 (a work to which many philosophers of my generation perhaps owe rather more than they would readily admit). More usually, comprehensive books on moral philosophy will contain a political section. Two of the twenty chapters of Brandt's *Ethical Theory* (1959) are about distributive justice and human rights, two of the eleven parts of Hospers's *Human Conduct* (1982) are about political ethics and justice, one of the five sections of Raphael's *Moral Philosophy* (1981) is called 'ethics and politics' and covers justice and liberty.

One indication of what I take to be the fairly far-reaching distinctness of moral and political philosophy is the large disparity between the lists of the classical contributions to the two disciplines in the post-medieval period. The major moral philosophers are Butler, Hume, Kant, Mill, Sidgwick and Moore. The major political philosophers are Machiavelli, Hobbes, Locke, Burke, Rousseau, Hegel, Mill and Marx. Mill is the only member of both lists. Hume and, in a smaller way, Kant contributed something to political philosophy. Hobbes and Hegel have some standing as moral philosophers. But the majority of these philosophers are either one thing or the other. In my experience, the same segregation is to be found among common or garden philosophers in the present age: those who teach one subject are seldom willing or able to teach the other. In the last few decades, however, the work of Rawls, in particular, and to some extent also that of Dworkin, has tended to bring the two subjects together.

II

These are fairly external considerations. To disentangle moral and political philosophy it will be best to go directly to a comparison of the nature and main problems of the two disciplines as they are ordinarily conceived. The disentangling of their objects, of morals and politics themselves, will be taken up later. The central issue of moral philosophy is that of how, if at all, moral beliefs, whether general rules or judgments of particular cases, are to be justified. That inquiry presupposes a clear conception of what makes a belief moral. But it is seldom adequately supplied with one. It is very commonly assumed without qualification that a belief is moral if its natural expression contains the words *good, right* or *ought*. That is an error and one that has undesirable consequences. The fact is that these words occur in all the varieties of practical discourse; in what Kant called 'counsels of prudence' and 'rules of skill', in bodies of guidance that do not fall comfortably into either of these categories such as the rules of healthy living, and, of course, in political reasoning and judgment. (There are some exclusively moral words—*obligation, virtuous* and *praiseworthy*, for example—but they are to be found in only a small fraction of recognizedly moral discourse.)

Whether preceded by an account of the domain of the moral or not, the central issue of moral philosophy is that of the justification of moral beliefs. To some extent that is a matter internal to morality, that of basing one kind of moral belief on another, as when the rightness of an action is derived from the goodness of the consequences to which it leads. The harder question, as we all know, is how ultimate moral beliefs, whatever form they have, are to be established. To make any headway in either of these types of inquiry it is essential to be clear about the meaning of the terms involved.

Political philosophy, as ordinarily practised, does, or should, begin with a delimitation of its scope, and is to that extent parallel to moral philosophy. Usually that concentrates on the problem of defining the state, often by way of an investigation of the notion of sovereignty. That way of proceeding assumes that politics is activity related to the state: obeying its laws, securing control of it for oneself or others, actually running it. Other institutions have their politics too; businesses, clubs, churches, trade unions, professional associations and so on, even perhaps families. But the convention of taking activity related to the state as literal or primary politics is a reasonable one.

But at this point the two philosophical disciplines diverge. There is no identifiable field of study which inquires into the justification of political beliefs. They are far too various for it to be a coherent undertaking. That is because the varieties of political activity are so varied. They can be classified without too much squeezing under four heads. First, there is the activity of obeying the law, expected of one who may be called, with only the appearance of paradox, the passive citizen. Secondly, there are the characteristic activities of the active citizen: voting, first of all, in constitutional systems where it is provided for and equipping oneself to vote effectively by acquiring the relevant political information. (Even where there is no voting or it is merely an empty ritual it is worth becoming politically informed. Voting is not the only way of bringing pressure to bear on governments and it is a good thing anyway for the passive subject to have some idea what they are likely to do.) Thirdly, there is the activity of the politically involved: persuading, organizing, running for or otherwise seeking office. Finally, there is the work of ruling or governing proper, most conspicuously as legislator or policy-maker, but also as administrative subordinate.

The traditionally central problem of political philosophy concentrates on the passive citizen. It asks why the citizen should obey the state and conform his behaviour to its laws, poses, in other words, the problem of the grounds of political obligation. To describe the problem in that second, more polysyllabic way begs the question in favour of an answer in moral terms. There can be, and obviously are, several good reasons of a non-moral character for thinking that one ought to obey the state, a matter that I shall look into more fully later.

Anthony Quinton

Since Locke, at any rate, the theoretical function of the problem of political obligation has been to set limits to the legitimate activity of the state by laying down conditions for the citizen's obligation. These take the form of retained natural rights which the state may not infringe on pain of forfeiting its legitimate authority. These natural or 'human' rights are in current political philosophizing argued for directly. They are still seen as limits to the authority of the state but are not arrived at by an argumentative circuit through a mythical agreement. The instances usually concentrated on are liberty, justice and its close associate: equality, property, the political right of democratic participation. The most important of all, namely security, seems to be taken for granted. That can be explained, but not entirely excused, by the fact that a state that does not provide a fair measure of it does not simply lose its legitimacy, it ceases to be a state altogether. That is the point made by the reference to 'habitual obedience' that occurs in the definition of sovereignty given by the nineteenth century John Austin. More attention could be paid to the right, or any rate value, by which ordinary citizens seem to set most store: prosperity.

Moral and political philosophy, then, should both start with an explicit demarcation of their respective fields. When they do, the demarcations, however, are of very different kinds of thing. Moral philosophy needs to pick out moral beliefs from other practical beliefs (prudential, technical and so on) and from beliefs generally. Political philosophy needs to pick out political from other forms of activity or, more usually, state-related activity.

The traditionally central question of political philosophy, that of the grounds of political obligation, or, less question-beggingly, of why citizens should obey the state, has a parallel in moral philosophy: the question—why should I be moral? But while the political question seems to be a substantial one, although, I shall argue, not a mainly, let alone exclusively, moral one, the moral opposite number is either a prudential question or it is empty. Of course I morally ought to do what I morally ought to do.

Up to this point, then, there are parallels between moral and political philosophy, but they go no way towards showing that the second is part of the first. That is clearly shown by the fact that there are same parallel elements in the largely hypothetical discipline of prudential philosophy. There is, of course, a great deal of prudential thinking, much of it stored in works of practical wisdom. Prudential philosophy, were it to come into existence, would need to delimit its field, to judgments or actions directed towards the long-term interest of the agent, and to confront the question: why should I be prudent?

After these first two, more or less parallel, elements moral and political philosophy begin to diverge. Philosophers who explicitly assimilate them tend to conceal the fact by various emolliently general formulae. Both, says D. D. Raphael, are concerned with 'beliefs about what is right and good for man and society'. Something a bit less efficient in covering up the differences is Joad's claim that moral philosophy deals with the nature of the good life for the individual, political philosophy with the principles that should govern the association of individuals in societies. The assumption behind these quotations seems to be that because both deal with what is right and good or with what is good and with what should be done they are, therefore, fundamentally the same. But counsels of prudence and rules of skill also deal with what is right and good and should be done.

The moral appropriation or requisition of the words *good, right* and *ought* is particularly blatant in J. L. Mackie's *Ethics: Inventing Right and Wrong* (1977). He says 'if ethics is the general theory of right and wrong in choices and actions . . ., then political actions and aims and decisions come with its scope'. The antecedent of this conditional is false; it is not ethics, understood as moral philosophy, that is the general theory of right and wrong in actions but a more general discipline, the theory of value. Political activity does, indeed, come within the scope of morality, it can properly be condemned in appropriate cases as wicked, dishonest, cruel and so forth. But so, equally, can actions motivated by prudential consideration or chosen as instances of technical skill. It does not follow from the fact that political activity can he morally judged that the politically right and good are the morally right and good.

III

I shall turn now to a comparison of morality and politics, understood as state-related political activity. Both are, certainly, forms of decision and action. In both there is the preferred decision, which is the right one or the one one ought to make, and it is, typically, intended to bring about a good result. But that, for reasons I have given, does not subordinate the second to the first.

An initial difference is that morality is universal, in the sense that its rules are taken to apply to everyone. Or nearly everyone: its rules are not incumbent on infants, the insane or the mentally defective. We do not always do even what we think right, let alone what really is right (if there is such a thing). But we all have some idea of what is right, which has more less influence on our decisions. In politics there are very various levels of activity, involving various proportions of the population as a whole (with much the same exceptions as in the case of morals). The only comparably universal one to morality is passive citizenship, obedience to the law.

Against that it might be objected that in a democratic state in which citizens are not legally obliged to vote, they have a moral duty to do so. But that is far from obvious. If they have no definite political opinions and are politically uninformed it could just as well be said that they have a moral duty to abstain from voting. Well then, the objector might go on, they then have a moral duty to acquire some political knowledge and to base some political opinions upon it. I can see that it might, in some large sense, be a good thing if all sane adult citizens of a state had enough political knowledge to vote reasonably (by which all I mean is that they have some idea of what they are voting for and against) and voted. But the fact that in most states many have not does not strike me as an obvious moral deficiency on their part. The fully politically involved, at any rate, are, and in a large state must be, a fairly small minority and rulers, who are not mere functionaries, a smaller one still.

Another marked difference is that where moral convictions are comparatively uniform, at least as regards a broad array of fundamental principles of conduct, political convictions typically clash. There are two ways in which this apparent difference could be played down. The first is that in democratic systems of government that are organized on party lines political disagreement is institutionalized and exacerbated. Moral disagreement does not have to be settled in the way political disagreement does. I can drink and you can abstain. We may deplore each other, but go our own ways. In the business of government a single decision, binding on everyone, has to be arrived at. As it happens, sensible governments do not push the opposition too far, but go some way to meet them with a compromise. The stark collision of party is, it could be said, part of the game of democratic politics, like a vendor's exaggerated initial price which gets the bargaining going.

That leads to a second consideration that tends to weaken the contrast. Just as there is a central core of morality which no one seriously challenges in principle. whatever they may do in practice— you should not kill or injure people, steal from them, lie to them, cheat them, break promises you have made to them—so there is a central core of agreed political beliefs: that there should be a government, that it should enforce the central core of morality by legal sanctions for the security of citizens from their neighbours, that it should protect the nation as a whole from attack by foreigners, that it should come to the assistance of the seriously disadvantaged by transferring to them some of the wealth of the better-off.

But despite these two diluting considerations the difference of nature and scale between moral and political disagreement is still substantial. It can be best brought out by the fact that people are not so indignant with those with whom they disagree politically as with those with whom they disagree morally. And the more professional political disagreers are, the less indignant they are. That is more true of politicians proper than of those I have called the politically involved, who tend to have the ferocity of football supporters. To the extent that it is so it is because these last, of all kinds of people in some way touched by politics, most ardently identify politics with morality.

It is an aspect of the universal application of morality that it does not require more than common knowledge. A moral agent could benefit from special knowledge, of psychology, for instance, but is more likely to benefit from a natural sensitivity to the feelings of others. But above the level of passive obedience to the law political activity requires uncommon knowledge. Another way of making the same point is that there are really no experts in morals as there are in politics. Priests were long supposed to be moral experts. That may have been in part because they were thought to have the power of absolving and remitting sins. The discharge of that function, particularly where it was tied up with individual confession, caused them to spend a lot of time thinking about moral problems and to equip them with a large and varied, if mainly vicarious, moral experience. Their training, however, exerted an influence in the direction of legalism, both in identifying the wrongs done and in the imposition of penitences. Many humane priests have always risen above this. But priests are primarily experts in theology and ritual. Political expertise, on the other hand, is an evidently limited acquisition.

A final difference will prepare the ground for a later discussion of morality in the relations between states. I imagine that most people are utilitarian enough to agree that morality is, in an ultimate, if not exclusive way, concerned with the interest or well-being of all humans, even all sentient creatures. Politics, except in very unusual circumstances, is concerned with the interests or well-being of a particular group. That group, ordinarily in the modern world a culturally coherent nation, is, and is seen to be, in competition with other groups like itself. That competition can be of varying levels of ferocity. But it is always present in a ruler's mind. His task in managing the relations between his own country and others is that of pursuing and protecting the national interest.

Politics, as the pursuit of national interest, is, then, impersonal like morality, but it is inevitably not universal in a world where there is a plurality of states. Let me repeat that, generally, it is not my purpose to deny that morality has a place in politics, only that politics is a part of morality, to be wholly guided and appraised by moral principles and to be directed exclusively towards moral ends.

IV

The idea that politics is a department of morals rests to a great extent on the identification of what is taken to be its central issue—why should one obey the state?—with the the pursuit of the ground of political obligation, that is of the moral duty to obey it. These are, as I have argued, by no means one and the same.

It is not directly to the purpose that in determining why people in fact obey the state any moral obligation they recognize to do so does not bulk very large. At the crudest level they obey it because they fear it, because it has the power to apply painful sanctions where obedience is not forthcoming. That is prudence at its most primitive. But there is another good general reason for obedience of a prudential kind. This is that the state provides security and protection of one's life and property which would be in constant danger without it. As things have turned out it does a number of other valuable things as well, but security is the fundamental consideration without which the other things it provides are barely worth having. Now this reason for obedience is essentially self-regarding. It is not exclusively self-regarding, except in the case of an emotionally isolated person. It derives much of its strength from one's concern for those, inevitably a minority, to whom one is linked by ties of personal affection. Even if it extends in some degree to one's compatriots at large it still falls short of the human or sentient community as a whole, which is the essential moral constituency.

The fact that this prudential consideration in fact weighs much more strongly than any strictly moral motive for obedience cannot be ignored in any inquiry into the reasonableness of obedience. The alternative, anarchist, option is to suppose that most people's obedience is unreasonable. There is an argument, the free-rider argument, which holds that it is. So long as most people obey the state, it is said, although, on some particular occasion or occasions, I do not, the protective power of the state will not be seriously or even perceptibly undermined.

Hume argued that what he called allegiance, obedience to the state, is, like promise-keeping and respect for property, something that is advantageous only if the principle involved is generally adhered to. I cannot reasonably allow my private desires to override it unless I am prepared to admit that others may reasonably do the same in similar circumstances. In that case, of course, the protective capacity of the state dissolves. That is not a moral argument, however; it still turns on the advantage to me and to those I care about. As it happens, people are not always reasonable in this way. That is where the other self-regarding consideration comes in, the directly prudential consideration of fear of the state's sanctions.

To say that is not to say that there is not also a genuinely moral reason for obedience. That is dependent on the fact that the law, or more accurately the criminal law, forbids or requires conduct that is ruled out or dictated by morality. The state is fundamentally in the business of the enforcement of morals. The main content of the criminal law coincides with the principal requirements of what is generally recognized as morality: the prevention of harm to others by killing or injuring them, stealing from them, breaking promises to them (the law of contract), defrauding them, defaming them, and so on.

It does not enforce the whole of morality, although it comes near to doing so in theocratic states. It limits itself, ordinarily, to those offences which are large enough to excite the sort of revengeful impulse which leads to violence and, it might be added, those which it is practicable to identify and penalise. It is morally objectionable to be impolite. The law confines itself to the much more narrowly defined offence of insulting behaviour.

Those who have discussed the enforcement of morals recently have curiously neglected its central place in the content of law. Hart, in his *Law, Liberty and Morality* (1963), enumerates four questions about the relation between law and morals. There is, first, the question of the causal influence of morality on law. Secondly, there is the question of whether some reference to morality must enter into any adequate definition of a law or a legal system. Thirdly, there is the question of whether law is open to moral criticism. Finally, there is the question of whether conduct which is by common standards immoral ought to be punishable by law.

In connection with the second of these he makes the peculiar remark, 'is it just a contingent fact that law and morality often overlap (as in their common prohibition of certain forms of violence and dishonesty)?' The suggestion here is that the prohibition of 'certain forms' of violence and dishonesty is somehow a comparatively minor aspect of morality and of law. In fact it is the central and crucial part.

What helps to conceal that fact is the cavalier way in which moral philosophers approach the phenomenon they are investigating. For the most part they take it for granted that we all know what the main types of conduct which are morally enjoined or prohibited are. When they do address themselves directly to any kind of descriptive survey of common morality the results are unpersuasive. W. D. Ross, for example, lists five kinds of *prima facie* obligation: keeping promises, telling the truth, being grateful for benefits received, making restitution for injuries done and, as a kind of utilitarian bedspread, designed to cover the very large area of the field left uncovered, doing as much good as possible. It turns out that this list, apart from its last item, is derived from Grotius and is not the outcome of any independent inquiry.

If one actually looks at the range of widely accepted moral beliefs the inadequacy of the Grotius–Ross list is obvious. Making restitution is parasitic on the far more important matter of not inflicting the injuries in the first place. Do not harm or injure others is, in actual moral life, the bedrock and first principle of morality. It embraces truth-telling and promise-keeping. Next in order of importance is what may be broadly described as charity (but in a narrower sense than that of the Charity Commission). The imperative here is to minimize suffering caused, not by oneself, but by other people or nature. The conferring of positive advantage on others (the leading implication of the phrase 'doing as much good as possible') is not, I would maintain, a requirement of morality at all. Mr Wardle of Dingley Dell was a very nice man, but one might feel that his beneficence could have been more thoughtfully and productively distributed.

Everyone knows that the ten commandments, a kind of moral archetype for western civilization, are almost exclusively negative, a matter of prohibitions, of thou shalt nots. The first four are of a purely religious nature: the ones about no other Gods, graven images, taking the name of the Lord in vain and not working on the Sabbath. The remaining six—forbidding murder, adultery, theft, false witness, coveting and requiring one to honour one's parents—are all, with the exception of the last, negative. They are also much the same as the varieties of harm to others which I have said it is the common purpose of law and morality to prevent. It is interesting that there is no reference to charity or alms-giving in this list, but it makes an appearance later on in Deuteronomy.

Now the fact that law has as its first aim the enforcement of the fairly universally accepted core of morality is the best reason I know of for believing that one morally ought to obey it. For I have not denied that there is good moral reason for obeying the law and more generally the government that upholds it. I have been concerned only to deny that it is the only good reason for obedience, as if the reasonableness of obedience stands or falls with the moral appeal it has for its citizens.

But the politician, or, to use a politer and in this connection more relevant term, the statesman or ruler, is not a moralist. He does not discover or invent the moral principles it is the primary purpose of the law to enforce. For the most part they are a traditional, customary inheritance. He will seek to change the law from time to time in accordance with shifts in the prevailing moral consensus. He needs. to be successful, to be sensitively perceptive about doing so. If not he will cause social disasters like Prohibition in the United States.

As a ruler, furthermore, his motive will not be principally the moral improvement of the citizenry but the preservation of public order. As I said one of the prevailing limitations on the amount of commonly accepted morality he will call upon the law to enforce is that only offences liable to excite violent reaction should be legally prohibited. Just like anyone else he ought to guide his personal conduct by basic moral principles, but he does not have to be a crusading moral enthusiast to perform his task well. In areas of lively moral controversy it is perfectly proper for him to sustain a law with whose moral correlate he does not agree, on the ground that it is necessary for the preservation of peace.

In fact, not much of the legislation of a modern state is concerned with moral, rather than administrative or procedural matters. That is even more the case with the business of government in general. That is partly administrative, where the criteria are convenience and efficiency, and partly assistance to the nation's prosperity, which is not a matter of morality, being neither harm-prevention nor the relief of suffering (although it may indirectly contribute to the second of these). As the supplying of positive benefits, it is, rather, a matter of collective prudence. A further aspect of the government's business, which will need some special consideration is the provision of national defence and the conduct of foreign relations.

Some of those who are acknowledged to have been great statesmen have been moral enthusiasts. Cromwell and Gladstone stand out in British history. Walpole and Disraeli are at the opposite extreme, along with Palmerston and Churchill to a less insistently non-moral extent. On the whole it would probably be agreed that the more non-moral (but not conspicuously immoral) rulers do

105

less harm than enthusiastically moral ones. The main tasks of the ruler are three: internal and external security and prosperity. Only the first of these is a moral purpose, although strictly defensive military policy is harm-preventing. And it is not the moral aspect of these tasks that should preoccupy a ruler. A good ruler is not a moral teacher or pioneer, he is the skilled practitioner of a technique, that of preserving public order, protecting the community against its rivals or enemies and enhancing its prosperity.

In the matter of conducting a country's relations with others, peaceful or belligerent, the ruler claims to be pursuing the national interest. That does not mean that he should repudiate treaties whenever he thinks he can get away with it. But he will abstain from doing so in the spirit of A. H. Clough's lines about adultery: do not adultery commit, advantage rarely comes of it.

A different idea of the moral responsibilities of a ruler in international relations has, of course, often prevailed in practice. In our day the leading moral imperialist is, or has recently been, the United States. The policy has had two large apparent successes, the imposition of liberal-democratic institutions by force of arms on Germany and Japan. Our own predilection for the same sort of thing in the past has one large disaster to its discredit: the post-colonial regimes of sub-Saharan Africa, and one slightly unstable success: the still surviving democracy of India.

To question the wisdom of this kind of thing is not to rule out there being good moral reasons for assistance to countries in desperate need in other parts of the world. But the provision of relief for the destitute must be realistically tailored to the balance of altruism and self-interest in the population who have to foot the bill. And there are also good prudential reasons for such policies, to prevent distress taking the form of a violent reaction. In any case, the moral grounds for aid do not suffice for a complete resolution of the problem.

In seeking partially to disentangle morality and politics I have not been aiming, in a Machiavellian spirit, to separate them altogether. I have agreed that the state has a moral function, even if it primarily pursues it in the interests of public order. But it has other functions as well. Again, although there are good moral reasons for obedience to the state, they are supported by prudential ones, which are probably in practice the stronger. I have left much undiscussed: for example, the validity and strength of the moral claim for what is called social justice, conceived as the establishment of some kind of economic equality. But I hope I have gone some way towards showing the usual assimilation of moral and political philosophy is a mistake.

106

Duties and Virtues

ONORA O'NEILL

Duty versus Virtue

Duty and virtue are no longer the common coin of daily conversation. Both terms strike many of us as old-fashioned and heavy handed. Yet we incessantly talk about what ought and ought not to be done, and about the sorts of persons we admire or despise. As soon as we talk in these ways we discuss topics traditionally dealt with under the headings of duty and of virtue. If we no longer use these terms, it may be because we associate them with heavily moralistic approaches to life, with obsolete codes and ideals, with 'Victorian' values and attitudes, rather than because the concerns our predecessors discussed in these terms have vanished from our lives.

Moralizers in each age latch on to established moral vocabularies to confine them for their own purposes; in doing so they may make those vocabularies less useful and less appealing to others who do not share their views. Those who want to think more critically or openly about the same topics then often find it useful to adopt a new or extended vocabulary which is less freighted with attitudes they reject. So it is not surprising that today when people talk about the topics that traditionally fell under the heading of duty, they seldom use the term. Instead they discuss moral requirements using the vocabulary of right action, indeed often specifically of rights, of norms, rules and principles of action, of conceptions of justice and of legal, professional and moral obligations, and of promises and commitments, of autonomy and of respect for persons. Nor is it surprising that we have come to talk about topics traditionally associated with virtue using a variety of other terms. Although explicit use of the term *virtue* has become more common in philosophical writing in the last decade, contemporary discussion of good lives, characters and communities often concentrates on particular traits or dispositions, or on the tact, care, sensitivity, perception and responsiveness to difference which such traits demand. Questions about duty, about what we are required to do, have been recast in discussions about right action; questions about virtue, about what it is good to be, have given way to discussions of character, relationships and communities.

Onora O'Neill

It is surely not surprising that concern with these topics has out-lasted various traditional ways of approaching them. Presumably we will always have reason to be interested both in the right and in the good, both in what is required and in what is excellent. The two concerns have been linked throughout Western traditions of philosophical, theological and popular writing since classical antiquity. Virtually everybody who wrote about what ought to be done also wrote about the sorts of lives it would be good to lead. Yet recently this has changed. Many philosophers writing in English in the last two decades apparently assume that we must approach the moral life *either* through the categories of duty, obligation and right action, among which they think justice of prime importance, *or* through those of good character, hence of the virtues, and that these two approaches are not complementary but incompatible.[1]

To some extent these two groups of writers lay claim to differ-ent territories. The advocates of justice and right action—of duty —dominate political philosophy and jurisprudence, as well as applied ethics, which has dealt mainly with areas of life that are most regulated by law and state. The friends of the virtues are most concerned with the ethics of personal life and of relation-ships; their conception of the more public side of life centres on the notion of community and does not engage much with ques-tions of state or legal order. Contemporary partisans of duty and of virtue at least agree on one matter: they do not see these differ-ences as mere division of labour. Many from both camps see writ-ing of the other sort as both philosophically and morally defective, *a fortiori* as dispensable. At the limit some hold that a serious con-cern for duty precludes us from saying anything about the virtues, and vice versa.

For example, some recent theorists of justice contend that we can establish no objective account of the good life; we can hope to establish only an account of the principles of justice (of course, even these are hotly disputed).[2] Although people will have concep-tions of the good, these must remain subjective and contentious. Philosophical writing can only be 'agnostic about the good for man', so must see the domain of life not constrained by obligations

[1] For recent comments on the traditional links between duty and virtue see Schneewind, 1990, 42–63; on the recent denial of these links see Onora O'Neill, 1992.

[2] Claims about the impossibility of an objective account of the good are particularly prominent in the work of leading theorists of justice, includ-ing in particular that of John Rawls and Ronald Dworkin.

of justice as available for the pursuit not of virtue, but of preference. In so far as they discuss recent philosophical work on virtue
ethics, the theorists of justice criticise it as lacking sound principles and rigorous argument, as failing to establish which life or
lives are good or best, as alarmingly casual about justice, and as
giving unwarranted weight to community standards, traditions, or
to ordinary processes of deliberation or moral perception, whose
moral authority (rather than corruption) they blandly assume
rather than demonstrate. At the limit, they see much recent work
in virtue ethics as condemned by its communitarian commitments
to relativism, and at its worst as a repository of conservative, ethnocentric and often elitist prejudice.

Virtue ethicists[3] have correspondingly sharp objections to make
against those who think that the moral life is centrally a matter of
justice, right action and of principle, rather than of good character.
They charge (with some truth) that contemporary advocates of
duty and right action are in fact narrowly obsessed with rights—
that is specifically with those duties that can be claimed of others.
They allege that the arguments which supposedly establish universal principles of duty, and specifically of justice, are not merely
inadequate but deeply misguided. The conception of life as guided
by rules or principles is ethically crippled, and perhaps ultimately
incoherent. The ethical deficiency of rule-based ethics is supposedly its rigorism: it cannot take account of differences and always
prescribes with rigid uniformity, so denying the sensitivity and
perception which virtue ethics treats as central to the moral life.
The deeper incoherence, which I shall not address directly here, is
supposedly that the very idea of following a rule overlooks the
unavoidable indeterminacy of rules, whose interpretation is always
open, which therefore can offer no guidance. (The charges of
rigidity and of incoherence are, of course, incompatible: if rules
prescribe nothing determinate, they won't prescribe with rigid
uniformity.)

Principles of Duty and of Virtue

The writers whose positions I have been sketching make varied
further claims. Here I shall pursue neither textual accuracy nor
case by case criticism. My aim is rather to suggest that without

[3] Prominent writers who make some or all of these claims include
Alasdair MacIntyre, Michael Sandel, Bernard Williams and Carol
Gilligan.

some rather extraordinary assumptions the claim that we must choose between duty and virtue because they are incompatible is wholly implausible. The clusters of ethical concerns which we associate with the two terms are close allies rather than irreconcilable rivals. Both clusters depend on viewing action as informed by principles which constrain but do not and cannot wholly determine what ought to be done and what it would be good to be.

I shall first argue for this central claim in a rather spare and elementary way and then sketch an alternative picture of some of the differences between concern for duty and for virtue. Of course, even if the arguments are convincing, they will not show that or how we can vindicate an integrated account of the right and the good. But they may at least show that it would not be foolish to aim to produce such an account.

Consider first the central objections aimed at theories of justice by some of those recent critics who take virtue to be the heart of ethical concern. These criticisms start from the fact that any account of what is ethically required (of the right, of justice, of duties) must focus on rules or principles. For example, such positions may claim that justice permits each to speak freely, or that we have a duty to rescue those whom we can easily help, or that we have a right that others be prevented from injuring us. In each case, *modal* claims are made about action informed by certain principles: action of a specified type is said to be required or permitted some agent, with the corollary that others are required not to prevent enactment of that requirement or permission; treatment of a certain type is said to be a matter of entitlement, with the corollary that some or all must be obliged to meet those entitlements. Principles of right—above all of justice—constitute a modal web of requirements, permissions and entitlements which must be internally consistent. The articulation of these modal consistency requirements for sets of principles that are to hold universally for some domain of agents—e.g. citizens of one state, or human beings —has been the focus of much of the most acute writing on justice, rights and obligations in recent decades. Universal permissions would be incoherent without universal obligations to respect those permissions; universal entitlements are nonsense unless there are counterpart obligations to meet those entitlements.

Many critics of theories of justice object to the very idea of universal rights, obligations or entitlements; more generally they object to the idea that there are universal ethical principles, often on the grounds that universal principles will demand action that is uniform, so necessarily enjoin lives of numbing rigidity, in which the particularities of persons and predicaments are systematically brushed aside. At the least, the result is insensitivity; at worst a callous inhumanity.

Yet is it true that any ethical conception which takes universal rules or principles as central must prescribe with rigid uniformity? There is, to be sure, a common use of the notion of a rule, which associates it with rigidity, and with uniformity. However, there is no reason at all to suppose that ethical rules—principles of duty or of justice, for example—have to be rules of that sort. Plenty of quite important and widely accepted moral rules do very little to impose rigid uniformity on life or action. All of us who refrain from perjury and injury keep within the requirements of two rather important moral rules: but unsurprisingly we can nevertheless lead rather varied lives. Evidently rules that state permissions will leave much open; but even those which prescribe or proscribe do not rule out varied response since they prescribe or proscribe only some aspects of what is to be done or shunned. Since rules are basically practical principles, incorporating certain act descriptions, and act descriptions are intrinsically indeterminate, it should not be surprising that rules too underdetermine action, and that any application of a rule requires judgment, and that judgment may well differ when cases differ—or even when they do not. Rules are universal provided that all cases within a certain domain fall within their scope; they prescribe uniformly when they demand that the treatment of those cases be the same in all respects. Any universal rule which is indeterminate will demand no more than that some, perhaps very minor, aspects of action be uniform, and will leave other matters open, hence in particular open for non-uniformity.

Of course, some rules incorporate a lot more detail than others, and perhaps those who worry about the rigidity of moral rules— of principles of duty or of obligation—fear that the only moral rules that can be vindicated are of this type, and so must mandate regimented action. Perhaps they fear above all that those who advocate any sort of ethics of rules or principles will in some way be recommending a particular sort of algorithmic rule. There are two points to be made here. First, strictly speaking, algorithms belong in formal systems, and there can be no algorithms for action precisely because there cannot be exhaustive descriptions of action. Second, less strictly speaking, there can of course be heavy handed and intrusive rules, rules that demand too much or regiment life excessively, which we might think of as quasi-algorithms; and I have offered no argument to show that ethical rules are not of that sort. Nor on the other hand do those who insist that duties and rights must prescribe uniformity prove that ethical rules must be of this type.

The fear that the principles of ethics are heavy-handed quasi-algorithms which threaten a stultifying uniformity of life has various sources. One may be consequentialist line of thought which, if taken to a theoretical extreme, suggests that ethics can be reduced to calculation, hence to quasi-algorithms. For example, the rule 'maximize utility' would (if it could be operationalized) point to one, or at most very few, permissible actions in any situation. However, such reasoning is (in principle, at least) sensitive to minute variation of circumstances—consequentialists often prize sensitivity to empirical circumstances—so there is little reason to suppose that its quasi-algorithms must regiment life by mandating uniformity of action where situations differ. The quasi-algorithms of felicific calculation for varied circumstances can hardly fail to map onto highly differentiated action. Quasi-algorithms need not regiment. The way in which utilitarian or other consequentialist reasoning may more plausibly be thought to regiment is rather that, since it takes sub-optimal action as wrong, any optimal act will be not merely permitted but required, so that once it has been performed another optimal act may loom up, which once again is required. The so-called 'overload of obligations' problem, which erodes the merely permissible, is instantly generated.[4] A burdensome sense that all of life is divided into the forbidden and the required may then fuel a fear that such reasoning leads towards a moral gulag. But these reasons for thinking that utilitarian or other consequentialist reasoning demands too much have nothing to do with the fear that principles or rules regiment: indeed, this sort of excess demand is a more troubling feature of act than of rule utilitarianism. Rule utilitarians have long pointed out that within a consequentialist framework a focus on rules and rights rather than on acts provides a superior framework for withstanding the domination of life by utilitarian demands.

Despite these theoretical points, there is little reason to fear that consequentialist reasoning *as it actually gets done* will tend to commend uniform solutions. Actual consequentialist reasoning is much less ambitious. Since it is impossible to generate a complete list of 'options', from which an optimal act is to be chosen, it has to work within the assumption that there are certain available or attractive options (real options), and it is only among these that consequences are to be reckoned and optima computed. Since options will differ with situations, the starting points for real life

[4] See Fishkin, 1982.

consequentialist reasoning will always be adapted to actual situations, so that fears of uniform prescription are, at the least, exaggerated. This may detract from the purity and ambition of consequentialist reasoning—but it at least puts worries about its supposed demand for uniformity into context.

However, worries about the structure of consequentialist thought are not the decisive context for understanding whether duty and its allies regiment life. Consequentialists see good results rather than duty and right action as morally fundamental. It is a standard complaint of those who take the right, and with it the web of moral requirement, as the central ethical category that consequentialist reasoning subverts what they take to be most central to the moral life by subjecting it to a calculus of tradeoffs between expected results.

If it were true that an ethic of rules must regiment, that it demands uniformity, then this would have to be because, as it happens, the ethical principles advocated by those who think duty and rights fundamental prescribe rigid uniformities. But why should we think this likely? It is true that the advocates of duty and right action commend universal principles: but universality does not entail uniformity. For principles to be universal is simply for them to apply to all cases that fall under the agent description they embody. In the case of negative prescriptions even a rather demanding principle will not get far towards imposing uniformity: in not committing perjury, or not coercing others, we conform to demanding moral proscriptions, and yet our lives become uniform only in very minor ways. However, it is theoretically possible that a positive prescription of a very specific character might impose far more in the way of uniformity (although strict uniformity would not, of course, be mandated even by quasi-algorithms, since even these are unavoidably less than fully determinate). If the most fundamental moral principles were, for example, to *require* marriage between cousins, or to *require* tithing of income, or *require* adherence to sumptuary laws, a considerable degree of uniformity at least for certain aspects of life would be prescribed. However, contemporary work on fundamental moral requirements, and indeed modern moral philosophy in general, does not advocate specific fundamental requirements. On the contrary, it has advocated rather indeterminate prescriptions and proscriptions for the construction of institutions, rather abstract human rights and the equally abstract obligations that are their counterparts. (This abstraction is not denied by those who worry lest rules and principles mandate uniformity: the very same writers often object that duty and rights provide too abstract an approach to ethics.)

113

These indeterminate principles are put forward as the framework within which more specific and more constraining requirements (laws, institutions, roles, practices) may be identified as required in particular situations. However, these derivative, more specific requirements are not to be taken as holding without variation for all situations or for all moral agents: we cannot simply infer uniformity of requirement from the fact that a certain universal principle forms the backdrop for judging the diversity of cases occurring within some domain. Background principles may do no more than define a context for debate about the construction of institutions, the framing of laws and the forming of practices, within which particular cases will be handled. The elaboration and interpretation of such principles may lead to quite determinate requirements in some cases, or even to uniform treatment of certain ranges of cases; but it can also lead to diversification of treatment of other cases. The inference from universal moral requirement to required uniformity of practice can fail at *many* stages.

At this point it is clear that the gap between the sort of practical reasoning that supposedly underlies moral requirements and that which underlies judgments about good lives and characters is greatly narrowed. Given that principles of action, and with them moral requirements, are not algorithms, practical reasoning that refers to principles can never dispense with judgment and sensitivity to the varieties of cases. Some of the central concerns of contemporary virtue ethics, including its emphasis on judgment and discrimination of cases, are not therefore alien but indispensable to a consideration of duty. This should surprise nobody; Kant, the greatest exponent of an ethics of duty, was also the first to insist that rules cannot determine their own application and that judgment is indispensable in all following of rules.[5]

Looked at from the other direction, I believe it is equally clear that judgments about good characters and good lives cannot be solely a matter of responsiveness to the particularities of cases. None of the virtues is a matter of *mere* responsiveness to the particularities of situations. Virtuous lives show *principled* responsiveness to situations, not mere registration of differences. To be courageous or caring or honest is not just to respond with discrimination and sensitivity to the variety of life and situation, but to do so in distinctive, characteristic, in short, principled ways. Of course, this is not to suggest that virtuous action is uniform: here too there can be principle without uniformity. The point is only

[5] The *locus classicus* is in the Schematism chapter of The *Critique of Pure Reason*, esp. A133–6/B172–51 (Kant, 1929).

that virtue is never unprincipled—just as duty is subverted rather than completed without elements of perception and judgment, so virtue is subverted by lack of principle. This is not, of course, to say that the virtuous can formulate or are conscious of their virtuous principles: they are more likely to have them well internalized. Nor is it to say that each good act is proof of virtue: on the way to embedding principles in character many good acts may, as Aristotle insists, precede the achievement of virtue.

In order to sustain the view that concern with the right and with the good are incompatible we would, it now appears, have to take a surprisingly divergent view of practical reasoning in the two domains. We would have to view reasoning about moral requirements not merely as informed by principles, but as wholly determined by those principles and as by-passing judgment and sensitivity. In short, we would have to suppose that the practices of interpretation and debate that we take to be part and parcel even of those domains of life which are most explicitly rule governed, such as legal and bureaucratic life, are dispensable in favour of mere, sheer uniformity of response. On the other hand, we would have to suppose that the sorts of responsiveness to cases and particularities which is most admired by those who are concerned with the virtues wholly dispenses with principles or standards, and is guided by unmediated apprehension of cases, so that there is no principle behind the various categories of virtue which we distinguish and discuss.

Conflicts and Consistencies between Duties and Virtues

It may seem that this rapprochement has gone too far. I said at the beginning that I would argue that concern for what is morally required and for what is excellent might be compatible, by showing that certain recent depictions of their incompatibility were illusory. It appears that I have now argued that both the right and the good must be understood as expressed in action informed by principles which underdetermine judgment of cases, hence underdetermine action. Yet there is surely a difference between these two domains of moral concern. In the rest of this paper I want to suggest some useful distinctions between duty and virtue.

Part of the difference is I think, simply one of modality. As soon as we raise questions about duty, or any of its contemporary derivatives, we raise questions about what is morally required. Our basic question has to be put modally. It may be the Kantian 'What ought I do?', or a less individualistic 'What ought we do?', or a more impersonal 'What is to be done?' Alternatively the question may be posed from the point of view of the recipient rather than the agent: 'What are my rights?' or 'What are we entitled to?' However, in every case the question has a modal structure. The answers to such questions must therefore be answers that speak to systems of requirements for pluralities of agents. If we either ought or are permitted to do X, others cannot be permitted to prevent us from doing X. If we have a right that Y be done to or for us, then there must be others who have the counterpart obligations so to do. The modal character of deontic claims—of claims about obligations and rights—means that they require us to think about systematic structures that mesh together the moral lives of many agents. If we are to call duty into question, we must call into question not principles and universality, but the claim that part of what is morally significant has this systematic, deontic structure.

This structure has indeed been called into question. So-called 'conflicts of obligation' will, it is argued, undermine any would-be account of moral requirements. By contrast, the less exigent structure of claims about what is good or excellent, which do not or need not interlock with claims about what is good or excellent for others, may seem less problematic. Classical discussions of the different 'lives' illustrate the less demanding structure of claims about virtue. We can grasp and appreciate both the life of honour and the life of contemplation as excellent lives, although they are incompatible in the sense that nobody can live both fully at the same time. In more contemporary terms, we can grasp and appreciate that both modesty and assertiveness, both care and fairness, can be virtues without thinking that both can be manifest in one life at all times. If we thought that both members of such pairs of virtues were matters of requirement in the same situations, our grasp of what an ethical requirement could be would collapse. Here at least is a clear difference between claims about the right and the good: the latter do not consist of deontic claims, and so there can be a plurality of good lives, no one of which is required.

It has sometimes been suggested that the modal structure of claims about right action and duty not merely differentiate these concerns from concern with virtue and excellence, but lead to conceptual shipwreck. Since any set of ethical requirements will generate conflicts of obligation, the underlying constellation of ideas to which notions such as duty, right and justice belong, will, it is said, prove irredeemably incoherent. It is certainly the case that, for any two principles stating ethical requirements, cases will arise in which it is impossible to honour both. For example, I may in a particular situation be able to save a life only by telling a lie, or to keep a promise only at the expense of causing great grief. Worse still, in some situations we will find that we cannot live up even to one principle without also violating that very principle. Conflicts of loyalty may reveal that we can honour one promise only by breaking another, sustain one relationship only by harming another. Does this show that although the idea of principled action is coherent, the idea of principles of moral requirement is not? I believe that it does not. The only case in which a conflict of moral requirements would be intrinsically incoherent is the case where the act descriptions embodied in the two requirements *cannot* be simultaneously satisfied. Anybody who aims to be both popular and a recluse, or to eat both abstemiously and gluttonously, or to be both celibate and sexually active, makes claims that, taken literally, are incoherent. No possible course of action can sustain both sides of these claims. However, in such cases the incoherence has nothing to do with the modal structure that is distinctive of duty and its cognates: it arises quite simply out of the attempt to combine commitments that are intrinsically incompatible.

It is quite a different matter to try to combine requirements that are not intrinsically incompatible. We constantly find ourselves committed to principles that may contingently rather than intrinsically come into conflict, and although this is a source of pain and difficulty in many lives, it is in no way incoherent. Principles generate conflicts in certain situations; even commitment to a single principle can do so. Conflicts of moral requirement may lead us to revise our plans and even plunge us into anguish: but they do not show that the principles (or principle) involved are senseless, dispensable or worthless. To take a well known example, Sartre's student had to choose between filial and patriotic duty. In his actual situation, unlike many others, these two were in sharp conflict. But it does not follow that both principles, or either principle, is worthless or to be discarded. Since principles are indeterminate, they can be lived up to in many ways, and unsurprisingly some ways of living up to them will conflict with some ways of living up to other principles. Often we are fortunate and find adequate ways of meeting the requirements of a plurality of principles. In a fortunate life all fundamental moral requirements can be met without great difficulty or sacrifice, in a well lived life action that lives up to all fundamental moral requirements is discerned and taken even when not easy or obvious. In an unfortunate life there may be deep, perhaps irresolvable, difficulty in finding any way of living up to all fundamental moral requirements, although these are intrinsically coherent. In short, the possibility of some cases of irremovable conflict does not make the idea of moral requirement incoherent or redundant. Only those sets of requirements which could never be lived up to are incoherent. These considerations show, I think, that there is no basic incoherence in the idea of a set of principles which state moral requirements. Of course, they do not show that moral requirements can be justified or what they are or whether they are all that is morally important: they just show that it is hard to live up to principles, even when these principles are matters of requirement.

Moreover, the very same considerations about conflict and consistency will arise in any account of virtue. In many situations it will prove hard to manifest both of two virtues: it is often hard to show justice and mercy, to combine fairness and solidarity. But it is not always impossible, and when it is done we admire the doing. What would, by contrast, be impossible is adopting two dispositions which always and by their very nature pulled in contrary directions. It is not an option to be secretive and open, to be taciturn and loquacious, to be firm and pliable in all situations: at best we can manifest one of these conflicting tendencies in a one situation and the other in another. An account of the virtues, like an account of duty and right, has to argue for a coherent set of virtues. However, coherence is not a matter of contriving a world in which the demands of all virtues are readily enacted in all situations. There is no such world. Coherence is only a matter of commitment to virtues which could be enacted, given good fortune and good judgment. One way in which that commitment is expressed is in shaping our lives so that intrinsically coherent moral requirements do not contingently come into conflict, for example, by making no promises or commitments that will clash,

Perfect and Imperfect Duties

The fact that the demands of consistency and coherence weigh on duty and on virtue in parallel ways shows that it is not specifically the modal structure of the requirements of duty that makes the two different. However, an important difference between duty and virtue lies in a feature closely connected to that modal structure. A significant feature of deontic principles is that they *link pluralities of agents in structures of requirement*. Our duties are mirrored in others' permissions and rights; our permissions and rights in their duties. There may indeed be duties to self; but, these apart, every right, duty and permission implies a constellation of rights, duties and permissions in others. It is this feature of moral requirement that leads us to distinguish duty from virtue, and to link discussions of some important duties closely with the ethics of a legal order and social structure in which reciprocal requirements are tightly specified, in particular with the ethics of public life and of social roles; it is the absence of this feature which makes it possible to think of virtue as embodied at least in large measure in character, and even of some virtues as lying outside social relations and reflected in matters such as personal style, intellectual or spiritual commitment and aesthetic orientation.

However, this contrast between duty and virtue should not be exaggerated or oversimplified. While some duties define tight and symmetrical links of moral requirement between agent and recipient, others define less exigent structures. If A has a right, then either all others or specified others (depending on the sort of right) must have an obligation to respect that right. Where duties have counterpart rights we may think of them as completely specified, or, using an older vocabulary, as *perfect duties*. Unless rights have counterpart obligations, which are allocated either to all or to specified others, they amount to nothing more than rhetoric, and at worst to a callous and dangerous rhetoric which ascribes entitlements but is vague or cavalier about what it would take to meet those entitlements. At best such a proleptic proclamation of rights might be used to urge people to seek to secure rights by determining some allocation of the corresponding obligations.

However, not all duties exhibit this strong modal structure: some are reflected in a less complete structure of ethical requirements and are often thought of as being virtues as well as duties. Unlike rights, certain sorts of duty require no fixed allocation among recipients. Duties of charity or beneficence are often construed like this: the duty is universal in that it is ascribed to all, but its allocation remains at each agent's discretion One use of the traditional term *imperfect duty* has been to distinguish duties that are unallocated in this way.[6] Some contemporary advocates of justice hold that there are no imperfect duties: they think that duties are always the mirror image of rights, so that those who are obliged have no discretion in the allocation of their duty. In the stark and simplified accounts of duty offered by some libertarians, we are obliged only to respect the rights of others, and everything else is a matter of preference.

However, in more traditional accounts of duty, two types of ethical requirements are often distinguished. *Perfect duties* will be matched by rights to have those duties performed. They will form a tight network of moral requirement which links agents and

[6]   See Campbell, 1975.

recipients in a web of reciprocal ties. Imperfect duties will not be matched by rights to have those duties performed. Although they are duties, hence required of agents, they lack counterpart rights: nobody can lay claim to performance. Many of the duties traditionally classified as imperfect have often also been classified as virtues. Kant, for example, was merely following tradition when he wrote on *duties of virtue*. Like many others he sees the social virtues as a matter of duty, but of duties without counterpart rights or entitlements.

The fact that duty and virtue can be seen as closely linked in these ways does not show that the good can be reduced to the right, or that virtue is simply duty without rights. The argument shows only that we can coherently speak of duties that are also virtues, in that both are matters of differentiated enactment of principle, that neither mandates uniform or rigid action. However, there may well be many other virtues which are not moral requirements at all. It may be that there are many ways of leading good lives, which are compatible with but go far beyond the limits of ethical requirement.

The fact that some recent writers on justice have been sceptical about establishing any account of duties without rights, and others sceptical about establishing an account of virtues which are not duties, shows that it will not be a simple matter to establish an integrated account of duty and of virtue. However, recent claims that this traditional ambition is not merely difficult but intrinsically incoherent cannot be sustained: in large measure it is based on no more than a wholly unlikely conception of the sort of rules that are most important in human lives.

The Definition of Morality*

JOHN SKORUPSKI

I

We use such terms as *good, bad, right, wrong, should, ought,* in many ways other than moral: good evidence and bad argument, right answers and wrong notes, novels which should be read and policies which ought not to be adopted. The moral is a sphere of the practical and the practical itself only a sphere or the normative. Norms guide us in all we believe, feel and do. Do these normative words then have a specifically *moral* sense? If so can it be defined?

I think they do have a moral sense. That calls for some supporting argument, but I shall not go into it here. (An alternative view is that they are univocal but always implicitly relativized to some contextually understood practice, project or objective. I am taking it, in contrast, that their moral use at least is categorical.) I want rather to consider an attempt to define that sense. It is not a definition which illicitly reduces the normative to the non-normative. It purports rather to define *moral* senses of goodness, rightness, wrongness and obligation in non-moral but still normative terms. 'Definition', however, will turn out not to be quite the right word. We shall see, I think, that 'moral' is strictly speaking indefinable, and why it is undefinable. Nevertheless, I shall defend the spirit of the definition; even though 'moral' cannot be defined I shall argue that we can still *construct* its sense (as one might say) using only non-moral normative concepts.

These issues of definition and construction are not my sole topic. I shall also broach (but no more than broach) deeper philosophical questions which lie behind them and give them their interest: questions about how morality is to be situated within the larger sphere of the practical, how it is related to such categories, putatively distinct from it, as the ethical, or the rational; what bases moral judgment has in reason and feeling. I shall also discuss some particular questions about the nature of moral punishment and blame. But it is with the issues of definition and construction that I begin.

*I am grateful to Berys Gaut, A. Phillips Griffiths, Matthew Kieran, Dudley Knowles and Christopher Martin for comments on this paper.

John Skorupski

II

The definition I have in mind is to be found in Mill[1]. The relevant remarks are to be found in his discussion of the concept of justice in chapter V of *Utilitarianism*. Having observed that the idea of something which one may be constrained or compelled to do, on pain of penalty, is central to the idea of an obligation of *justice*, he observes that this idea nevertheless 'contains, as yet, nothing to distinguish that obligation from moral obligation in general':

> For the truth is, that the idea of penal sanction, which is the essence of law, enters not only into the conception of injustice,. but into that of any kind of wrong. We do not call anything wrong, unless we mean to imply that a person ought to be punished in some way or other for doing it; if not by law, by the opinion of his fellow creatures; if not by opinion, by the reproaches of his own conscience. This seems the real turning point of the distinction between morality and simple expediency. It is a part of the notion of Duty in every one of its forms, that a person may rightfully be compelled to fulfil it. Duty is a thing which may be *exacted* from a person, as one exacts a debt. Unless we think that it might be exacted from him, we do not call it his duty . . . we call any conduct wrong, or employ, instead, some other term of dislike or disparagement, according as we think that the person ought, or ought not, to be punished for it; and we say that it would be right to do so and so, or merely that it would be desirable or laudable, according as we would wish the person whom it concerns, compelled, or only persuaded and exhorted to act in that manner. (J. S. Mill, *Collected Works,* 1965, X, 246)

These brief remarks of Mill will lead us into a good deal of analysis and discussion. But before taking up more subtle issues, including subtle issues about circularity, let me remove the impression of blatant circularity which may seem to lurk—to be almost explicit—in Mill's words.

If I define 'X *ought* to do Y' as 'X ought to be punished in some way for non-performance of Y', I use the word I am defining in my *definiens*. Mill does not quite put it this way, since what he

[1]It has recently been refurbished by Alan Gibbard, in his book, *Wise Choices, Apt Feelings,* Oxford 1990, ch. 1, pp. 40–45, ch. 7. For a comprehensive discussion of Mill's view see Lyons, 1976.

defines is 'duty', 'right' and 'wrong'[2]. But he clearly takes it that 'X is (morally) right' = 'X (morally) ought to be done', and 'X is (morally) wrong' = 'X (morally) ought not to be done'.

The apparent circularity is avoided if the 'ought' in the definiendum is a moral one, while the 'ought' in the definiens is not. It's pretty plausible that this is Mill's position. Thus in the *System of Logic*, 1879, VI xii 6&7 he says that general utility is the first principle of Teleology, or Practical Reason—the normative doctrine which, in combination with 'laws of nature', produces the Art of Life. Morality is one 'department' of this Art, the others are Prudence and Aesthetics (the 'Right, the Expedient, and the Beautiful or Noble'). So general utility stands outside Morality, as the final source of practical-rational oughts. (The position is still consistent with there sometimes being a *moral* obligation to act directly on grounds of general utility. General utility can play a bit-part within, as well as being the ultimate animator without.)

III

The distinction between the moral ought and a more fundamental practical ought is plainly indispensable to anyone who seeks to define morality in the manner of Mill. Further issues about this practical ought, however, can remain open. Obviously it is not essential to agree with Mill that its determining principle is general utility. A contractualist, for example, who based his practical ought on self-interest, limited sympathy and self-interest, instrumental rationality, or whatever, could still adopt the Millian definition as an account of what makes an ideally agreed rule a *moral* rule. Since there can be ideally agreed rules which are not moral rules (e.g. to purely co-operative co-ordination problems), a contractualist criterion of the moral is required, stronger than that of simple ideal agreement.

Again, the definition can be adopted whatever view one takes on the epistemological status of the practical ought. One may hold that it is grounded in a structure of objective norms, or like

[2] He differs here from those contemporary consequentialists who follow Moore rather than Mill, by defining 'morally right action' and 'moral duty' directly in terms of optimal consequence—with predictably disconcertlng results (Moore, 1903, section 89). If consequentialism is *defined* as a view which accepts these Moorean definitions, then the classical nineteenth century utilitarians, Bentham, Mill and Sidgwick, cannot readily be classed as consequentialists.

Gibbard (1990) one may believe that it expresses the attitude of the person who issues the ought, and is not constrained to reflect any such structure. One may identify it with the ought of practical rationality as such, or one may take some other view, involving, for example, a broad notion of the ethical and a narrow notion of the moral.

The last distinction is made by Bernard Williams, in *Ethics and the Limits of Philosophy* (1985, ch. 10, 'Morality, the Peculiar Institution'). He treats the moral as a particular form—a somewhat pathological one—of the broader category of the ethical. We shall consider later whether the institution of morality is as peculiar as he makes it (section IX). But for the moment note only that, while Williams offers no *definition* of morality, his view is like Mill's at least in this, that he thinks morality's central concept is moral obligation—and its fundamental assumption is that penalty, specifically, the penalty of guilt and blame, is appropriate for non-compliance with moral obligation.

Where Williams usefully reserves the word 'moral' for the narrower notion, and the word 'ethical' for a broader one, Mill uses 'moral' itself, and its cognates, in broader and narrower ways. The definition he provides is of *narrow* morality, as one may call it, corresponding to Williams' 'moral', as against his 'ethical'. But when Mill speaks, as he often does, of the processes of moralization his concern is ethical—for example, in this remark: 'the moralization of the personal enjoyments we deem to consist, not in reducing them to the smallest possible amount, but in cultivating the habitual wish to share them with others. . .' (*Collected Works*, 1965, X 339).

Our conceptions of moral education and moral life go well beyond narrow morality. Much beyond the simple carrying out of duties attracts an admiration which is still *broadly* moral. In this broader sense, moral education, as Mill pre-eminently understood, is an education of the affections as well as of conscience and will, transcending 'the notion of Duty'. Narrow morality itself— the system of practices to which adherence should be exacted on penalty of blame—is conditioned by the state of ethical development of a society:

> the domain of moral duty, in an improving society, is always widening. When what once was uncommon virtue becomes common virtue, it comes to be numbered among obligations, while a degree exceeding what has grown common, remains simply meritorious. (*Collected Works*, 1965, X 338)

So while the test of utility is not in Mill's view in any way itself relative, the historicity of social forms and human dispositions, on which he placed great stress, means that narrow morality inevitably is so.

He thinks that in an improving society its domain widens. One might think in contrast that it narrows, for example because the general good no longer requires the sanctioning of various classes of action with moral penalties. On a sufficiently utopian view of present or future human nature, its domain could shrink to zero. Another attitude to morality, distinct from this, though it can be combined with it, is that of the subversive thinker (by now a somewhat jaded character) who views morality as a device of repression and self-delusion to be thrown off by the strong spirit. The utopian and the subversive can agree on the *definition* of morality while asserting its present or eventual nullity.

One might even, consistently with the Millian definition, hold morality to be null on conceptual grounds. Thus, while holding that the moral is defined in terms of guilt and blame, one may also hold that guilt and blame presuppose pure voluntariness, or 'autonomy', and that these are incoherent concepts.

These various views of morality have this much in common: they all take what I shall call below an 'external' view of it. (That is not quite true of the last—one could hold morality to be incoherent without viewing it from any other normative standpoint, or holding any other such standpoint to be coherent.) I shall defend this externalism, and the spirit at least of Mill's definition, even though I shall reject it as a strict definition. As to the philosophical context which I shall sketch out for the definition, that will be Millian in three further respects—in envisaging a domain of ethical, or ethical-aesthetic ideals which are relatively independent of (narrow) morality; in agreeing that the fundamental ought is that of practical reason as such: and in holding further that the standard of practical reason is impartially conceived general good. (But this is not to accept the utilitarian's notion of *aggregate* or *average* utility as the right account of that good—those classical utilitarian notions of distribution are determinate and disputable versions of the more general, determinable, concept of distributive impartiality.) I shall not defend these Millian features: they will be provided simply as a backcloth which I find persuasive and against which the concept of the moral, together with its distinctive concepts (blame, penalty, moral freedom) can be viewed in their true proportions and proper role.

125

John Skorupski

In the passages I quoted, Mill's most usable words are that

> We do not call anything wrong, unless we mean to imply that a person ought to be punished in some way or other for doing it; if not by law, by the opinion of his fellow creatures; if not by opinion, by the reproaches of his own conscience.

Let us drop the reference to law, and concentrate on the reproaches of conscience and the opinion of our fellow creatures. We lose nothing by doing so, and we leave space for the possibility that something not morally wrong should nevertheless be punished by law. The key notion then is that of punishment by guilt and blame. Allowing further that guilt—the reproaches of one's own conscience—is identical with self-blame, the single notion involved is that of blame. This identification will do for the moment; but it would be more accurate to identify guilt with what I call below the 'blame-feeling', directed at oneself. (We *feel* guilt.) Blame in general will shortly be considered in more detail. But for the moment we have two central thoughts, The first is the definition of the morally wrong as the blameworthy. The second is that blame, whether by self or others, is itself penal. They need not go together, but they do in Mill, and I shall be discussing both; but we begin with the first.

Consider then the following definition:

> M. x is morally wrong if and only if the agent ought to be blamed (by himself and others) for doing x

This will also furnish a definition of 'x is morally obligatory', given that the latter means 'not doing x is morally wrong'.

As it stands this isn't even right extensionally. There may, in special circumstances, be good reasons why an agent ought not to be blamed, even though he acted morally wrongly. (It will drive him to breakdown, or will be bad for the over-censorious blamer, or whatever.) Judicious insertion of something like 'in normal circumstances' or *prima facie'*, or more ambitiously, of a clause taking explicit account of such special circumstances, is required. A related though distinct point is noted by Alan Gibbard, (1990, 44). He holds that an action may not be blameworthy even though it is morally wrong—his example is speaking rudely to a friend out of a paroxysm of grief. So he proposes the following definitions: 'An act is *wrong* if and only if it violates standards for ruling out actions, such that if an agent in a normal frame of mind violated those standards because he was not substantially motivated to conform to them, he would be to blame. To say that he would *be to blame* is to say that it would be rational for him to feel guilty and for others to resent him' (p. 45). (Here again the last sentence needs something like an 'in normal circumstances' clause.) I am not sure whether in Gibbard's example we *would* say that the speaker acted wrongly. Another response, which maintains the equivalence of wrongness and blameworthiness, is that though speaking rudely is in general wrong, the speaker envisaged by Gibbard did not in that particular case act wrongly.

At any rate I shall keep to my simpler definition, M (in which the variable, x, ranges over token actions); the points made in what follows would not be affected if one substituted Gibbard's definitions. The crude form I have given is enough to raise the question —whether we have here something that at least could be *refined* into a definition of the moral.

M, it may be said, is (subject to such correction) an *a priori* truth; but that leaves open the question of why it is. That it is so by definition of 'morally wrong' is only one possibility. Another is that it is so by definition of 'blame'. Blame, it may be said—the characteristic moral penalty we are considering—has a definitive object— it is directed to that which is (believed to be) morally wrong. There is indeed also a wider sense. One can *blame* the dud calculator-batteries for a mistake in the bill, blame the weather for the train delay, etc. But in that wider sense M is simply false. Perhaps one ought to blame the weather, rather than British Rail, for the train delay. But the weather didn't act morally wrongly, though it did delay the train. And if British Rail was in *that* sense to blame, it still wouldn't follow that British Rail acted morally wrongly—though it might be appropriate to seek compensation. One can say such things as that Mary was to blame for the misunderstanding, but that one can't really *blame* her—she was understandably distracted by something else that was happening. Narrow blameworthiness turns on whether the agent could have helped doing what he did—a point we shall come back to.

Narrow blame is the concept invoked in M. But once that is clear, is it not also clear that the primitive term is 'morally wrong'? The agent of course (morally) ought to blame himself if his action is morally wrong. So M is true by definition—but by definition of (narrow) 'blame'. The moral itself is indefinable. At least it is not definable in this way.

V

There is a particular perspective from which this response has special force. It is reached only when morality is clearly disentangled

127

from nature and divine command. But it goes beyond that crucial separation in asserting the *irreducible* reality of moral law, the *indefinability* of moral concepts in non-moral terms. There can be, it adds, no external critical standpoint on morality. *Morality is* the governing normative standpoint. I will call this internalism. It is internalist also in that it does not allow as meaningful the question why I ought to do what I morally ought to do. On the definition of morality under consideration, that question can in principle arise. (It raises issues which will not be treated here.) Internalism stands in contrast to a secular-naturalistic perspective which is shared by philosophers as opposed in other respects as Mill and Nietzsche. This naturalism also makes the crucial separation, so it does not commit Moore's naturalistic fallacy. But it views morality externally. It sees it as an institution criticizable from some ethical or rational standpoint outside it. (So it is not 'value-free'—it is a position *within* the philosophy of value.) And it looks for a genealogy of the moral and of moral phenomena such as conscience and blame. This is the perspective to which the Millian definition belongs.

(I shall not consider here a third view, that the moral ought is a perspective irreducible to other oughts, but that neither it nor any other ought is the *governing* normative standpoint. That would make the moral ought incommensurable with non-moral oughts in a way that neither the internalist nor the externalist allows.)

The internalist holds that the concept of the moral is indefinable in non-moral terms. I will now argue that he is right, but that internalism does not follow from the indefinability of moral concepts. The external perspective can be maintained, even if 'moral' cannot be defined.

VI

The charge against the Millian definition, M, is that it involves a subtle circularity (the 'second' naturalistic fallacy, as one might say). Blame is a response whose justifying base requires that the object be something that has been done or brought about but morally ought not to have been done or brought about. It requires it in the way that fear requires that the object be dangerous. One can feel guilt about something one does not really believe to be morally wrong, just as one can fear something which one does not really believe dangerous, but in these cases the response is pathological.

The externalist may reply that there is a disanalogy between blame and fear. The dangerous (as against the fearsome) can be characterised independently as that which is liable to harm or damage. But in the case of blame no *independent* characterization of its justifying base—'moral wrongness'—can be given. To say that the object must be morally wrong for blame to be justified is not to give an independent characterization of the object, any more than to say that the object must be boring for boredom to be justified is to give an independent characterization. Saying that something is boring—boredom-worthy—is saying that the proper or just response to it is boredom. Likewise, saying that something is morally wrong—blameworthy is saying that the proper or just response to it is blame.

But can the logic of 'morally wrong' be aligned in this way with the logic of 'boring'? To examine this more closely we will compare the concepts 'boring' and 'red', and then see how 'morally wrong' fits in.

At the semantic level 'visual experience of red' is roughly definable as 'visual experience of the kind which a suitably sized red thing, optimally displayed to a relevantly normal observer, would cause that observer to have as part of his perception of that thing'. (Various refinements could be added.) This is analytic on the meaning of 'visual experience of red'. Thus 'red' is semantically primitive, and 'visual experience of red' is defined in its terms.

At the constitutive level, in contrast—the level of cognitive role, as against semantic content[3]—we have a norm partially constitutive of the concept red. That norm is something like this:

> When it visually appears to me that there is there an item which is red (a feature of the visual appearance is that an item looks red), then, in the absence of counter-evidence, I am justified in asserting 'There's something red there'.

So here the sensation of red (a feature of the total visual experience) primitively provides a defeasible warrant for a verdict about the world—that it contains something red.

Compare 'boring'. At the semantic level, 'x is boring' is definable as 'x has properties to which the proper or just reaction is a feeling of boredom whose object is x'. Thus unlike 'x is red', which is semantically primitive, 'x is boring' is definable. It is defined in terms of '(feeling of) boredom'. So it's certainly analytic

---

[3] The distinction between cognitive role and semantic content underpins the distinction I make between a constructon and a definition of the concept of the moral. I discuss it in 'Anti-realism, inference and the logical constants' (1993).

that a feeling of boredom is a feeling of the kind which boring things, optimally displayed to a good judge, would cause that judge to have. But that is in virtue of the definability of 'boring', not in virtue of the definability of 'boredom'. The latter is the primitive expression.

Whereas at the semantic level there is this asymmetry, at the constitutive level there is at least some symmetry. There must also be asymmetry, if the semantics of expressions is fully fixed by the concepts, that is, cognitive roles, they express. Presumably it will lie in the *location* of the two concepts in the more general fabric of concepts—in particular in the fact discussed below, that judgments about what is red are accountable not only to phenomenology but to a wider theoretical context. But the symmetry is that the norm which partially constitutes the concept of the boring is something like

A feeling of boredom with x, in the absence of countervailing considerations, justifies the verdict 'x is boring'.

A further point will be of importance to us: in both cases the verdict incurs the *convergence commitment*. In issuing the verdict I commit myself to holding that qualified judges would either converge on the same verdict or would be suffering from some discernible error or failure of relevant information which would explain their disagreement. Now this commitment is a general feature of the act of assertion[4]. With any assertion, if we acquire reason to think that this kind of convergence cannot be expected to occur, i.e. that fault-free divergence can perennially persist, we acquire reason for withdrawing, or in some cases—perhaps—relativizing, the assertion. But, despite the existence of this general convergence commitment, the response itself—the sensation of red or the feeling of boredom—defeasibly justifies the appropriate judgment. (The commitment is incurred by the act of judgment, not its content.)

Now we come back to the difficulty for the Millian definition. It is this: semantically, 'morally wrong' does not behave like 'boring' —instead, it behaves more like 'red'. If there is a connexion between blame and moral wrongness at the semantic level, it is that 'blaming' (in the narrow sense) in part means 'considering to be morally in the wrong'. So '(morally) wrong', like 'red'. and unlike 'boring', is the semantically primitive term.

We must conclude that Mill's account fails as a literal defitnition, at the semantic level. But it can still survive as what I call a

[4] See Skorupski, 1985–1986.

construction of the concept of the moral. To see this and to see why blame is a penalty, we must consider the emotional core of blame.

VII

Blaming someone can be a performative act. Like welcoming someone or apologising to them, the act of blaming has an emotional core. The welcome-emotion is feeling happy or good that you have come, the apology-emotion is feeling sorry for something I've done to you. I can often sincerely welcome and apologize without *feeling* the emotion, but the act always *invokes* the emotion —accepts its appropriateness. And sometimes it isn't enough to do the performance without having the feeling. You may not feel genuinely welcome, and you may feel that I am not as sorry as I should be. Blame similarily has an emotional core. I shall simply call it the *blame-feeling*, without broaching the many interesting questions about its relationship to other emotions. (A little more about it will be said in Sections VIII and IX.) As with apology or welcome, the act of blaming can be effectively performed without the emotion being felt—but not always. A child, for example, may not feel blamed if the blaming is too evidently formal.

Though blame can be an act it doesn't have to be—unlike apologizing or welcoming. Whereas having the sorry or the good-to-see-you feeling is not itself apologizing or welcoming, having the blame-feeling—when one has the appropriate moral concepts, and is not seeking to check the blame-feeling as inappropriate—*is* blaming. (These qualifications are required because, on the account I will give, the blame-feeling is a more primitive phenomenon than fully developed moral blame.)

With blame, as with apology and welcome, the core feeling has a justifying base—a set of beliefs without which it doesn't make sense for you to have the feeling. The question is whether the concept 'morally wrong' features intrinsically in that justifying set of beliefs. Compare feeling sorry. Here the thought that I have injured or offended you in some way features intrinsically in the justifying base. But it needn't have been a morally reprehensible way, and it needn't have been a voluntary or even an avoidable way.

With the blame-feeling, similarily, the thought that what was done was *morally* wrong need not enter the justifying base, though some more basic notion of wrong-doing must. Nor need the wrong-doing involve wronging someone, as apology requires injuring or offending someone. However a more important contrast with feeling sorry, for our purposes, is that the act which arouses the blame-feeling must be thought of as one which the agent could have *avoided* doing. It is not quite the voluntary that is here in question. For one can blame a person for things he did not do voluntarily—spilling the coffee, running someone over. These are still things that he could have avoided doing, with proper care. So I shall use the term 'avoidable' to cover all such doings, including those which are not in the full, intentional, sense. acts (and including omissions). A doing was avoidable when the agent could have done otherwise. Thus one constraint on the intelligibility of the blame-feeling is that its object must be a doing which is taken to be avoidable. We shall consider later what sort of constraint it is.

Another constraint on the intelligibility of the blame-feeling, of course, is that the doing must be thought to be wrong. But 'wrong' here is still pre-moral. At this pre-moral level wrong-doing is simply a doing which properly arouses the blame-feeling—a 'blame-feeling-worthy' doing—in the way that the boring is simply the boredom-worthy. 'Blame-feeling-worthy' is here a more basic concept than our actual, moralized, notion of the blameworthy.

A third constraint is that one must believe that the agent knew or could have known what he was doing. This condition will be relevant only in one of its aspects—that he knew or could have known the action to be wrong (see Sections VIII and X).

What makes a space for the distinction between having an emotional response and judging it justified? It comes from the discipline set up by criteria grounded in experience of that response, reflection on it and inter-subjective comparison. Those criteria are in play when we judge that what bored or amused us, or what aroused in us the blame-feeling, is not after all boring, amusing or blame-feeling-worthy. Let us call them 'hermeneutic' criteria, and the discipline they impose hermeneutic discipline, since their ground is what can intelligibly, understandably, produce a given emotional response. Not only emotional responses are disciplined hermeneutically—aesthetic responses and impressions of validity would be other examples. But it is with emotional responses that we are concerned here. The understanding in question is an understanding from within—a matter of *verstehen*. ('I can't understand why you find that funny.' 'I used to find that funny, but I really can't see what's funny about it any more.') So judgments which are disciplined hermeneutically, and in no other way, are finally accountable only to spontaneous response—but the spontaneity in question is that which emerges from experience, reflection, and intersubjective comparison and agreement. The criteria formed in that process are enough to allow a distinction between what seems to me a just response and what is a just response, and thus to underwrite the judgments as *judgments*. But they are internal criteria—they do not shape the judgments by any controls other than those which flow from appeal to the ideal of an undistorted, 'adequate' or 'well-tuned' convergence on a spontaneous emotional response. Let us call such hermeneutically disciplined normative judgments 'response determined', and the concepts which they predicate 'response determined' normative concepts. On the analysis, so far, 'That was a wrong-doing' would be an response-determined judgment.

However the judgment 'This is (morally) wrong' is not an affectively-determined normative judgment. And as we have seen, in a certain semantic respect 'morally wrong' behaves like 'red' rather than like 'boring' or 'amusing'. Similarily, in so far as 'blameworthy' in its actual use is definable in terms of the morally wrong, it cannot be detached from the normal syntax that goes with that and aligned, as I aligned 'blame-feeling-worthy' in the last but one paragraph, with 'boring' and 'amusing'. The concept that stands to the blame-feeling as the concept of the boring stands to boredom is a simpler concept than the concept we actually have. The externalist needs to explain this point. Whether the externalist view is reductive will depend on the explanation it gives. It will be reductive if it explains the asymmetry between 'boring' and 'morally wrong' in a way that does not at the same time justify it.

An analogy would be this. Someone who reflects on the intentional content of amusement may conclude that it is always some kind of incongruity that causes amusement. He may think of this as a substantive theory—incongruity being some independent relation in the objects. But we find, when we examine, that incongruity is not characterizable in a way that is at all independent of what we spontaneously find amusing. The alien who felt no emotion of amusement could not focus this alleged phenomenon of incongruity. Incongruity is simply a response-determined concept in disguise. An explanation of 'morally wrong' which treated it in the same way, as a response-determined concept in disguise, would be reductive.

So we need to show why 'morally wrong' is not a response determined concept, and that may in turn give us the material for a nonreductive construction of the morally wrong. The material is indeed available—it lies in the fact that verdicts about what is morally wrong, unlike verdicts about what is boring, are accountable to criteria which are independent of, and *externally* regulate, the blame-feeling.[5] Boredom, amusement, irritation, etc. generate criteria internal to the response, which regulate verdicts about its propriety, set up the ideal of what well tuned judges would feel, and in turn make space for judgments about whether a person is, say, irritable, or lacking in discrimination or sensibility (and thus in a particular context disqualified as a judge). But moral judgments are not disciplined *solely* in this hermeneutic way. They are, in this respect, comparable to verdicts about redness. These latter judgments are indeed accountable initially to perceptual experience. But they are accountable also to criteria of theoretical reason. Those latter, external, criteria are mediated through a context of physical theory, a body of beliefs which can retrospectively override a judgment that something is red, even when that judgment is default-justified by perceptual experience. If, for example, we find that atmospheric conditions, or the relative speed of a body to the perceiver, can affect its apparent colour, then we may withdraw colour judgments which perceptual experience would otherwise have justified by default. At the limit, indeed, we could discover that nothing is red, even though we have sensations of red. That doesn't seem possible with 'boring' (i.e. that we have the very same feelings of boredom but 'discover' that nothing is really boring). But it does seem possible with 'morally wrong', precisely because 'morally wrong' is not a response-determined concept. The institution of morality might be shown, by criteria external to the hermeneutics of the blame-feeling as such, to be redundant. Blame-feelings might never justify judgments of blameworthiness, that is, moral wrongness. And the construction of the concept of the moral must illuminate the ways in which that is *possible*— though I shall argue in Section X that no such undercutting takes place.

VIII

But let us first go back to the blame-feeling, which is primitive to the construction of the notion of the morally wrong. It has a justifying base, which places hermeneutic constraints on its possible objects. These constraints, as with other feelings, are hermeneutic in that they limit what we find intelligible. One cannot intelligibly, for example, be bored or amused by a car tyre. There must be something about it which makes it boring or amusing—and it is that total context (appearing at the fancy-dress ball wearing a car tyre as a hat) which is boring or amusing. A car tyre in itself cannot be the total object of boredom or amusement.

[5] Kant classes moral judgments as 'logical' rather 'than 'aesthetic' for related reasons. See Kant, 1928.

It is at this level, I believe, that we find the connexion between blame and avoidability. It rests on a hermeneutic constraint, which limits the objects of the blame-feeling to (what are taken to be) avoidable doings. That constraint underlies the central principle of narrow morality: the blameworthy agent could and *ought to* have done better. The ought here is the moral ought; so the principle's aprioricity is in part owed to the definition (or rather, construction) of the moral ought. But only in part, because the principle also requires that the agent *could* have done better. It may be suggested that the aprioricity of this stems from 'ought implies can. But this only pushes the question back to why *that* principle is *a priori*. On the view I am suggesting its foundation is the hermeneutic constraint on the blame-feeling—the object of the blame-feeling must be an agent who could have done better. Not every such agent is blamed, but nothing can be blamed which is not such an agent. To blame anything else is unintelligible, in the way that being bored by a car tyre is. (The connexion between blame and avoidability here proposed thus differs from views which derive it from the *pointlessness* of blaming the unavoidable.)

This unintelligibility is not to be further explained at the level of *reasons*. One might try to explain, in biological or psychological terms, why human beings have the blame-feeling, and one may also try to resolve the feeling into other feelings. But insofar as such explanations go beyond the hermeneutic domain, the domain of the directly or intrinsically intelligible, they address non-philosophical questions (perfectly good ones of course). In contrast, one can simply seek greater understanding of the blame-feeling at the hermeneutic level, by placing it in a wider group of hostile or disparaging emotions, such as anger, disdain, contempt, suspicion, scorn, horror, frigidity. In all of these cases the object is something whose doing is thought to fall short, or expected to fall short, of what good doing of that kind would be. It *should* have been better, though this 'should' does not imply 'could'. (I can feel angry with a bent nail—it shouldn't have bent, it was faulty.) Anger, disdain and the rest can certainly be aroused, quite intelligibly, by doings which the agent could not have bettered. Blame cannot. We may or may not feel there are moral grounds for inhibiting such feelings, when the agent couldn't have helped it, and may be hurt by them. But still these are not *hermeneutic* constraints, on the intelligibility of the feelings. In contrast, if someone expresses the blame-feeling towards a doing which he also claims not to think the agent could have bettered, our understanding is strained.

John Skorupski

IX

It is by reference to the blame-feeling that we should understand the penal nature of blame. Emotions are aroused by characteristic objects—but they also give rise to characteristic dispositions. To what then does the blame-feeling dispose? To exclusion of those towards whom it is felt from the moral community, to a withdrawal of recognition, however partial and temporary. That community is the community of agents who live by, observe, intelligible norms. Hence the ethical significance of the effort to understand other persons and cultures from within. Here lies the connexion with avoidability: what prompts exclusion is the failure to avoid something which should have been recognized as proper to avoid, if one was freely responding to relevant norms. The wrong-doer is discredited, dishonoured as a 'self-legislating' member of the kingdom of ends.

The blame-feeling does not dispose, like anger, towards attack, like fear, towards flight, like frigidity, towards withdrawal of love or like feeling sorry, towards reparation. It disposes towards ostracism, the cutting off of solidarity, the reduction of respect. There is an overlap here with disdain. But the blame-feeling *presupposes*, and then imperils, the wrong-doer's standing as a free self-legislator. while disdain does not suppose it in the first place. At the limit, the withdrawal of recognition becomes the attitude taken to a being which must be, not reasoned with as autonomous, but trained, or deterred, by external penalty and reward. At this limit the blame-feeling ceases, since its object must be thought of as a member, however errant, of the moral community. Without moral membership ostracism, withdrawal of membership, makes no sense. Blame is a penalty in itself, an internal penalty, in as much as it gives rise to this sense of threatened recognition, of casting out into the liminal region between the village and the bush, the social order and the outer hermeneutically unintelligible, world.[6] Guilt is self-exclusion, one's own withdrawal of recognition from oneself.

[6] 'No more fiendish punishment could be devised, were such a thing physically possible, than that one should be turned loose in society and remain absolutely unnoticed by all the members thereof. If no one turned round when we entered, answered when we spoke, or minded what we did, but if every person we met "cut us dead", and acted as if we were non-existing things, a kind of rage and impotent despair would ere long well up in us, from which the cruellest bodily torture would be a relief; for these would make us feel that, however bad might be our plight, we had not sunk to such a depth as to be unworthy of attention at all.' (James, 1890, vol. 1., 293–294.)

As an act, blame puts this disposition to exclude overtly, even formally, on the record (though perhaps only between blamer and blamed), in the same way that overt greeting, welcome or apology puts on record the corresponding disposition to make at home, or to make amends. Interestingly, the same sort of putting on record is not possible with anger or scorn. One can of course make one's anger or scorn explicit, but there is no socially recognized vehicle, instituted in forms of language, for being (performatively, so to speak) angry with someone or scorning them. And if one by-passes blame by saying 'I'm rather angry with you', one is in fact soft-pedalling, ducking past the judicial-penal element in blame, staying on equal terms with the other, being 'non-judgmental'. On the other hand, the old-fashioned habit of snubbing people one didn't approve of (cp. James on 'cutting dead') was a close cousin of the practice of blame: it implied withdrawal of respect. Its withering is an aspect of our increasing focus on the morality of action and blame as against the ethics of character and approval—a natural development of the decline of status distinction. (The interaction of character and ethical approval with breeding and social status, as in the very meaning of words like 'gentle', 'noble', is insufficiently explored by 'virtue theorists', though they were clear enough to Aristotle. The abstraction from social realities can give their discussions a somewhat innocent air.)

The judicial-penal element, internal to blame as such, consists in loss of recognition. External punishment, in family, school or law, at least sometimes functions to restore recognition (not least by oneself). This aspect of the matter picked up by those who say that external punishment is the wrong-doer's right; though recognizing it does not force us to deny the obvious deterrent function of external punishment.[7] And the inherently penal character of blame is the key to understanding how blameworthiness comes to be detached from the blame-feeling; how it transcends the primitive, responsive determined concept of blame-feeling-worthiness. It is *because* blame is penal that one can rationally raise the question of what *should* be penalised by means of it. Spontaneous blame-feelings thus come under the regulation not only of their own hermeneutic discipline, but also of external regulative forces—ethical ideals and practical reason as such. The content of these is not our main concern here, though I shall sketch out a view of them in the final section. The main constructive claim of this paper is that the concept of the moral emerges from this inter-

[7] Hegel is a source of this view, as of the notion of recognition which I have made use of in this section.

action—between hermeneutic criteria regulating the blame-feeling from within, and external criteria which come from sources independent of it and which seek, more or less successfully, to shape its penal effect to a larger context. This interaction is an important phenomenon on any view of what those external criteria are. Their presence explains why the concept of the moral cannot be reduced to the internal, affective criteria which partly constitute it, any more than the concept of redness can be reduced to the phenomenal criteria which partly constitute it. But to see the interaction one must recognize, as the externalist does, that there are indeed standards regulating blame other than those affectively determined by the blame-feeling itself.

X

If we accept that there is this interaction we must then also accept the logical possibility that morality might be superseded. External criteria might convince us that it is never rational to allot blame. We might become convinced, like the utopian and the subversive thinkers of Section III, that the penal element which is incipient in the blame-feeling—the element of exclusion, which morality accredits and institutionalizes into a mode of social control distinct from formally prescribed external penalties—should, on the contrary be discredited and, so far as possible, decommissioned. More effective methods of pursuing our ethical ideals or practical-rational goals might be found. Blame-feelings might persist, being grounded in human nature—but instead of being harnessed in a social institution they would become surplus to requirements. They would be seen as non-rational survivals, unhelpfully 'negative' and 'judgmental' in their accompanying disposition to withdraw recognition and to exclude.

All of this is indeed *abstractly* possible. but perhaps it only has to be spelt out explicitly to seem unreal. It could also happen, however, that the supersession of morality arose out of a deeper analysis of the hermeneutic of blame itself—it might be that that itself rested on some confused picture of things. The blame-feeling might be irrational in the same way as fear of unlucky omens, or disgust at taboo substances, or belief in the magical power of symbols. It would be prone to undercutting from rational reflection on its justifying base as such, irrespective of the efficiency or otherwise of harnessing it in a social institution.

The blame-feeling would be undermined in this way if there was philosophical reason to conclude that nothing is avoidable. The notorious argument here, of course, is from determinism—

but this will not sway those of us who regard *that* alleged incompatibility (of 'free will and determinism') as either an irrelevancy or a confusion. Is there, though, some more subtle incoherence in morality's dependence on the notion of avoidability?

Bernard Williams notes that blame, 'the characteristic reaction of the morality system' (1985, 177) is 'directed to the voluntary' (178). He highlights what I have also highlighted, that when we blame we blame for what the agent should have *recognized* as something to be avoided. We take it that the agent is responsive to the norms to which we also respond. But Williams thinks the agent would only have had reason to act otherwise if doing so would have promoted projects or concerns he in fact had—there are no reasons grounded in concerns which he is rationally *required* to have. So 'The institution of blame is best seen as involving a fiction' (*ibid*. 193), the fiction that there are reasons for acting which apply to all agents, irrespective of their already existing motives. Now this fiction does not concern the voluntary, that is, avoidability, as such. It lies rather in the assumption that wrong-doer and moral judge respond in common to categorical norms, which transcend their possibly divergent motives. Williams rejects such 'absolutely "external"' reasons—ones that do not 'speak to any motivation the agent already has' (*ibid*. 223–224, n. 19)

Here he represents Humean or Nietzschean presumptions, rather than Kantian or Millian ones. Autonomy, or (in Mill's less transcendentally-charged phrase) 'moral freedom', involves something more than the instrumental notion of practical rationality. Moral freedom is, precisely, the disposition to respond to reasons whether or not they 'speak to any motivations the agent already has'.[8] Thus when Williams predicts that if we achieve a 'reflective

---

[8] Williams is wrong in holding that Kant also thinks every reason must 'speak' to a '*motivation* the agent *already* has' (*ibid*. my emphases). It is truistic, of course, that a reason must engage with *something* 'already' in the agent, if it is to affect his belief or his action. It must engage with a capacity to recognize reasons and a disposition to respond to them. but it is not true, and Kant does not hold, that it must engage with an already existing *motivation*. To identify the formal, place-holding, notion of a disposition to act or believe on reasons, with the psychologically robust notion of a 'motivation'—a desire to act or believe on them—is to beg the question against the believer in what Williams calls 'external reasons'. Let me add here that in equating Kants autonomy and Mill's moral freedom for the purposes of this paper I do not mean to suggest that they are identical. They have in common the idea of rational mastery of one's desires; but Mill, of course, does not identify the moral with the rational—as the passages quoted in Section 11 suffice to make clear.

and non-mythical understanding of our ethical practices', 'the practices of blame, and more generally the style of people's negative ethical reactions to others, will change' (*ibid.*194), his prediction is grounded on the idea that what cannot survive non-mythical understanding is the (Kantian/Millian) ideal of autonomy or moral freedom—the capacity to recognize impartial claims of reason as authoritative, and to act from that recognition.

I do not agree. Moral freedom does not require the idealist underpinnings Kant gave it; nor is it the case that to be a naturalist one must be a Humean. On the contrary, a *properly* naturalistic, non-mythical, understanding of our hermeneutic notions would, among other things, scrap the mythopoeic 'science' of 'desire-belief psychology'.

This is not the place to defend such convictions; but if I am right then neither determinism, nor the supposed impossibility of giving an account of categorical reasons without idealism, nor the Humean doctrine of motivation, is the problem. However Williams presents a further, independent, and important, line of thought. 'To the extent that the institution of blame works coherently', he suggests, 'it does so because it attempts less than morality would like it to do'. Morality, he thinks, tends to seek more than the practices of blame require:

> There is a pressure within it to require a voluntariness that will be total and will cut through character and psychological and social determination, and allocate blame and responsibility on the ultimately fair basis of the agent's own contribution, no more and no less. It is an illusion to suppose that this demand can be met. (*ibid.* 94)

It is indeed an illusion that suppose that *this* demand can be met. I further agree with Williams that 'the institution of blame' does not require it. But then what is morality other than that institution? A firm distinction should be maintained here, between the principle of avoidability, which is both central to morality and defensible— that I cannot be blamed for what I could not have avoided—and, in contrast, the pressure which Williams identifies towards 'total' voluntariness. The former is deeply rooted in the hermeneutic of the blame-feeling. The latter arises not from anything essential to morality itself, but from that least compelling aspect of the Kantian legacy—its rigoristic moral egalitarianism.

To impose such rigoristic egalitarianism is not what morality 'would like to do' but what Kantians and many other modern moralists would like to do, under the influence of two governing ideas: that worth cannot reside in acts or qualities outside the agent's control and that all agents must be equal in their possession of that control, the control on which worth depends. It is this ideal, the ideal of pure egalitarian desert, which forces them towards the idea that all worth traces back to the transcendental exercise of moral freedom—and to the fetishism of morality that goes with it.

XI

Blame presupposes moral freedom. You cannot be blamed for what you could not have *recognized as* something you should not do, and were able not to do *on the basis* of that recognition. But it is not true that all worth presupposes moral freedom. A quality of character or an action can have worth even though it is not the product of an exercise of moral freedom. A person's generosity and moral courage, for example, have value even if they are natural to him and do not result from any choice or effort on his part. And his generous and brave acts are admirable even if they are products of spontaneous inclination rather than conscientious principle.

The reluctance to accept that stems, as Williams suggests, from a yearning for 'ultimate fairness'. This remains even when other misconceptions, as that all inclination is selfish, are removed. Natural qualities are unequally distributed, and the inequality does not stem from the efforts of the agents. Hence the attractiveness of transcendentalising autonomy, and giving it the monopoly of worth. If every agent is transcendentally equal in autonomy, and nothing except autonomous action has worth, worth maps onto 'the agent's own contribution' in the way that pure egalitarian desert requires. But in fact autonomy—in the shape at least of its demythologised correlate, moral freedom—is also, just like generosity or moral courage, a natural quality of human agents. As with natural generosity and courage, its worth does not depend on its resulting from an exercise of moral freedom. We can to some. but only to a limited extent, make ourselves more morally free, by our own effort. But that requires some moral freedom in the first place, not itself resulting from the agent's own effort. It is not required, for being free, that you should freely have made yourself free, nor is it a condition of your freedom having ethical worth.

If moral freedom is a natural quality, then, as with generosity or moral courage, it is entirely expectable that some should have it more than others. This does not itself cause problems for the institution of blame. Diminished moral freedom means diminished blame. Neither the practice of blame, nor the institution of morality based on it, require 'ultimate' equality in the degree of moral freedom moral agents have. It is only required that they have some. But while that does not undermine morality, it does undermine those modern ideals of it according to which, we are all, in respect of moral agency, equal—and which base our equal worth or dignity entirely on that. It is those ideals, rather than anything within morality itself, which produce the pressure to 'cut through character and psychological and social determination', to identify ethical worth with autonomous action, and to hold that all agents are—transcendentally speaking—equally autonomous. Seeing morality non-mythically certainly forces one to give up that, and thus for example, to rethink those varieties of the liberal ethic which rest on it.[9]

In eliminating the fetishism of morality, the external, genealogical, point of view on moral phenomena comes into its own. It dismantles the monopolistic concept of 'moral worth', replacing it by the diversity of valuations connected with admiration and blame. But it too has its characteristic dangers—the antipode of moral fetishism. It is pretty obvious (other than to the last discoverers of Nietzsche) that shallow suspicion of the supposed 'illusions' of morality is presently a much greater danger than fetishism. We need to find a way between fetishism and modernistic subversion, a way of redirecting suspicion from the innocent, and pre-eminently human, institution of morality to the rigoristic-egalitarian modern distortions of it. If we direct suspicion to its proper target, we shall not think that dismantling 'moral worth' is dismantling morality. And we shall better appreciate the relations between morality and other systems of human valuation. also rooted in spontaneous feeling, and disciplined hermeneutically.

As well as morality, whose emotive core is the blame-feeling, there is the system of *ends*, whose affective core is liking or desire. Then there is the system of *character-ideals*, whose core is admiration. Like morality, these systems are controlled by the ideal of undistorted, well-tuned convergence referred to in Section VI. Objective ends, such as happiness, or insight, or recognition and respect, are resilient categories under which we continue to desire objects—after experience, reflection and discussion—despite the

[9] It is however easy to overstate the importance of autonomy in the ethics (let alone the political economy and political sociology) of classical liberalism. See my 'Autonomy in its Place', in Knowles and Skorupski, 1993, and my 'Liberal Elitism', 1992.

tensions which this plurality of categorial ends creates, and the perennial disagreements as to their relative importance. Objective character-ideals are constituted by what is in the same way, through the same tensions and disagreements, *admired*.

There is interaction between these three systems, one kind of value spilling over into another. In particular, there is interaction between morality and the system of character-ideals. Not all ideals of character are virtues—not, for example coolness, wit, or sheer vitality; the admiration we feel for them is in some cases ethical, in some cases aesthetic, in some cases a mixture of the two. Note the asymmetry here which is obscured by the notion of 'moral worth': blame is a penalty, but admiration should not be moralized into a reward. We admire many character-traits and performances whose absence is not *blameworthy*—though it may become disestimable. We naturally admire physical courage and style. But we do not blame those who could have done something to reduce their timidity or frumpishness, but haven't bothered—though we may well, if we are honest with ourselves, admit that we think less of them.

In contrast, someone who could have done something to overcome his natural cruelty, but has not bothered, is blameworthy. A virtue is something narrower than the general notion of a character-ideal. It is a quality of character which we admire or can come to admire, and failure to develop which in oneself, where it is possible to do so, is—other things being equal again—blameworthy. Our notion of virtue draws on the resources of the system of character-ideals, and its core-sentiment of admiration. The moral shades into the ethical and the ethical into the aesthetic, along a spectrum with the blame-feeling at one end and simple admiration of human excellence at the other.

Behind these systems of valuation lies the background framework of practical reason. This is the larger structure of which Mill thought that morality is only a department. My division into morality, character-ideals and ends corresponds fairly obviously, if only roughly, to his division into Morality, Aesthetics and Prudence. But to call these only departments is misleading. They are more like fiefdoms, coming under the loose sovereignty of reason, but animated by their own independent spirit, without which reason would have nothing over which to rule. If the fundamental idea of practical reason is impartially conceived good, it is an idea that would remain empty without them; just as truth, the idea of theoretical reason, would remain empty without substantive valuations, similarly grounded in convergence, about what reasonings are justified and what explanations good.

This highlights a final point. One can be a rationalist about practical reason, without being a rationalist about moral judgments—judgments as to the blameable—or indeed about judgments as to the admirable or the desirable. *Their* material is drawn from various modes of feeling. That, I should add, is to reflect a rationalist, but not a cognitivist, view of them. They are genuine judgments. The point is that even where reason regulates and modifies them, as in the case of the blameworthy, it does not give them their primitive grounds. But to pursue this meta-ethical issue, or to map out general relationships between the various aspects of human valuation and practical reason, is no task for today. I have been concerned here only with sketching how the moral fits in.

Ethics, Fantasy
and Self-transformation

JEAN GRIMSHAW

In this paper I want to discuss an issue (usually perceived as an ethical one) which has generated a great deal of feminist discussion and some profound disagreement. The issue arises as follows. One of the most important targets of feminist action and critique has been male sexual violence and control of women, as expressed in rape and other forms of violent or aggressive sexual acts, and as represented in much pornography. Pornography itself has been the subject of major and sometimes bitter disagreements among feminists, especially around the issue of censorship. But it is not that with which I am concerned here. The issue which I want to discuss involves the question of sexual desire and fantasy, and their apparent potential incompatibility with political and ethical principles. This is by no means, of course, an issue of exclusively feminist concern; but I shall focus on some recent feminist argument, since it is that with which I am most familiar.

There is a great deal of evidence that women's sexual fantasies often involve various forms and elements of domination, submission, humiliation; even rape itself. Women can find pornographic literature such as *The Story of O* erotic; this famous pornographic novel involves the ritual rape and repeated beating and humiliation of the heroine, who is reduced to being nothing but a total sexual slave of her masters. Less obvious but more widespread ways in which women can find pleasure in scenarios involving violence and humiliation can be found in many genres of romantic massmarket fiction. These may rarely involve an actual rape, at least between the pages of the book, but they routinely involve the mistreatment, humiliation and near-brutality of the hero towards the heroine, until the last pages when it is revealed that he really loves her. Ann Barr Snitow (1979) has argued that mass market romance may be seen as a kind of pornography for women.

But it is also clear that such fantasies can exist in women who have a strong commitment to sexual equality, who abhor male violence or sexual domination of women. And the question of what our response should be to this fact has generated some profound disagreements. There is a range of views on the question. I shall outline some of them, and then go on to consider what seem to me to be some of the philosophical and ethical issues involved.

There are two responses to the existence of these sexual fantasies in women which seem to me to represent two ends of the spectrum. At the first end is the kind of view which suggests that the person who has the fantasies should just learn to live with them and accept them. They are harmless; there is no necessary connection at all between fantasy and real life. Any attempt to make those who have such fantasies uneasy or guilty about them is divisive and coercive. In addition, the supposition that fantasy or desire could ever be made to toe a politically 'correct' line is pointless, since fantasies can never be controlled in this way. Furthermore, even if acted upon in controlled ways (such as in various sado-masochistic sexual practices), they do not in any sense necessarily compromise political principles, or make women less likely to wish to condemn rape and real-life sexual violence. In addition, it is a good thing that sexual desire and fantasy is freed as much as possible from structures of guilt, fear, shame and psychic distress.

At the other end of the spectrum is a radically different view. A fairly extreme statement of this view can be found in a book by Sheila Jeffreys, *Anti-Climax* (1990). The book offers a powerful indictment of the ways in which both much twentieth century literature about sexuality and the so-called 'sexual revolution' and increased sexual 'permissiveness' of the decades since the 1960s have been premised on sexist views of women and phallocentric views of sexuality. But Jeffreys view of sexuality and of sexual fantasy is nevertheless one that I find troubling and problematic for many reasons. Jeffreys argues that far from heterosexual intercourse being something that all women 'naturally' like or enjoy, it is something into which many of them are pressured by the power of ideology and social sanctions. She does indeed show how concepts such as those of 'inhibition', 'frigidity' and 'repression' have been used in large numbers of books about sexuality to disallow any kind of response from women that was unhappy with a model of sexuality totally dominated by intercourse and male pleasure. But her own view of women's sexuality runs something like this. Women's sexuality as currently constructed, including many of their sexual fantasies, is almost wholly adapted to, or colonized by, male needs and desires. Even many ideas of a more 'autonomous' and active female sexuality are, she argues, constructed on models of male sexuality—as continuously capable of sex and always desiring it, for example, or as capable of separating sex from loving emotion and making use of all sexual opportunities.

But male sexuality—and heterosexuality itself—is a ruling class sexuality, constructed around the domination and subordination of women. Heterosexual desire is eroticised power difference; men's desire for women is based on eroticising the powerlessness, 'otherness' and subordination of women. And women's desire for men is based on the same structures; they too have been conditioned to think that inequality and subordination are sexy. Women's sexual response to men has been based partly on the material need to cope with male power and their own frequent dependence; but they have also learned the 'deep structures' of their own eroticism in a male dominated society. The reason why women have such things as sadomasochistic fantasies is that they are born into, and conditioned by, a system of subordination, which has a 'negative' effect on their sexual feelings and responses.

Jeffreys argues that we need to move away from the assumption that all forms of sexual arousal or fantasy should be seen simply as 'pleasurable'; we need to be able to describe sexual responses in a way that firmly sees some of them as negative and as destructive. And women need to 'unlearn' their sexual and emotional responses; to develop sexual responses and fantasies that are not premised on subordination and inequality. We need to democratize desire; to learn to eroticise sameness, equality and mutuality. Women need to monitor and try to change the responses of their bodies to those things which indicate their own oppression. Thus, writes Jeffreys (1990, 305) :

> If we listen to our feelings about sex sensitively instead of riding roughshod over them through guilt or anxiety about being prudes, we can work out what is positive and what is negative. The negative feelings are about eroticized subordination or heterosexual desire.

We should therefore try to shut down those responses which are are about subordination, rather than 'pleasure'. Jeffreys suggests that we should forget about 'surrendering' or 'letting go', about 'submissiveness' and 'giving in'—all those words which according to her, carry connotations of passivity, dependence and subordination. Instead, we should learn to eroticise the meeting of 'equals'.

Jeffreys admits to not knowing what desire or fantasy might look like in a world in which it was not premised on 'subordination'; but she also thinks that it is a moral task for women (with no shirkers allowed) to try to change their sexual feelings and fantasies. Nor, she implicitly suggests, is this as difficult to do as one might think; association with other women in a feminist environment might do the trick. But if we cannot do it, then perhaps it is so much the worse for sex. Sexual desire and fantasy as we know them are incompatible with freedom; if forced to choose between freedom and sex then we should choose freedom. We should of course also change our sexual behaviour and practices; but the 'inner' is as important as the 'outer'. Jeffreys sees the persistence of certain sorts of fantasy, I think, as one of the strongest marks of the colonisation of women's sexual life and imagination. Without eradicating what she sees as the negative forms of this imagination, there can be no freedom for women. Women need to try to shut down those responses which in any way eroticise their subordination.

However, not at all those who argue that women might try to change their desires and their fantasies believe, like Jeffreys seems to do, in sexual voluntarism; any woman can change her desires and fantasies if she tries hard enough. In an article, 'Feminine Masochism and the Politics of Personal Transformation' (1990), Sandra Bartky considers the issues in a much more complex kind of way. She presents us with the case of an imaginary protagonist, P, who is prone to various desires and fantasies of a sadomasochistic nature, yet is also an active and committed feminist and a believer in sexual equality. P, as Bartky presents her, feels shame and anxiety at the persistence of these fantasies, which do not seem to be in line with her politics. There are two possible courses of action, Bartky suggests, which P might think of adopting; she could try to get rid of her shame, or she could try to change her desires.

Bartky argues that whilst P should not be *made* to feel shame by others, she is nevertheless entitled to her shame. Those sexual liberals who argue that anything goes in the matter of sexual desire and fantasy (provided, of course, that they are not acted on in such a way as to harm others), have simply failed to respond to radical critiques of female subordination. They do not recognize how deeply the female psyche and imagination has been colonized, or the extent to which sadomasochistic fantasies may both be an expression of a woman-hating culture and distressing to those who have them. Bartky concludes that it is a good and sensible project for P to try to change her desires, *if* she can. But there is the rub. Bartky argues that sexual voluntarism—the idea that people can, with sufficient will-power, simply change their fantasies—is inadequate on many grounds. First, it fails to recognise the ways in which many fantasies may be extremely deep-rooted in the psyche; they may, for example, be mechanisms for psychic survival or well-being whose nature and motivation is highly obscure. Second, (but related), Bartky argues, correctly I think, that the view of the sexual voluntarists is often based on a wholly inadequate view of the ways in which patterns of sexual behaviour and desire are learned. Jeffreys, for example, will have no truck whatsoever with any psychoanalytic view of the nature of desire and fantasy. Instead she adopts a view that sexual mores and sexual desire are learned by a process of 'conditioning', in which notions of female subordination are imprinted on a relatively passive subject. Hence the implausible notion that simply substituting a different 'input' (in this case a feminist one) might be enough to bring about processes of radical change of the deep structures of fantasy and eroticism. Third, the supposition that all fantasies ought to toe a morally and politically correct 'line'—even supposing that this were possible—is bound to be judgmental, divisive, and coercively alienating of those who seem to fall short of a (mythical) ideal.

So whereas Jeffreys would set P the moral task of changing her fantasies and her desire, Bartky suggests that whilst this is a reasonable goal for her to have, it is unlikely that she will get very far in doing so. Bartky's arguments against sexual voluntarism seem to me to be on the mark; but they leave P in an apparently unfortunate dilemma. And I think that despite Bartky's disagreements with many of the sorts of arguments put forward by writers such as Jeffreys, the whole debate is underpinned by some unexamined presuppositions and key terms; and it is these that I should now like to explore a little further. I want to offer some thoughts about fantasy and desire, about the nature of eroticism, and finally about the whole project of self-transformation envisaged both by Bartky and by Jeffreys.

Fantasy and desire

The first thing to note here is that there is at times what I think is a problematic conflation between fantasy and desire in Bartky's argument. Bartky writes in what seems to be an undifferentiated way about fantasy and desire—about sado-masochistic sexual practices and about the fantasies of humiliation and the like which she ascribes to P. But 'desire' is a difficult term here, since it is plain that there are elements in many fantasies which are not connected with desire in the sense that one would like them to happen in real life. The connection between desire and fantasy is a complex one. Thus fantasies (of the kind which one would not like actually to happen) may prompt or facilitate desire for that which one would. So the notion that P should

Jean Grimshaw

'change her desires' is not at all as clear as it may seem at first sight. Suppose that a fantasy involving bondage or humiliation leads not to a desire to be bound or whipped but to a desire for more 'conventional' sex; what is it exactly that Bartky supposes should be changed?

Even more interesting and problematic, however, is the concept of 'fantasy' itself. Many writers on the subject of sexual fantasies do not stop to explore what they mean by 'fantasy'. Most commonly, they seem to assume that having a fantasy always involves a clear conception of one's own desires in relation to the fantasy, and a clear conception of one's own role in it; what one imagines doing, or having done to oneself. But this view of fantasy needs challenging.

In an essay entitled 'A Child is Being Beaten', Freud (1979) described a fantasy experienced by one of his patients. The interesting thing about the fantasy—indicated in the title itself—is that it was not clear to the patient *who* was being beaten or who was doing the beating. Sometimes, the patient might appear in the narrative as the child; sometimes as the person doing the beating; sometimes as a third party watching the event. In other words, the fantasy presented a scenario, but one in which the role of the person having the fantasy could shift or be quite unclear. I speculate here—but perhaps it is the case that in this kind of fantasy scenario, the persons involved are more likely to be 'strangers', anonymous, ciphers even, who interchange in the particular narrative. The point I am making is that the nature of fantasy, and its connection with desire, is often highly indeterminate; fantasies commonly offer open, rather than closed narratives, or hints of narratives, in which the question of identification with the position of victim, agent, voyeur, etc. may be undecidable or shifting. Empirical studies which try to establish whether or not there is a connection between fantasy (e.g. whilst reading or watching pornography), and what people then go out and do, frequently tend to miss this point. They assume without argument, for example, that if a man watches or fantasises a pornographic scene he is automatically 'identifying' with the man in the picture or the narrative, and desiring to 'do the same', or have the same done to him. Recent critiques of certain earlier psychoanalytic theories of the positioning of film viewers have also noted that one cannot assume that men will 'identify' with the male heroine, or women with the female heroine.

I am inclined to think that the term 'fantasy' should be reserved for such narratives or scenarios in which the question of 'identification' may be shifting or indeterminate. Sometimes, however, the

150

term 'fantasy' is used to refer to things such as passing thoughts which may indeed involve another specific person; imagining momentarily, for example, that someone whose voice one cannot stand is being smothered. Even here, however, I speculate that it is more likely that the fantasy (if it is one) will be of 'the person being smothered', rather than of I myself doing the smothering.

But there is another extremely important consideration. It should not be supposed that all fantasies have a clear and obvious meaning which can just be read off from some account of the salient features of the narrative. Apart from the complexity of the structures of identification that may be involved, and the undecidability of the positioning of the characters in the scenario, if we are to give any credence at all to psychoanalytic (or poststructuralist) views of meaning, then the unconscious or psychically important meaning of a fantasy may not be that which a naive reading would suggest. It might, in fact, even be its complete opposite. When considering the 'dreamwork', Freud argued that the latent meaning as opposed to the manifest content of a dream could only be arrived at by a process of considering the elements of the dream and discovering the ways in which their meaning was subject to processes of condensation and displacement. One thing might symbolise something else, or several other things; the manifest content might conceal the latent dream wish; in the process of displacement, meaning is 'shifted' from one thing to another. Condensation and displacement may be thought of, in a more linguistic turn, as metaphor and metonymy. Given the constant slippage of meaning, there is no way in which the 'real meaning' of a fantasy can simply be read off from a first account of the narrative or scenario. And in fact, some psychoanalytic uses of the term phantasy (spelt with a 'ph' to distinguish it from conscious fantasies), suggest that there are phantasies which are wholly unconscious, and whose meaning is radically inaccessible.

The indeterminacy of fantasy is linked, I think, to the profoundly unsettled, disparate and often decentred nature of sexual desire. An obvious point to make, for example, about Jeffrey's analysis of sexual ideology and pornography as wholly orientated towards male dominance and female submission is that she does not even seem to note the importance of the fact that many men, too, have masochistic fantasies involving various forms of domination (often by women), and of pain and submission. Flagellation was, apparently, one of the most common Victorian male fantasies (and practices when visiting prostitutes). And, given the indeterminacy of fantasy as well as evidence from women's sexual practices, it is plain that women may fantasise themselves in a dominant role. Jeffreys, and to some extent Bartky, seem to write as if there were no ambiguities and tensions around identification with 'subordinate' or 'dominant' roles in fantasy scenarios, and as if it can normally be assumed that the man will identify with the dominant role and the woman with the subordinate one. Jeffreys, in particular, writes as if the *sole* things that turn men on are having power over women and women's submitting to that power. This seems to me plainly false. Even Freud, for example, who, despite his own critique of the identification of masculinity with sexual activity and femininity with passivity, in the end consigns women to what he describes as 'passive' aims in intercourse, nevertheless constantly stressed the ways in which human desire is never irrevocably 'fixed' on any one set of aims, and the ways in which 'normal' heterosexuality and desire for intercourse is only precariously achieved.

Jeffreys would I think say that in so far as women had fantasies of or desire for domination in sex, this would merely show that they had accepted the dominant ideology and were behaving like men. I've suggested, rather, that identifications in fantasy are often radically indeterminate, and that the prevalence of any set of sexual aims or desires in any human being is always precarious.

Eroticism

I would now like to make some tentative suggestions about the nature of eroticism . Jeffreys' view of sexual desire and sexual fantasy is that it is learned in a process of indoctrination or conditioning; she is totally sceptical, for example, of all psychoanalytic or other models which trace some of the deepest sexual impulses of human beings to the experiences of childhood. The result is, I think, that her view of sexuality is curiously disembodied. Sexual desire is simply a matter of social 'conditioning'—and we might be able to reprogramme it by substituting a new sort of conditioning. Now indeed the extent to which specific adult sexual proclivities and fantasies can be traced directly back to particular childhood experiences seems likely to remain a contentious issue. Nevertheless, it seems to me that without a background of early infantile experience and embodiment, it would be difficult to make much sense of adult human sexuality at all.

There are two aspects of human sexuality which are, I think, particularly interesting in this context; issues of power and issues concerning selfhood and the loss of self. Eroticism, in one sense, does indeed involve power; the power to give pleasure, to dominate the senses of the other, temporarily to obliterate the rest of the world; the power involved in being the person who is desired, the power to demand one's own pleasure. And along with this power go forms of 'submission' (of surrendering, letting go, receiving), or of self-abnegation, of focusing entirely for a while on the pleasure of the other. I suggest that these things are among the constitutive elements of human eroticism. In addition, the erotic seems to me frequently to involve some sense of 'loss' of the boundaries of self; the temporary erosion of the bodily boundaries between one person and another, and the temporary obliteration of one's normal or everyday sense of oneself. One reason for the banality (and lack of eroticism!) of many sex advice manuals is that they treat sexuality as if it were a matter of 'button-pushing' between two wholly self-conscious human beings who simply 'do' things to each other; they miss the dimension of sexuality in which one gets lost and the frontiers of one's self temporary dissolve.

Jeffreys suggests that we should rid sexuality and sexual desire of all overtones of power, or of domination and subordination. But this fails to recognise either the crucial slippages and tensions in the meaning of a word like 'power', or the ways in which, I have suggested, certain forms of power and submissiveness seem constitutive of human sexuality and sexual desire. This constitutive sort of role of submission and powerfulness can all too easily get overlaid, however, with more malign structures of gender, class or race-based forms of domination and exploitation. But in the desire to purge sexuality of the oppressive features of certain kinds of power, I think it is important not to lapse into a vision of 'mutuality' which seems unable to analyse the power of human eroticism adequately at all.

Some accounts of human sexuality have suggested that all adult human sexual desire aims unconsciously to 'replay' aspects of early infancy; the early symbiotic relationship to the (all-powerful) mother, or the first stages of life in which consciousness of self as separate was not really developed. Whilst I am suspicious of the reductionism of such accounts, it is nevertheless true that long before 'social conditioning' of the sort envisaged by Jeffreys can seriously come into play, our lives are often governed by, or at the mercy of, strong and often painful bodily desires and longings, and profound ambivalence towards those who are our caretakers. These surely form a background to adult human sexuality. No human being is totally without the desire to hurt and harm those whom he or she both loves, but may also at times perceive as threatening or engulfing. No-one is wholly without the desire at times to have others in their power, if only to be the object of their desire; or without the desire to regress, to submit, to be protected and overwhelmed by the power of the other. The problem in thinking about sexuality, eroticism and power is how to give an account of these kinds of 'power' and 'submissiveness' which both recognizes their constitutive role but does not build into that constitutive role the sorts of power that come along with other forms of exploitation and domination.

The project of self-transformation

I now want to return to P's dilemma, as expressed by Bartky; should she or should she not attempt to change her desires and her fantasies, and should she feel shame at them?

The above discussion has suggested, I hope, that the dilemma is not quite as straightforward as it may at first have appeared to be. The meaning of P's desires and fantasies, the role she plays in them, and the significance they have in her life may itself not be clear at all. Barky in fact recognizes herself, in her critique of sexual voluntarism, that when it comes to the roots of sexuality in the human psyche, self-knowledge often fails, and we are pretty much in the dark. But if this is acknowledged, then it should also be acknowledged that precisely *what* should be changed, and why, is also highly unclear. In the light, too, of the fact that that the relation between fantasy and desire is a highly complex one, setting out to 'change her desires' is not at all a clear project on which P could embark, since their nature and meaning may be very obscure to her. So my own first piece of advice to P would be not to assume that there is an obvious 'meaning' to all her fantasies, or that their narratives indicate in any way at all what her 'real' desires or the deep structures of her own eroticism are.

Nevertheless, it might be argued that despite all the ambiguities and unclarities surrounding the interpretation of fantasy, surely there are *some* cases which are clear enough for P to be worried about and to want to try to change. Suppose, for example, that she persistently has a fantasy involving a scenario of a gang rape—even if it is unclear whether she is a participant or a voyeur—and that she can at times find this fantasy erotic. Suppose, even, that she finds it difficult to get sexually aroused with her partner at all if she does not fantasise such a scenario? Might she not feel morally guilty at such a fantasy and want to get rid of it? I want to end by asking whether she can and whether (and if so why) she should.

On the grounds that 'ought' implies 'can', P can only sensibly be advised to try to change her desires and fantasies if it is possible for her to do so. Here I think one has to steer a course between two paths. The first is the crude kind of sexual voluntarism which suggests that all that is needed is to keep away from men, acquire a feminist circle of friends, and use your will power. At a certain level, it may well be possible not to 'dwell' on fantasies that irrupt into one's mind; unless they are hopelessly obsessional, it may be possible to exercise control and to prevent them from lingering too long. But the 'deep structures' of human fears and human desires are both so opaque and so deep-rooted that the notion that one could voluntarily change them, as the result of a short-term effort of will-power, is surely wrong. Nevertheless, one wants also to say that the structures of human eroticism, whilst owing much to the general conditions of human infancy and human embodiment, also owe a great deal to the particular ways in which our desires and our imaginations are formed by the social relationships that help to create our personalities. Surely, if we saw the world differently, and if the social relationships under which we live were different, it might be expected that the structures of human desire and fantasy would be somewhat different?

In *The Sovereignty of Good*, Iris Murdoch (1970) writes about the ways in which we might attempt to change our feelings about someone, by a process of learning, painstakingly and sometimes painfully, to see someone differently. Thus, if I learn more about a person's situation, I might come to see them as downtrodden and oppressed, and the anger I felt at their behaviour might shift in the direction of tolerance or pity. Similarly, if I learn about the ways in which I have been exploited myself, or about the ways in which certain social practices have worked against my own interests or those of other women, I might come to feel angered rather than flattered, say, by certain forms of male attention. Changes in one's emotions are frequently a result of changes in one's perceptions of the world, and in some circumstances these changes in perception may only result from a sustained collective endeavour to understand things differently, in which one is supported by others. Similarly, perhaps, it might be that new ways of seeing and understanding the world (which themselves could probably only come about in the context of changed social practices), could result, eventually, in profound shifts in patterns of desire and fantasy. We could, I think, only wait on events to know.

But suppose that we had some reason to hope and believe that in a different world, and with different understandings of our situation, our erotic life and our fantasies might be rather different. Why should this be a matter of concern to us? Provided that exploitation and harm to others are avoided, what does it matter what fantasy scenarios people play out in their heads; given that the meaning of these is in any case so unclear?

More than one answer might be given to this question. The first might be that even though many fantasies are unclear and difficult to interpret, some are *so* horrible that one would not want to countenance them as harmless in any human being, since the harm they envisage being done to another is so intolerable. One might instance here, for example, some of the fantasies described by Klaus Theweleit in his book *Male Fantasies* (1987) where he gives an account of the sexual fantasies he analysed in the letters, diaries and novels of a group of mercenary soldiers, the Freikorpsmen, in Germany between the two world wars. These frequently involved the violent murder and mutilation of 'The Red Woman'—a mythical and over-sexualized figure of the communist woman whom the Freikorpsman wanted to obliterate to a bloody pulp. The fantasies are indeed horrifying, and closely related to a transparent fear of female sexuality. Theweleit speculates rather unsatisfactorily on the social background to these exaggerated fears of women, which spawned such hatred and desire for vengeance; but beyond doubt the fantasies are troubling and horrifying.

Perhaps if a person was prone to dwell obsessionally on fantasy scenarios such as those described by Theweleit, it might be a cause for alarm. But the sorts of fantasies that Bartky envisages P as having are not as extreme and horrifying as this. Nor does Bartky suggest that having them is likely to make P commit acts of atrocity or violent harm to others. Why, then, should P attempt to get rid of them (even if she is likely to fail)? Part of the answer is that Bartky sees them as causing her suffering and feelings of shame. I've suggested that one way of coping with the shame, if it is painful, might be to overcome it by recognising the complex and indeterminate nature of fantasy, and not letting oneself assume that there necessarily *is* any deep conflict between one's desires and one's politics. But this is only part of the answer because at bottom, I think the reason why Bartky would like P to embark on the project of changing her desires is what I shall call an ethical vision of self and community. Bartky writes (1990, 51):

> liberals ignore the extent to which a person may experience her own sexuality as arbitrary, hateful and alien to the rest of her personality. Each of us is in pursuit of an inner integration and unity, a sense that the various aspects of self form a harmonious whole. But when the parts of the self are at war with one another, a person may be said to suffer from self-estrangement. That part

of P which is compelled to produce sexually charged scenarios of humiliation is radically at odds with the P who devotes much of her life to the struggle against oppression. Now perfect consistency is demanded of no one, and our little inconsistencies may even lend us charm. But it is no small thing when the form of desire is disavowed by the personality as a whole.

In addition, in what I think is a telling comment, she says (1990, 61):

> The order of the psyche, here and now, in a world of pain and oppression, is not identical to the ideal order of a feminist political vision. We can teach a woman how to plan a demonstration, how to set up a phone bank, or how to lobby. We can share what we have learned about starting up a women's studies program or a battered women's shelter. But we cannot teach P . . . how to decolonize the imagination.

The problem with the imagery of decolonization is that it suggests that somewhere there might be an 'authentic' female imagination, free of all the influence of male domination. But this is to fall too far back into the coercive language of political 'correctness' of which Bartky herself is critical. It also supposes that we have some clear means of telling what is and is not politically 'correct'—that the meaning of desires and fantasies is, as it were, written on their face, and that we can clearly separate those which are authentically feminine from those which are masculine, or the effect of social subordination.

There is a need here to look critically at Bartky's vision of coherence, integration and unity. It has two aspects. First, Bartky envisages a (utopian) situation in which the structure of the human psyche might 'mirror' the ideal form of a community. I am not entirely clear what this might mean. If it means that all the desires of all individual members of a community might simply reflect or be wholly in tune with the larger political goals which a community set itself, then I can see no reason for supposing that this could be possible. One important reason for this is that I can see no possibility of a final elimination of potential conflict between individual aspirations, desires and interests, and broader social goals. In this sense, the personal can *not* always sit happily alongside the political. To suppose that it might seems to me to amount to imagining a kind of Platonic Utopia of the most coercive kind.

The other kind of 'incoherence' that Bartky sees as a fundamental human goal is a coherence *within* the psyche. It would need another paper to explore this idea adequately, and I do not have space to discuss here, for example, Lacanian versus other psycho-analytic views of the 'fragmented' or 'split' nature of the human psyche. But even supposing (which I am inclined to do) that there *is* some sense of 'coherence' or 'integration' which is of central importance to human life and selfhood, it is also important not to assume that one can easily identify 'parts' of the personality or make quick judgements about what coheres or conflicts with what, or what the nature of the conflict is. For this reason, my second piece of advice to P, if she is distressed about what she feels to be a conflict, and if she desires more coherence within herself, would be this. Don't assume that 'conflict' can easily be identified, or that the only possible meaning of 'coherence' in one's life must be the impossible dream that all elements of thought, fantasy, imagi-nation, desire and action might fit together into a seamless whole.

How we do Ethics now

JAMES GRIFFIN

1. Piecemeal appeal to intuition

By far the most common form of argument in ethics nowadays is
what can be called piecemeal appeal to intuition. Any reader of
philosophy will know the kind of thing I mean. 'On your principle,
it would be all right to do such-and-such. But that's counter-intuitive. So your principle is wrong.' The word 'intuition' here is not
used, as it was in earlier times, to refer to a special way of knowing;
instead it is used to mean merely a moral sentiment or belief that
persons have independently of the moral theory or philosophy or
stance that they might adopt.

Philosophers now pretty much agree that piecemeal appeal to
intuition is a bad method, though, for lack of better, their belief has
not had the revolutionary effect on their practice that one would
expect to follow.

The case against piecemeal appeal to intuition has been made
fully and powerfully by others. [1] Briefly, the trouble with intuitions
is that, as a kind of belief, they do not have the standing that would
allow them to test anything. It may well be that some intuitions are
as sound moral beliefs as we shall ever get. Others, however, clearly
are not, and there are no internal marks distinguishing the first lot
from the second. Intuitions, despite the misleading suggestion in
their name of a special sort of perception into moral reality, are just
beliefs. Some of those beliefs have been drummed into us in our
youth by figures of authority and are no more reliable than those
figures were. Some are social taboos that, if we understood their
origin, we would see are now obsolete. Some are edicts of the perhaps unfortunate super-ego that emerged from our private battle
with our own aggression. And so on. What knowledge we have of
the origins of our moral beliefs hardly leads us to grant them a lot
of authority. [2] Causal explanations are not equally corrosive. Some
leave us hesitant when before we were confident; some make us

---

[1] I have in mind particularly the attacks of R. M. Hare and R. B.
Brandt. See Hare, 1971, and 1981, ch. 8; Brandt, 1979, ch. 1. See also
Singer 1974.

[2] On, e.g., psychological causes, see Freud (1957, 138): 'Ethics must be
regarded . . . as a therapeutic effort: as an endeavour to achieve something through the standards imposed by the super-ego which had not

drop what before we held; some actually strenghthen our beliefs. For the most part, though, we do not know the causes of our moral beliefs. Even perfectly natural, nearly universally distributed sentiments and attitudes may not be in order as they are. For instance, it is natural—indeed characteristic of human nature generally—for our sympathies to be warmly engaged by nameable persons whose lives are at risk and not by merely statistical lives, but it is not at all clear that governments are right to spend, as they usually do, far more on saving one missing yachtsman than it would take to save dozens of unknown lives through wider detection of cancer. And moral sentiments, attitudes, and beliefs are—like certain observations of supposedly brute facts—theory-laden, and the theory can be poor. For instance, much of our moral vocabulary in English has a certain—to my mind wrong-headed—model of moral relations built into it etymologically: the terms 'ought', 'should', 'duty', 'obligation', 'retribution', 'merit', 'rights', 'contract', all come originally from commerce or commercially-oriented law and have to do with owing, paying, binding, and so on. In Old English 'ought' was the past tense of the verb 'to owe' and was used in that way until quite recently (e.g. Shakespeare). 'Should' comes from a Teutonic root meaning 'to owe', and in Middle English there was a transitive use of 'shall' and 'should' meaning 'to owe'. A 'duty' is what is owed, from the latin 'debere', a sense it still retains in Customs Halls. 'Merit' comes from Latin 'meritum', meaning 'price', 'value', 'service rendered'. To 'retribute' is to repay. 'To oblige' is to bind or to make indebted. And so on. It is natural for us to reach for relations that we understand to explain those that we do not, but there is no guarantee that we have always reached in the right direction. True, etymology is not meaning, and all of these words, despite their origins, have taken on a life of their own. But their origin still makes itself felt, and

---

been attained by the work of civilization in other ways. We already know—it is what we have been discussing—that the question is how to dislodge the greatest obstacle to civilization, the constitutional tendency in men to aggressions against one another . . .' Freud ought to have inserted 'in part' between 'regarded' and 'as a therapeutic effort'. But he must have identified here an important cause of why one person inclines to one set of moral views and another to a different set.I myself suspect that often we find, through the workings of a mechanism of compensation, an overly strict super-ego associated with relatively unstrict moral intuitions, and *vice versa*. But the moral views of any reflective person will be shaped by vastly more sorts of causes than just the ones that Freud mentions. For an example of such psychological speculation, see E. Westermarck, 1932, chs. 8 and 9.

etymology can—and in this case does—shape our thinking in ways that we are often unaware of. We still talk, as if it were a far more decisive move in argument than it is, of *paying one's debt* to society, of not *owing* anything to nations of the Third World, and so on. It is no panacea even to take the most optimistic view about the soundness of some of our intuitions. Even if some are indeed perceptions of moral reality, we have also to wonder whether they are more than the merest glimpse of a fragment of reality, and whether therefore when reality's whole contour is eventually revealed, we might view the fragment quite differently.

That, in very summary form, is the powerful negative case. What it suggests is that the role that intuition should play in moral philosophy is no more nor less than the role that we are content to let it play in other branches of thought, in mathematics, in the natural sciences, and in other parts of philosophy. For instance, Russell's Theory of Types has strikingly counter-intuitive consequences for Boolean class algebra and the definition of numbers. Since the Theory restricts a class to members only of one type, it has the result that Boolean algebra can no longer be applied across classes but has to be reproduced within each type, and furthermore that numbers, defined on the basis of certain logical concepts, have similarly to be reduplicated for each type—consequences that Quine once condemned as 'intuitively repugnant'[3]. But no logician takes such repugnance as closing an argument. On the contrary, intuitive repugnance is just a spur to start looking for a good argument. It is especially in moral philosophy that intu-

---

[3] W. V. Quine, 1953, 91ff. On intuition in the natural sciences, see e.g., Newton-Smith, 1981, 197, 212–213. On intuition in philosophy, see e.g., Nozick, 1981, 546; Rorty, 1980, 34 . We find what seems to me the right sort of ambivalence about intuitions, the right mixture of scepticism and respect, much more commonly in these other departments of thought. On the side of respect, see Hintikka, 1967, Introduction, p. 3: 'An intriguing aspect of the completeness and incompleteness results is that one of their starting-points (viz. our concept of what constitutes completeness) is inevitably an idea which can perhaps be formulated in naive set-theoretic terms but which either is not formulated axiomatically to begin with or which (in the case of incompleteness) cannot even possibly be so formulated. Yet concepts of this kind are most interesting. We seem to have many clear intuitions concerning them, and it is important to develop ways of handling them.' On the side of scepticism, see Daniel Dennett's and Douglas Hofstadter's complaint about the 'intuition pump', the use of one sort of example to push our intuitions in a particular direction (say, in a debate about whether computers think), in Hofstadter and Dennett, 1982, 375, 459.

itions have risen so far above their epistemological station. That may be for the reason I mentioned earlier: where on earth are better arguments going to come from?

2. Purist view

A bold response to the inadequacy of piecemeal appeal to intuition is to become teetotal: to forswear all dependence on substantive moral beliefs, and to try instead to derive such beliefs from considerations that are themselves untainted by moral element. But is that possible?

Kant is the most famous purist—at least on a common reading of him[4]. On that reading, his aim is to derive substantive moral conclusions from formal features of rationality. What philosophers have in mind in speaking of reason and rationality varies greatly, from thin, irresistible, logical standards at one end to thick, contentious moral standards at the other. Kant looks like a purist because, at first glance, he seems to use the thinnest of conceptions, indeed only the notion of contradiction. His Categorical Imperative test involves first universalizing one's proposed maxim of action, adding this new law of human operation to a description of how the rest of the world operates, and then seeing whether contradiction results. But in some cases of even blatantly immoral maxims, it is very hard to uncover anything remotely approaching contradiction in the strict sense. But Kant explains that he has in mind either of two sorts of contradiction, contradiction in formulation and contradiction in the will. And his explanation of, in particular, contradictions in the will draws upon a quite rich account of rationality. There is nothing wrong in this. But both his rich account of rationality and his use of a much enriched notion of contradiction as a test of right and wrong carry a heavy freight of teleological views about human nature and, in the end, also moral views. A rich theory of rationality and a substantive moral theory come hand in hand. When accounts of rationality get rich in this way, they get contentious. People differ about what count as moral reasons. How do we decide who is right? The decision, in the end, will not be merely about rationality unmixed with moral matters; it will be a choice of substantive moral position. A widespread view—one that seems to me right—is that if Kant is read as

[4] Kant, 1948, esp. sect. 2. I explain my views about Kant's categorical imperative and its ethical content somewhat more fully in *Well-Being*, ch. X, sect. 4.

appealing only to a thin enough conception of rationality to count as a purist, he does not succeed in deriving substantive moral conclusions; and that if he is read as enriching his conception of rationality enough for it to yield substantive moral conclusions, then he is not a purist. Either way, we cannot point to Kant to show that purism is a live option.

There are modern purists, Hare[5] and Brandt[6] prominent among them, but unfortunately I do not have time to talk about them. To my mind, their forms of purism finally fail to work too. One cannot derive substantive moral principles from the logic of key moral terms (Hare) without the help of *some* substantive beliefs. Nor can one choose a reforming definition of ethics that will reduce it to a manageable factual project (Brandt) without some substantive beliefs guiding the choice. I cannot see any form of purism that works.

3. Have we been too hard on intuitions?

The claims commonly made for intuitions in the first half of this century were a good deal stronger than the ones we usually make now. W. D. Ross, for example, held that our considered moral beliefs provided the standard by which the truth of any moral theory had to be tested, instead of having themselves to be tested by reference to any theory. But he did not regard 'intuitions' as merely beliefs or sentiments or attitudes. Such beliefs, he wrote contain 'a considerable amount that we do not think but know' (Ross, 1930, 40). He says that because he regards intuition as a special mode of knowledge. Most of us nowadays find too many problems with that conception of intuition to want to use it. But one does not have to defend intuition in that older sense in order to mount some sort of defence of intuitions in our current sense. Perhaps intuitions should be seen as common-sense beliefs. Some of them will no doubt be faulty, but there may be a core of them that form the unshakeable framework for all our thought. After all, there have been defences of common-sense in the case of beliefs about the external world. Why not a similar defence of common-sense

[5] See Hare, 1952, ch. 11; 1963, chs. 2, 3, 6, 7; 1981, chs. 1, 2.5, 4.1ff., 8.1ff. For further discussion, see J. L. Mackie's objections in 'Rights, Utility and Universalization' and Hare's response in 'Reply to J. L. Mackie', both in Frey, 1984.

[6] See Brand, 1979, ch. 1 and his further thoughts in 'Criteria for Explications of Moral Language', in Copp and Zimmerman, 1985.

inethics? True, we have the large problem of how to distinguish unsound common-sense beliefs from sound ones; they can look exactly the same from the inside. But that some common-sense beliefs are dud should not, by itself, undermine our confidence in the whole lot. We do not conclude, because of the fact that our sense reports or our memory claims might occasionally be defective, that we must doubt them all. Instead, we trust the body of them, indeed use them to pick out the duds among them. If we did not, we should lose the framework within which our concepts must operate.

Now, a similar argument is worth considering about morality. A word has meaning only in virtue of there being rules for its use, rules that settle whether the word is correctly or incorrectly used. And Wittgenstein argues that the rules cannot, in the end, be satisfactorily understood as a mental standard—an image, say, or an articulable formula—but only as part of shared social practices. And these shared practices are possible only because of the human beliefs, interests, dispositions, sense of importance, and so on that go to make up what Wittgenstein calls a 'form of life'.[7] Our form of life provides the setting in which our language develops and only within which its intelligibility is possible. And a form of life seems to consist in part in a certain shared set of values. Donald Davidson has a similar argument. We cannot, he thinks, interpret the language that others use without assuming that we have certain basic beliefs and values in common with them—that, for instance, many of our aims, interests, desires, and concerns are the same.[8] If that is right, then general scepticism about common-sense values is self-defeating. The values are embodied in the language we use, which sets for us the bounds of intelligibility.

There is force to these arguments of Wittgenstein and Davidson; the difficulty is to say how far they take us. How many such basic beliefs are there? How much can we mine from them? I shall come back to that later. Still, some of our 'intuitions' are such basic beliefs.

4. Coherence

Even so, the negative case against intuitions as a class still stands. So if we are to use intuitions at all, we shall have to find a way of

[7] See Wittgenstein, 1953, *passim* but esp. sects. 1–38, 136–156, 167–238; 1967, sects. 338–391. For references to 'form of life', see 1953, sects. 19, 23, 241; 1969, sects. 358–359, 559.

[8] See, e.g., Davidson, 'Psychology as Philosophy', p.237, and 'Mental Events', p. 222, both in Davidson, 1980.

using them critically. That is what some people see the coherence test as doing.

In the natural sciences we cannot test an hypothesis by seeing whether it squares with pure observation. Observation is not pure in the sense needed; our reports of our observations are themselves theory-laden. In the case of a conflict between hypothesis and report of observation, therefore, sometimes the one and sometimes the other should give way. We have to be prepared to adjust each, going back and forth from theory to report, until the set of our beliefs reaches some sort of equilibrium. This procedure is not confined to the natural sciences; it also plays an important part in mathematics and logic. Axiomatic systems face the problem of showing that the axioms themselves are sound. If there can be no doubt about them, if they are, say, self-evident, then one has got a genuinely foundational form of justification: one can justify certain beliefs by deducing them from sound fundamental beliefs. But in at least much logic and mathematics, the starting points are not beyond doubt. As the system of belief develops, pressures can build up to amend the starting point rather than give up too much of the body of our beliefs. One might even find, in developing theories of meaning and truth, pressures building up to abandon, say, the Law of Excluded Middle.[9] This sort of holism has claims to be the deepest form of rational procedure in all areas of thought.

The best procedure for ethics, it is plausible to think, is the similar one of going back and forth between intuitions about fairly specific situations on the one side and the fairly general principles that we formulate to make sense of our moral practice on the other, adjusting either, until eventually we bring them all into coherence. This is, I think, the dominant view about method in ethics nowadays.[10]

But it is not much of a test to achieve coherence simply on a narrow front. Some general moral views look quite plausible because they address only issues our intuitions about which they are tailor-made to fit. Then it is not surprising, nor interesting, that one can bring that set to coherence. Coherence would be a testing requirement only if the set of beliefs were made to range over the whole domain of moral issues. Indeed, to be testing the coherence should be wider still. Beliefs outside ethics are often

[9] See, e.g., Lakatos, 1964. See also Michael Dummett's argument against the Law of Excluded Middle and in favour of an intuitionist mathematics; for a recent statement of the issue see Dummett, 1991, 9–11. See also discussion of these matters in Newton-Smith, 1981.

[10] John Rawls is its most influential proponent (1972, sects. 4 and 9). See also Rawls, 1951; 1975, esp. sect. 2; 1980.

James Griffin

more decisive against a moral view than beliefs inside it—for instance, that a moral view rests on an unrealistic factual account of how the human psyche, or of how society, works. The severest test would be to confront all plausible competing moral views and the grounds that can be offered for each and to make this larger set of elements coherent. This is, in fact, a particularly large set, because the grounds for various competing moral conceptions are likely to include psychology, sociology, anthropology, genetics, philosophical theories of personal identity, and so on. I shall take the coherence test in its widest, most attractive form. Indeed, when the coherence is made to reach across such a wide front, the test it provides seems impeccable; it seems no less than the requirement that all relevant reasons be duly considered and weighed against one another.[11] Who could resist that?

There is a second—but this time less obviously compelling—way to make the coherence test more testing. One could, as some philosophers suggest[12], put intuitions through an initial sifting, retaining only 'considered' ones; only they need enter the coherence. My considered intuitions, I could say, following John Rawls' lead, are those of which I am confident for a fair amount of time and which I formed in the absence of conditions likely to corrupt judgment—for example, I was calm, adequately informed, and my self-interest was not aroused.

But this preliminary sifting seems to me better avoided. Why confine ourselves only to intuitions of which we are relatively *confident*? Confidence in ethics has different psychological explanations, many of them not epistemologically reassuring. The confident ethical beliefs of a thoroughly conventional member of a privileged class might be his worst; his best might be his unconfident glimmerings of a different way of life. Some confident beliefs—for instance those basic ones that set for us the bounds of intelligibility—are indeed sound, but we cannot confine our attention to them at this early stage, since at first sight they seem too few to provide us with anything worth calling a test. And why confine ourselves to *calm* judgements? One's most penetrating moral judgements might be made when one is shaken out of one's quotidian complacency—when one is indignant, grief-stricken,

[11] See Scanlon, 1990. He speaks there of 'the method of Reflective Equilibrium': 'What "authority" do the conclusions of this kind of reflection enjoy? The short answer is that they are the judgements that seem to us to be supported by the balance of relevant reasons, and this is a kind of "authority" it is hard to top.'

[12] I have John Rawls particularly in mind. For his definition of 'considered judgements', see Rawls, 1972, 47–48; see also p. 20.

terrified by death[13] Many people's best moral thinking is reserved for their deathbed or their doctor's waiting-room. Anyway, to say that we should interest ourselves only in judgements formed in the absence of conditions likely to corrupt judgment begs the important questions. If we knew which conditions did that, and also knew that we were avoiding them, we should indeed be able to isolate a class of especially reliable judgements. One condition likely to corrupt judgment is heteronomy: that is, our judgements' being formed by social or psychological pressures rather than by our recognition of their intrinsic merits. But how does one tell that one has avoided heteronomy? Another corrupting condition is self-interest. But self-interest is a master of disguises. Think of the long road of discovery we had to travel to lay bare seemingly impartial norms of society as the entrenched protection of the rich, or of the male, that they really were. So we need a procedure that starts from where we actually are, and that is from a rather shakier state than appeal to 'considered' intuitions suggests.

I shall come back to 'considered' moral beliefs later; all that I am resisting is their introduction at this early stage. I see no case for an initial sifting of intuitions. If the sieve's mesh is made up of psychological standards (for instance, confidence or calmness), then it is better not to use it. If the mesh is made up of epistemological standards (for instance, reliable or uncorrupted judgment), then it is too early for us to be able to use it.

I said earlier that, if one is to use intuitions, one must use them critically. Does the coherence test do this satisfactorily?

Well, we know some of the enemies of soundness in ethics, and the thing to do is to ask how, or whether, the coherence test combats them. I have just mentioned two enemies,

1. *Heteronomy*: Many of our moral beliefs are formed by social and psychological pressures, rather than by our recognition of their intrinsic merits.
2. *Self-interest and self-deception.*

to which we could add

3. *Ignorance*: We form many beliefs on too little information, or on false information, or we do not represent things to ourselves vividly or imaginatively enough.
4. *Conceptual poverty*: We often do not have perspicuous concepts, or a rich enough set of concepts—at the extreme, our whole model of what morality is, and what moral standards are like, may be mischosen.

[13] A point made by Daniels, (1979, 258).

5. *Coarseness of feeling*: Our emotional life may not be full or subtle enough; our sensibilities may be dulled or underdeveloped.
6. *Over-generalization*: We have the failing, in all departments of thought, of jumping to conclusions, of taking part of the story as the whole story.

Suppose that we find ourselves faced with a conflict between two beliefs. There is always the option—an especially live one in morality—of deciding that we shall have to live with the conflict. But more often we do not. Then we are forced to resolve the conflict by dropping one or both of the beliefs. How do we choose? The mere fact of conflict tells us nothing; it only forces the choice. We might decide that the intuition in this particular case rests on no better ground than that a certain response was drummed into us as children, so our respect for it is shaken. Or we might begin to see all too clearly how a certain principle arose from nothing better than the wish of our social class to protect its privilege by dressing it up as a disinterested obligation, so our adherence to it stops. Or we might come to think, of either an intuition about a particular case or a general principle, that it does not employ the right, or a rich enough set of, value concepts. Or we might decide that a moral principle makes assumptions about human motivation that run up against observations so plain that they must be trusted. Any of these discoveries can suggest which piece of intellectual baggage it is wiser to jettison. But then what is going on in the resolution of the conflict is a judgment of the form *here is a fault* or *this is not well grounded*. Here we appeal to standards that are not derived from any simple sort of coherence; indeed it is these other standards that are doing the work of motivating successive resolutions of conflict and so of carrying us to better beliefs. Conflict raises a question. The new equilibrium constitutes the answer. But all the testing work is done between those two points. Does the notion of coherence capture that?

This brings us on to the well-trodden ground of coherence theories. The coherence theory of truth (a theory about what truth consists in) raises many of the same issues as the coherence theory of justification (a theory about how one distinguishes sound from unsound beliefs), but it is the second that concerns us now. The coherence theory of justification holds that ultimately a belief is justified by, and only by, its relation to other beliefs. The relation in question has been given many interpretations, ranging from the weak (consistency) to the strong (entailment of each by a conjunction of some of the rest) with positions in between (centring on a notion of 'mutual support').

Now, the word 'coherence' itself suggests something fairly weak, perhaps consistency. But consistency alone must be too weak. Consistency is a logical, not an evidential or explanatory relation. A pure consistency test would leave too many competitors in the field. Virtually any moral view can be made consistent, even on a wide front, by jettisoning a well-chosen belief here or there. Our freedom to produce a consistent set is too great. Passing the coherence test, if coherence is consistency, turns too much on psychological matters of what a person finds easy to believe or to stop believing. But none of this holds out hope of leading to sounder beliefs, only to more harmonious ones.

So by 'coherence' we should mean something stronger—something that brings in the idea of evidential fit. Instead of taking the coherence test as requiring only that the set of beliefs be consistent, we should also require that the set exhibit relations of mutual support: for instance, that one not believe a proposition P without also believing a sufficient selection of propositions that support it. But support comes in different strengths, and the requirement as I have so far stated it is still fairly weak. It requires only that if one thing is believed so must certain others be. It leaves our freedom to produce a purged set of mutually supporting beliefs still too great. We can produce sets of mutually supporting beliefs by purging a few recalcitrant beliefs. But this requirement, too, puts too much weight on the psychological matter of what one finds easy to believe or disbelieve. For instance, a moral view might fit into a fairly satisfying set of mutually supporting beliefs, except for one or two factual beliefs about the nature of human motivation. What is more, those beliefs about motivation might themselves be distasteful precisely to persons sympathetic to the elevated moral view in question and so be easily discarded by them. But those factual beliefs may also be of a kind to compel accommodation; they may more merit inclusion than just about anything else in the set. A satisfactory coherence test could not test only whether one can get one's beliefs into a set with the internal virtue of connections of support and explanation; it must also involve assessing the strength of a belief's claim on inclusion. And one cannot explain the strength of that claim in terms of the mere quantity of its supporting beliefs; in both ethics and the natural sciences, a firm enough general conviction can lead one constantly to see confirming instances. At some point the quality of the support must enter: some beliefs make a strong claim themselves on our acceptance. It is not that they can be justified without appeal to any other beliefs; it is, rather, that they can, none the less, be judged to be especially reliable. In the natural sciences, what we see with good eyes, close to, and in good light has just that status. Any single observation statement is defeasible, but as a class they are especially reliable.

The obvious move now is for coherence theorists to admit beliefs of special reliability. Need they? The idea of an especially reliable belief may seem, to some coherence theorists anyway, to smack too much of an anti-coherence conception of justification. It may seem simply to surrender to the view that justification consists, in the end, of a belief's corresponding to a reality independent of any belief. Instead of thus moving away from coherence and in the direction of correspondence, it might be said, we should fully exploit the coherence theory's own resources—for instance, such tests as whether a belief has predictive or explanatory power. I doubt, though, that predictive and explanatory power can themselves be understood properly without appeal to especially reliable beliefs. Predictive and explanatory power help to justify only because there are certain beliefs, such as observation reports, that are especially reliable and so have to be predicted or explained by any satisfactory scientific theory. The explanatory power of a belief matters to us only in proportion to the credibility of the beliefs being explained. In any case, our concern now is justification, not in the natural sciences, but in ethics. There is no analogue in ethics to the predictive power of a scientific theory. There is no really satisfactory analogue, I think, to explanatory power either. I would not deny that good moral theories have a kind of explanatory power; they can illuminate and organize our scrappy moral thoughts. But what they explain and illuminate are, precisely, our own central moral beliefs. The explanatory circle in this case is too tight to provide much in the way of justification. In the natural sciences, a theory that proves to have explanatory power thereby acquires some credence because what it explains is largely independent of the theory and is itself of a credibility that demands explanation. Ethics provides no analogue to that independence or to that credibility. Justification does seem to need beliefs of special reliability.

So let me return to where I was a moment ago. The obvious move is for coherence theorists to admit beliefs of special reliability. The question now becomes, Can they? Can special reliability be explained if justification takes the form simply of belief supporting belief, or can it be accounted for only by a structure with a place for a belief's correspondence to a reality independent of belief? Many coherence theorists think that they will have no trouble explaining special reliability.[14] For all that I have said so far, they may well be right. Whether they are raises large metaethical issues. For now, I want to make two smaller claims: first, that we have no method unless we can identify beliefs of special reliability; and, second, that the coherence test, as it has so far been developed in contemporary philosophy, does not satisfactorily do that. So let me set aside the bigger issues and speak to these smaller claims.

To help isolate issues, consider a view about justification that nearly all of us accept. Call it holism.

Holism is the denial of foundationalism. Foundationalism is the view that we may justify certain beliefs by derivation from foundational beliefs that do not themselves need justification, that are in some way self-justifying or self-evident. Holism is the view that no beliefs are so privileged that they need no justification, that all beliefs need, and some can get, support by leaning on other beliefs in one way or other. Holism can (and, for instance, in the natural sciences should) say that some beliefs have an especially high degree of credibility (for instance, what is observed in favourable conditions), that beliefs can be ranked as to soundness. Holism can allow that certain central beliefs form the necessary framework for the intelligibility of our language. It need only stop short of claiming that any single belief of high credibility can be finally justified all on its own. For instance, even beliefs about what is observed in favourable conditions are defeasible: part of what justifies them is that nothing turns up to defeat them. And part of what gives them their special weight are well-established theories about what perception is and how it can go wrong. Holism, so understood, is compatible with both a coherence and a correspondence theory of justification. Which is right will turn, for instance, on what, in the end, we decide is involved in establishing the special reliability of certain classes of belief. Holism is itself an especially plausible view; what it describes is, I think, the fundamental rational procedure in all departments of thought. But we must not let the coherence test cloak itself in the strength of holism.

To isolate issues further, consider another view about justification that most of us accept: there is no pure 'given'. All beliefs involve interpretation. We can never get behind our conceptual framework to confront naked reality. So even basic beliefs can be justified only by appeal to other beliefs; justification is confined to the circle of beliefs. That may look tantamount to the coherence theory, but it is not. The rejection of the pure 'given' is compatible with coherence and correspondence theories of truth and of justifi-

[14] For example, Brink, 1989, 135–139.

James Griffin

cation; it is consistent, in particular, with the view that, though we can never get behind our conceptual framework, parts of that framework are responsive to, are corrected by, a reality independent of it. Whether that is so waits upon answers to certain metaethical questions. But the coherence test should not be allowed to cloak itself, either, in the strength of the rejection of the idea of the pure 'given'.

We have no method for ethics, I say, unless we can identify beliefs of special reliability. But that, a coherence theorist might say, is exactly what the class of 'considered' beliefs that I brushed aside earlier is meant to be. So we should have a second look at them. The question I asked earlier, however, still stands: how do we pick out 'considered' beliefs? If the criteria are psychological (unhesitating, confident, calm, disinterested), then they are not strong enough to pick out beliefs of special reliability. If the criteria are epistemological (sound, free from distorting influences), then we cannot establish what they are without facing up to those large metaethical issues I alluded to a moment ago. Now, it may be objected that I am drawing too sharp a line between psychological and epistemological criteria, and that I am exaggerating how much theoretical work has to be done to arrive at rough but serviceable epistemological standards. Do we not, without the theoretical deliverances of metaethics, have some idea of what is and what is not trustworthy? In this respect, though, our situation in ethics is little like our situation in the natural sciences. Part of what enters the holistic balance in science is an account of what goes on in observation, because that is part of what is to be explained. We test our beliefs about how we are causally connected to what we observe, how we make perceptual mistakes and correct them. In the natural sciences, part of what is being justified holistically is our belief in there being certain sets of especially reliable beliefs. And it receives a lot of justification at quite early stages in our thought about the world, without much help from epistemology and metaphysics. We know that if our eyes and the light are good, and we are close up, and we take a good look, our belief about what we see is especially secure. There is nothing like that going on in reaching a wide coherence in ethics. Our reaching such coherence does not, as part of the process, help to make the set of 'considered' beliefs more reliable. It is not that a causal account of our normative ethical beliefs and an error theory for them are not available; rather, they will not be forthcoming unless we are able to answer certain metaethical questions in a certain way. Short of that, the signs available to us, psychological or epistemological, fall short of providing grounds for special confidence.

It is true that we should not need to appeal to metaethics if we

172

could assess competing moral views just by appealing to entirely non-moral matters of fact. All we should then have to do is to identify especially reliable factual beliefs. And facts about human motivation and about how societies work go a long way toward weeding out unrealistic moral views. This possibility raises a raft of familiar questions about the relation of fact and value, particularly about reductive naturalism—the view that ethical beliefs can be reduced to factual ones, on roughly Hume's understanding of the 'factual'. I find reductive naturalism implausible. And the 'facts' that do indeed provide tests for moral views are far from purely factual. For instance, some moral views rest on dubious conceptions of the human will. But we cannot determine the limits of the will independently of knowing what are plausible human goals and how inspiring they are. The capacity of the will is partly a function of its goals. So any 'fact' likely to get far in testing competing moral views will be partly constituted by beliefs about values; we shall not know whether it is specially reliable without knowing whether its constituent ethical beliefs are too. So we have not avoided metaethics.

Might the core values that Wittgenstein and Davidson speak of, the values that are part of the framework for intelligibility, be all the specially reliable beliefs we need? I doubt it. They, I take it, will be confined to a few basic prudential values—for instance, that we want to avoid pain and anxiety, that we have aspirations and attach importance to their being fulfilled, and perhaps also a few basic moral beliefs—for instance, that murder and cruelty are wrong, and that we must show respect of some sort for others. But we shall have nothing comparable to the rich set of observations that operate in justifying scientific beliefs. Those few unshakeable prudential and moral beliefs will do no more than rule out the craziest of moral theories. The notion of respect, it is true, is closely connected to more specific concepts, such as some form of loyalty and honesty, but even their addition does not provide much of a test. It could not seriously test the moral views that we now think of as seriously in contention. Those views share most of the same specific ethical concepts; they differ over where in deliberation these concepts figure.

There are various ways of enlarging the set of core beliefs necessary for intelligibility. They are not confined to ethical beliefs. Our core values are part of our being able to see others as persons. They are normative constraints on central notions in the philosophy of mind: to see an event as an action one must be able to see it as intentional, which requires seeing it as aimed at the good. But these mental notions are involved in the claims about intelligibility that we have already made.

One might, then, try adding to the core beliefs various specific ethical notions—what are now often called 'thick' concepts—such as 'loyal', 'honest', 'just', 'chaste', 'patriotic', and so on. If they are not quite part of what Wittgenstein calls our form of life, they are anyway much more deeply embedded in a culture, indeed in a particular period of a culture, than thin terms such as 'good' and 'ought'. But thickness is not reliability. Our thick concepts largely define our current common sense ethical outlook. They are many of the intuitions that I spoke of at the start. They are not the especially reliable beliefs that we are looking for.

Admittedly, we cannot know at the outset how conclusive a test ethics permits—whether, for instance, there is one that will fix on a single best among competing moral views. But a 'test' that decides very little between them loses its claim to be considered a test at all, especially if, by broaching some of the large metaethical questions, we might be able to devize something more deserving of the name of 'test'.

5. The independence of normative ethics from metaethics

I maintain: no method for normative ethics without answers to certain key metaethical questions. The most prominent proponent of the coherence theory in our time is John Rawls, and his special contribution to it has been to maintain: method is largely independent of metaethics.

His reason is this. Metaethics is concerned with such questions as whether and in what sense moral judgements are true, whether they are objective, whether values form an order independent of human belief and attitude, whether they can be known, and so on.[15] Normative ethics, in contrast, is the systematic and comparative study of competing general moral views—utilitarianism, Kantianism, virtue theory, and so on. The programme of normative ethics is to develop each view, probably much further than they have yet been developed, then to compare their features, and also importantly, on that basis, to decide on their relative adequacy.[16] For my own part, I decide their adequacy by bringing my own beliefs into wide coherence. Once the rest of you have also done this with your beliefs, we may find ourselves converging on

[15] See Rawls, 1972, 51ff; 1975, 5–7; 1980, 554.
[16] See Rawls, 1975, 8.

some of the same beliefs. If enough of us converge, then we may be willing to regard the beliefs converged upon as objective.[17] And we might then also be in a position to settle issues about the truth of moral judgements, the independent reality of values, and other metaethical difficulties as well.[18] In this way, Rawls argues not just for the independence of normative ethics from metaethics[19] but also for its priority.[20] At this stage in the history of philosophy, he says, we are not in a position to make much headway with metaethics, but we have just seen ways in which, with advance in normative ethics, we might eventually make advance in metaethics too.

Can we, though, describe a test capable of ranking competing normative views, while ignoring metaethical questions about objectivity, truth, or knowledge? The test at work in normative ethics must yield a ranking in a strong sense. It must yield not merely a preference between the competing views but a decision as to which has more reason on its side. It must guard against the quite ordinary ways that our moral beliefs go wrong. It must meet doubts about our beliefs that arise from our own past mistakes— that is, not extreme philosophical doubts about whether we can know anything, or at least anything about values, which is a prob- lem that we consign to metaethics, but entirely realistic doubts. Rawls agrees.[21] In describing the ranking, he regularly uses terms that carry considerable epistemic weight. We compare moral views, he says at one point, on the basis of, among other things, how well they accommodate facts about the human psyche and society; that decides what Rawls calls their 'feasibility'. Then given their feasibility, we look at their content in wide coherence; that decides their 'reasonableness'.[22] And, for Rawls, decisions about reasonableness have to come largely from each individual's reaching wide coherence; the further step of convergence between different individuals' beliefs adds little. Lack of convergence can, it is true, serve as a trip-wire. My lack of convergence with the rest of you on what I claim to see trips up my claim to see, but whatev- er special reliability reports of perception have rests primarily, not on convergence, but on what individual perception is. Similarly, convergence between you and me in ethics matters to the justifica-

[17] See Rawls, 1975, 9; 1980, 554, 570.
[18] See Rawls, 1980, 564–565.
[19] See Rawls, 1975, 9, 21.
[20] See Rawls, 1972, 53; 1975, 6, 21.
[21] See Rawls, 1972, 50, 53, 121, 452; 1975, 8–9; 1980, 534, 568–569.
[22] See Rawls, 1975,15; 1980, 534.

tion of belief only if it is what has been called 'principled' convergence—that is, convergence arising from your or my having separately applied standards of reasonableness to the formation of our own beliefs. Rawls agrees with this too.[23]

But his agreement just brings us back to old questions. It is not enough to say that putting our beliefs in wide coherence will distinguish the more from the less reasonable. It will do that only if we can identify beliefs of special reliability. And we cannot do that without broaching some key metaethical questions. So normative ethics cannot be independent of metaethics.

But can we, in the present state of philosophy, make progress in metaethics? There is a good argument that we cannot. We now know so little about the nature and structure of our substantive ethical beliefs that we do not know whether the best moral view will, in the end, recommend itself to us because it meets epistemological standards or because it meets practical ones, such as its meshing effectively with the human will or its providing a much needed social consensus for us here and now.[24] We may find that moral standards are what we agree between us to use as such, not what we discover independently to be such. Therefore, we cannot get far with metaethical questions about truth, objectivity, and reality until we have got clearer about the status that moral standards have in what turns out to be the best normative view. This conclusion seems to me undeniable. But there is a second argument. For the reasons that I have just given, we cannot get far with finding the best normative view until we have got clearer about what beliefs are especially reliable, and for that we need answers from metaethics. The combined effect of these two arguments is that sometimes the priority runs one way and sometimes the other. Normative ethics and metaethics have to advance together. The first is not independent of the second, or, since Rawls allows that the independence he has in mind is not especially strict (1975), there is nothing like the high degree of independence that he suggests.

6. What we need

Is what I am after just a beefed-up version of the coherence test? It may look as if it is—as if in acknowledging that justification in

[23] See Rawls, 1975, 9

[24] On the distinction between justification as epistemological and as practical, see Rawls, 1980, 554, 560–561; 1985, 224 n. 2.

ethics has to be holistic I have virtually accepted that the proper method will be some sort of coherence test. Have I done more than show that the requirements on 'considered' beliefs have to be stiffened? And with them stiffened, can we not proceed pretty much as before, slowly advancing towards coherence? I think that we have to wait for an answer to that question. What is missing in all of the versions of the coherence test that we have so far considered is any adequate explanation of 'mutual support'. One way to add that explanation would be to find the sort of beliefs that have special credibility, and then to identify the individual beliefs of that sort. Perhaps, when we have added that, we shall find that we have produced a sophisticated coherence test. But perhaps not. Reaching coherence, it is true, would be an acceptable characterization of the over-arching holistic nature of the justification. And that means, as well, that any individual belief that seems to have special credibility might collapse under the pressure of the rest of our beliefs. Even so, 'reaching coherence', without something built into that notion that explains 'mutual support', remains far too thin a description of how we should be doing ethics.

Justice without Constitutive Luck*

S. L. HURLEY

What fundamental aim should be seen as animating egalitarian views of distributive justice? I want to challenge a certain answer to this question: namely, that the basic aim of egalitarianism is to neutralize the effects of luck on the distribution of goods in society. I shall also sketch part of a different answer, which I think does a better job of supporting egalitarianism.

My arguments here are not presented in a way that is intended to win over those who have no sympathy with egalitarianism to begin with; they move within the compass of egalitarian concern. Moreover, it is difficult, for familiar reasons, to separate the question of what the basic aim of egalitarianism is from the question of what it should be. If one aim does a better job of supporting egalitarian results than another, then, even if few egalitarians recognize this, it may be regarded as a stronger candidate for what the basic aim of egalitarianism is. As with other essentially contested concepts, a new conception does not change the subject.

1. The luck-neutralizing aim and the regression principle

I'll begin by putting two pieces on the board, and considering the relationship between them. The first piece is *the aim to neutralize the effects of luck*. The thought that it is basic to egalitarianism to aim to neutralize the effects of luck on distribution is found in various places. It's perhaps at its most explicit in recent work by Gerald Cohen and by John Roemer. It also surfaces in John Rawls' *Theory of Justice* (1972), when he talks about the moral arbitrariness of the natural distribution. And the Robert Nozick of *Anarchy, State and Utopia* (1974) may be assuming that egalitari-

*I am grateful to the British Academy for its generous support of this work in the form of a Senior Research Readership (1990–1992). For helpful comments on and criticism of earlier drafts, I am indebted to Ruth Chang, Gerald Cohen, Ronald Dworkin, Derek Parfit, Joseph Raz, John Roemer, Paul Seabright, and Bernard Williams. I am especially grateful to Gerald Cohen, Ruth Chang and Paul Seabright for detailed comments and discussions; many of the objections to which I try to respond in the text are due to them. Needless to say, all remaining errors are my own.

anism fails in the absence of the luck-neutralizing aim, when he suggests that you don't have to deserve to be everything you are in order to deserve the results of what you do.[1]

The idea of neutralizing the effects of luck is tied very closely to the idea of responsibility, since luck and responsibility vary inversely with each other. I here assume that luck and responsibility are conceptual correlates of one another, in this sense: something for which you are not responsible is a matter of luck for you, and something that is a matter of luck for you is something you are not responsible for.[2] The more that is regarded as among the effects of luck, the less people are regarded as responsible for, and the more effects on distribution there are for the luck-neutralizing egalitarian to neutralize. Given the luck-neutralizing aim, exactly which effects on distribution demand egalitarian neutralization depends on what people can properly be regarded as responsible for. Gerald Cohen and John Roemer in particular have diagnosed the deep structure of contemporary debates about the metric of distributive justice—should it be resources, welfare, or something else—in terms of a presumed responsibility-tracking exercise. But it is important to make explicit the thesis that egalitarianism must view judgments of distributive justice as tracking judgments of responsibility. Why? Because this thesis should not be taken for granted. Indeed, I shall argue that egalitarianism should not be seen as depending on such a responsibility-tracking exercise at all, and that it is weakened by such dependence. Instead, I shall recommend that we conceive of egalitarianism as emerging from a cognitivist approach to political theory in general.

The second piece I want to put on the board is a principle about responsibility that is inspired by something like a Kantian view of these matters. This principle says: in order to be responsible for something, you must be responsible for its causes. I'll call this *the regression principle*. Thomas Nagel, for example, gives one clear expression of the regression principle in his well-known article on 'Moral Luck', in the course of expounding a broadly Kantian view about the way in which responsibility is negated by luck:

[1] See Cohen, 1989, 906–944; cf. Cohen 'The Pareto Argument for Inequality' (Oxford, typescript, 1992); see Roemer, 1985, 151–187; 1986, 751–784; 1987, 215–244; see Barry on Rawls on moral arbitrariness (Barry, 1989, 217–234, 393–400); cf. Scanlon (1988, 156) on moral arbitrariness; Nozick, 1974, 225.

[2] I say more about the relationship between luck and responsibility in *Justice Without Luck*, a book in progress that continues the themes of this lecture.

If one cannot be responsible for consequences of one's acts due to factors beyond one's control, or for antecedents of one's acts that are properties of temperament not subject to one's will, or for the circumstances that pose one's moral choices, then how can one be responsible even for the stripped-down acts of the will itself, if *they* are the product of antecedent circumstances outside of the will's control?

The area of genuine agency, and therefore of legitimate moral judgment, seems to shrink under this scrutiny to an extensionless point. Everything seems to result from the combined influence of factors, antecedent and posterior to action, that are not within the agent's control. *Since he cannot be responsible for them, he cannot be responsible for their results.* . . (Nagel, 1979, 25; my italics)

We need now to ask: what is the relationship between the luck-neutralizing aim taken as a basis for egalitarianism and the neo-Kantian regression principle? A clue is given by the idea of a certain kind of luck, which is often included within the scope of the luck-neutralizing aim. This is what Thomas Nagel and Bernard Williams call *constitutive luck*: luck in the kind of person you are.[3] Genetic luck might be an example. An egalitarian may regard constitutive luck as the source of 'morally arbitrary differences' between people, such as certain talents and handicaps, and may thus hold that the effects of these differences on distribution should be neutralized. But why is constitutive luck *luck*? The thought that your constitution may be a matter of luck, and hence something you are not responsible for, seems to be an expression of the principle that in order to be responsible for something you must be responsible for its causes. If the causes of your constitution are a matter of luck for you, so that you are not responsible for them, then your constitution itself is a matter of luck, and so are the consequences of it, such as abilities or actions that may make you better or worse off than other people. And an egalitarian who pursues the luck-neutralizing aim will try to neutralize these effects of luck on distribution. Thus the idea of constitutive luck illustrates a link between the aim to neutralize the effects of luck and the regression principle.

How tight is the connection between the luck-neutralizing aim and the neo-Kantian regression principle about responsibility? Can you pull them apart? Can you endorse the aim to neutralize the effects of luck but not endorse the regression principle? Much

[3] See Nagel, 1979; also 'Moral Luck', in Williams, 1981.

here depends on whether the luck-neutralizing aim is formulated as the aim to neutralize the *effects* of luck, or whether instead it avoids the appeal to effects.

Consider first whether the aim to neutralize the effects of luck can be pulled apart from the regression principle. Perhaps this is logically possible, but it would not make much sense to do so. Why? Because the aim to neutralize the *effects* of luck implicitly embodies a structural principle that the regression principle simply makes explicit: lack of responsibility anywhere back in the casual chain that leads up to some event propagates forward to that event. If we aim to neutralize the *effects* of luck anywhere back in the causal chain, then we are effectively refusing to hold people responsible for something unless they are also responsible for its *causes*.[4] If something that is a matter of luck for me and that I'm therefore not responsible for—say, some gene of one of my great grandparents—has effects on my constitution and hence on my choices and actions and hence on my share of goods, then the luck-neutralizing aim aims precisely to neutralize those effects. It operates so as not to hold me responsible for those *effects* just because I am not responsible for their *cause*, namely, the gene that was a matter of luck. The luck-neutralizing aim appeals to effects, and the regression principle to causes; but the practical upshot is the same. In this sense egalitarianism understood in terms of the aim to neutralize the effects of luck is a fundamentally Kantian project. It is not easy to pull it apart from the regression principle about responsibility. (In the next section I consider the possibility of reformulating the luck-neutralizing aim to avoid appealing to the effects of luck.)

Suppose someone objects that we can oppose choice to luck.[5] If we are willing to talk about luck this way at all, it is hard to doubt that factors that are a matter of luck have effects on our choices: via, for example, constitutive luck. But maybe we can hold choices to be exempt from the project of neutralizing the effects of luck, even when choices are among the effects of luck. Now this move would have to be given some independent justification. Perhaps it can be justified, but the result would not be an account that made neutralizing the effects of luck basic to egalitarianism, since many choices are among those effects. Rather it would be one that gave free rein to the effects of choice *even though* choices are among the effects of luck. So, for example, if the effects of constitutive luck

[4] Compare the claim of Roemer, 1987, 216.
[5] See and compare, for example, Cohen's treatment (1989) of the relationship between choice and luck.

182

include talents and handicaps that cause us to make certain choices that in turn affect how well off we are, the effects of those choices would be exempt from 'egalitarian' concern, on such a view. To spell this out: I may make a choice that is an effect of good constitutive luck (such as a talent for making certain types of choice) and you may make a choice that is an effect of bad constitutive luck (such as a handicap at making certain types of choice), and as a result of these choices you may be much worse off than I; but such a disparity would not be a matter of egalitarian concern, on such a view. This result, however, is not egalitarian in an intuitive sense: genesis *via* choice *per se* does not negate the egalitarian's concern with ill-being. My reply to the objection is then twofold: this kind of view does not make the aim to neutralize the effects of luck basic, so is not my target. Moreover, it is not clear that the distributions regarded as just on such a view would be recognizably egalitarian, in the sense just indicated: egalitarian concern with ill-being may survive recognition of its genesis *via* choice.

So far, then, I've claimed that there is a tight relationship between the aim to neutralize the effects of luck and the neo-Kantian regression principle about responsibility. Why does this matter? It will matter for present purposes because I want to challenge the thought that the basic aim of egalitarianism must be to neutralize the effects of luck. In fact, I want to argue that egalitarianism is better off without this aim. This is partly because the aim to neutralize the effects of luck is tied to the regression principle, and the regression principle makes both practical and theoretical trouble for egalitarianism.

As a pragmatic matter, egalitarianism is weakened if it is made hostage to the principle that you must be responsible for the causes of anything you are responsible for. It is weakened because most of our practices of praising and blaming and our reactive attitudes are inconsistent with this principle. If we adhered to this principle, we'd never hold people responsible for anything; but we do. In this sense the principle is deeply unnatural. Egalitarians shouldn't want our natural practices and attitudes to be fatal to egalitarianism—especially if, as I'll argue, egalitarianism can be supported in a way that is not tied to the luck-neutralizing aim or to the regression principle. We can take the ground out from under the feet of anti-egalitarians by showing that egalitarianism does not need this kind of unnatural basis. Imagine being able to say: '*Of course* the foundations underlying desert don't themselves need to be deserved, all the way down. *Of course* people can be responsible for choices that flow from their constitutions, even though they are not responsible for their constitutions. But you are mistaken in thinking that this undermines egalitarian schemes of distributive justice.' This position should be so attractive to egalitarians on pragmatic political grounds that they should try to see how to justify occupying it.

Consider the following objection. We sometimes exempt people from responsibility for something because they are not responsible for certain of its causes (consider the effects of brainwashing, or of a brain tumour); no justification can be given for not doing so consistently (in more ordinary cases). In the absence of an account of why we exempt people from responsibility only in certain special cases, we should fall back on the more general exemption from responsibility provided by the regression principle.[6] I find this argument unpersuasive for at least two reasons. First, the claim that no principled account can be given of why we exempt people from responsibility in some cases and not others is unwarranted.[7] Therefore there is no call to fall back on the excessively general regression principle. There may not be general agreement on any such account, but the regression principle itself is no less controversial. The regression principle is too simple and sweeping, too revisionary of pre-theoretical intuitions of responsibility that go with our natural reactive attitudes in many ordinary cases. Second, suppose for the sake of argument that the claim is correct that no principled account can be given of the differences between cases. Then we are faced with a conflict: we recognize responsibility in some cases, and refuse to in others, and we cannot account for the difference. There is still no reason to suppose that we should resolve this conflict one way rather than another. Despite the hard cases we disagree about, our intuitions recognizing responsibility in many ordinary cases are at least as strong as and even more entrenched than our intuitions refusing to recognize responsibility in unusual cases like cases of brainwashing. (At least until the regression principle has got a grip on us, that is.) If these conflicting intuitions cannot be reconciled, then it is not yet apparent why we shouldn't resolve the conflict in favour of our intuitions of responsibility rather than in favour of our intuitions of nonresponsibility.

Egalitarianism is also weakened theoretically by being made hostage to the aim to neutralize the effects of luck and to the regression principle. In a nutshell, this is because the regression

---

[6] See and compare Klein, 1990, ch. 4. On our conflicting intuitions about responsibility and the regression principle, see Strawson, 1986, 88, 96, 101, 106. Compare Nussbaum, 1986, 282–289; Honoré, 1988.

[7] See, for example, Scanlon, 1988.

principle makes responsibility impossible: no one can be responsible for the causal antecedents of an action or choice, all the way back.[8] Merely rejecting determinism does not suffice to restore responsibility. Given the regression principle, so long as one's acts have causes for which one is not responsible, then one is not responsible for those acts either, even if the links between cause and effect are not deterministic.[9] Now egalitarians may tend to assume that the global defeat of responsibility by luck provides a universal equal baseline for egalitarianism to build on. But this assumption is unjustified. If no one is responsible for anything, it doesn't follow that we all have equal claims. That no one is responsible for anything itself provides no reason to regard equality as a default position or normative baseline. If we neutralize the effects of luck, but ultimately everything is among those effects, then we are left not with a baseline of equality but rather with indeterminacy. Perhaps considerations independent of luck-neutralization could justify an equal baseline. But again my target is the view that luck-neutralization, not something else, is the basis of egalitarianism. If luck-neutralization is the basis of egalitarianism, then it seems necessary to recognize some residual equal immunity to the effects of luck in order to warrant assuming an equal baseline. Now Kant himself gave us that residual equal immunity to the effects of luck in the shape of a noumenal self. But if we don't believe in anything like a noumenal self, then the effects of luck run rampant and nothing escapes them. This provides no justification for assuming an equal baseline.

2. The luck-neutralizing aim without the regression principle

Return now to the question of whether the luck-neutralizing aim can be reformulated to avoid the appeal to effects.[10] My previous points associating the luck-neutralizing aim with the regression principle depend on its appeal to effects. But it may be objected that the luck-neutralizing aim can be reformulated in a way I have not yet considered, which dissociates it from the regression principle by eliminating its appeal to effects altogether. Perhaps the luck-neutralizing aim should not be construed to aim to neutralize the *effects* of luck on distribution. Rather, it might be construed as

[8] See and compare Strawson, 1986, 26–30, 49–50, 56.

[9] See and compare Scanlon, 1988, 152–153.

[10] As I understand the position Cohen would take in response to my arguments, it would fall in this category.

requiring us to judge directly of the relevant distributions themselves, rather than their causes, whether they are a matter of luck for the persons concerned. That is, we judge whether each person's distribution is something he or she is responsible for directly. We 'neutralize' the distribution just if responsibility for it is lacking, but we studiously avoid building the regression principle and a neo-Kantian view of responsibility into our account implicitly, by avoiding the appeal to effects. The right account of responsibility is left open: perhaps luck does not run rampant; perhaps responsibility can be understood along compatibilist lines.

The role of *effects* within the luck-neutralizing aim as it is usually construed is what associates it with the neo-Kantian regression principle. There is no way that I can see to appeal to the effects of luck without this consequence, unless one appeals to them only selectively, in which case the aim to neutralize the effects of luck is not doing the work. We are now considering the possibility that, in order to avoid this association, the luck-neutralizer may abjure concern with the *effects* of luck on distribution. Instead, he may simply require us to judge directly whether distributions themselves are a matter of luck, leaving it open what our grounds for these judgments are. This position makes a theory of distributive justice depend directly on judgments of responsibility with respect to distribution, but does not involve us in a particular way of making those judgments. This would be a way of adhering to the general responsibility-tracking/luck-neutralizing conception of egalitarianism, but without going further to aim to neutralize the *effects* of luck and thus effectively building in the neo-Kantian regression principle.

However, the luck-neutralizing aim understood this way, shorn of any appeal to effects, is a very unattractive basis for egalitarianism. It would make judgments about distributive justice depend directly either on case-by-case judgments of responsibility, or on some successful theory of responsibility. Both sorts of dependence would weaken egalitarianism practically. Case-by-case dependence would be hopeless. While there may be at least pre-theoretical agreement about many ordinary cases of responsibility and nonresponsibility, there is disagreement about hard cases. Moreover, as I shall argue below, our determinate judgments about responsibility simply do not extend as far as would be needed to work out the details of what luck-neutralization demands. We should thus not welcome an understanding of justice that runs directly into the morass of our judgments about responsibility, if there is an alternative. Furthermore, there is no positive theory of responsibility that is widely agreed upon. Why make distributive justice hostage to these theoretical disagreements about responsibility, if there is an alternative that does not? We will be in a better position to obtain agreement about egalitarianism if it is freed from the responsibility-tracking conception. The alternative, cognitive account of justice I favour assumes the denial of the regression principle and hence is compatible with our normal practices and reactive attitudes in ordinary cases, but it does not aim to track responsibility and it depends on no detailed positive theory of responsibility for direct judgments about particular distributions.

Notice also that the direct-dependence view will not necessarily result in egalitarianism at all. Consider the natural distribution of talents and handicaps and its consequences for the distribution of resources in the absence of interference. Suppose someone believes that, even if people do not deserve their talents and handicaps, they do deserve most of the effects of their talents and handicaps on the distribution of resources. Such a person illustrates one way of believing that the foundations of desert don't themselves need to be deserved, all the way down. Hence he believes, however implausibly, that the distribution of resources that results from the natural distribution of talents and handicaps is largely just, even though very unequal. He is happy for society to alter distributions of resources in the few cases he recognizes to be a matter of luck, but he just doesn't recognize very many. Such a person adheres to the luck-neutralizing aim, yet it would be strained to regard him as an egalitarian. Thus the luck-neutralizing aim by itself, in the absence of certain specific judgments about responsibility, isn't particularly egalitarian.

Moreover, this direct-dependence reading of the luck-neutralizing aim runs into theoretical problems. Earlier I claimed the global defeat of responsibility does not support assuming an equal baseline. Now we should consider whether the partial defeat of responsibility takes us back to some equal baseline. If someone is responsible for her distribution, fine; we leave it alone. But what do we do if someone isn't? What baseline do we go back to? Presumably to a baseline determined by what the person is responsible for. But there is no particular reason to suppose there is a default position or responsibility baseline that is the same for all people, or that the results of going back to the baseline determined by what each person is responsible for will be egalitarian. Suppose many people are not responsible for their distributions at all; where does that leave us? *How can we say what other distribution they would be responsible for?* And why have we any reason to say it would be the same for everyone? After all, equal distributions may be no less matters of luck than different distributions. If we presuppose that there is a

possible equal distribution for which people are all responsible, as
well as that some of them are not responsible for their actual distributions, we get an equal baseline to go back to. But in the
absence of neo-Kantian selves, it is not evident that any such positive judgments of responsibility for an equal distribution are forthcoming—at least, unless we have already presupposed the very
egalitarianism our judgments of responsibility are supposed to be
supporting. If so, however, our egalitarianism is underwriting our
judgments of equal responsibility, rather than the other way
round.

It may be objected that we do not need an equal baseline but
only judgments about whether differences between the distributions people enjoy are a matter of luck or not. If they are, we eliminate them; if they are not, we do not. My reply is that we may not
need an equal baseline, but we need more than merely judgments
about whether actual differences are a matter of luck or not, and
that the more that is needed is just as problematic as an equal
baseline, and for similar reasons.

Consider how to work out the consequences of dispensing with
an equal baseline and depending merely on judgments about
whether or not differences are matters of luck. Consider four persons who have four different distributions of whatever it is we are
concerned about: A is better off than B, who is better off than C,
who is better off than D. Suppose we judge that the difference
between A and B is ot a matter of luck, say because A and B have
made different choices in the same type of circumstances and we
regard them as equally responsible for the distributions that have
resulted from their choices. Similarly, we judge that the difference
between C and D is not a matter of luck, because C and D have
also made different choices in the same type of circumstances and
we regard them as equally responsible for the distributions that
have resulted from their choices. However, the type of circumstance in which A and B have made their choices is very different
from the type of circumstance in which C and D have made their
choices; the circumstances in which A and B have chosen are more
favourable than those in which C and D have chosen, and we
judge this difference to be a matter of luck. So we judge that all of
the following differences are at least in part matters of luck: that
between A and C, that between A and D, that between B and C
and that between B and D.

Given these judgments about luck and nonluck, whose distributions do we equalise? We cannot eliminate all of the differences
that are at least in part matters of luck, while leaving alone the differences between A and B and between C and D, which are not

matters of luck. We then face questions of the following type: should we eliminate the difference between A and C or between B and C? Again, we cannot do both while preserving the difference between A and B. But since A and B are equally responsible, *ex hypothesi*, for their respective distributions, it seems arbitrary to decide either way. We have no reason to regard C as 'responsible' for a distribution equal to A's distribution instead of B's or vice versa. We can say that the difference between A and B is not a matter of luck, and that the difference between C and either A or B is, at least in part, a matter of luck. But these judgments do not solve our problem. We need some way of correlating C with either A or B. This is not a correlation of degree of responsibility, since A and B are *ex hypothesi* equally responsible, but simply make different choices and hence are *responsible for* different results. It is rather a correlation of the distributions that people choosing in different circumstances are ideally regarded as responsible for. To solve our problem, therefore, we need to find a reason for a judgment such as the following: A and C are responsible for the same distribution and B and D as responsible for the same distribution, but the first distribution is better than the second. This *particular* judgment, of course, is not necessary; it merely illustrates the *type* of judgment that is needed to solve our problem. But if we do implement this particular judgment, notice, we reverse the positions of B and C: B was better off than C, and is now worse off. Presumably this difference reflects a judgment not only that it is a matter of luck for B to be better off than C but that it would not be a matter of luck if C were instead better off than B.

The point is this. In the absence of an equal baseline, we cannot get by merely with intuitions that certain actual differences and not others are matters of luck. To work out the implications of luck-neutralization, we would need judgments about just what nonactual differences would *not* be matters of luck, given that actual differences *are* matters of luck. That is, we've got to say not just that some people are *not* responsible for what they have actually got; we've got to go further and specify some other possible state of affairs they *would* be responsible for. But our real-world judgments of responsibility simply do not extend this far.

An equal baseline would give the same default position for everyone. If there is no equal baseline, then we replace differences between people due to luck not necessarily with equality but in some cases with *different differences*, for which they presumably *would be* responsible in some ideal sense. The complaint about an equal baseline was that it was unjustified: there is no reason to assume, when differences between people are due to luck, there is some equal distribution that people are nevertheless responsible for. But the complaint applies with at least as much force to the different differences we may suppose people to be responsible for in the absence of an equal baseline. There is no reason to assume, when actual differences between people are due to luck, that we can identify different differences between them that would not be a matter of luck. It is hard enough to judge whether people are or are not responsible for what they have actually done or have actually got. There is no reason to believe we could in general also specify, even in relative terms, different possible distributions for which people are responsible, when they are not responsible for their actual distributions. In terms of my example: it is hard enough to judge that B's actually being better off than C *is* a matter of luck. I see no nonarbitrary basis for specifying in addition that a different possible state of affairs in which C was better off than B would *not* be a matter of luck. More generally, I suggest that the question of which possible differences between people would not be a matter of luck, when the actual ones are a matter of luck, is either indeterminate in many cases or has only arbitrary answers. But a luck-neutralizing or responsibility-tracking conception of distributive justice, even one freed of association with the regression principle, would require us to deny this.

John Roemer suggests a way of dealing with this kind of problem. I am much indebted to his illuminating formulation of the problem, even though I do not agree with his solution. Consider all the factors judged to show a person not to be responsible for some type of behaviour. For some fixed values of these factors, consider the population of people to whom those values apply. Presumably there will be a range of behaviour within it. For example, among all those smokers with a given occupation, income level, gender, etc., some will have smoked for 2 years and some for 20 years. Now consider a different population, to which different values of these factors apply: a different occupation, income level, etc. Again, there will be a range of behaviour within this population. Roemer suggests that we focus on the median behaviour within each type of population. '. . . [S]ociety has already accounted for, in the definition of type, all the circumstances affecting smoking behaviour which it takes to be beyond a person's control. Now let us compare two people of different types, both of whom are at the median of their respective type-distributions of years of smoking. Although it might not make sense to say they have taken the same degree of responsibility, we can say that, given their type, each has exercised a comparable degree of responsibility, by comparison to what others in his type have done' (Roemer, 1993).

Roemer thus supports an egalitarian ethic that requires these two people, at the medians of their respective types, to be equally indemnified by society.

My disagreement with Roemer's proposal comes to this. We cannot normalise a measure of degrees of responsibility by using the range of behaviour within each type, simply because within each type everyone is equally responsible for his or her distribution. The type is defined so as to ensure that differences of distribution within types are differences for which people are responsible, since all differences for which they are not responsible are used to distinguish the types. Because of this, we cannot nonarbitrarily use the median within each type to establish comparable degrees of responsibility across types. It might be assumed in some cases that the median position in each type involves the same comparative degree of will power, and Roemer may not intend his proposal to apply unless this assumption is made. This assumption may be justified in the smoking example. But it is not in general justified, since for many relevant kinds of behaviour it may not be correct to presume that behaviour at one end of the range within each type ought to be resisted. Moreover, we already know that existing differences across types are due at least in part to luck. What we need to know is what different differences across types would *not* be a matter of luck, given that we cannot equalize all differences across types so long as differences within types are to be respected as not a matter of luck. That is, we need to know what people *are* responsible for, when they are not responsible for existing differences. This is just what I have claimed may often be indeterminate, or admit of no nonarbitrary determination.

One way of apparently avoiding these difficulties is the following. Simply take the monetary value of the differences that are a matter of luck, and redistribute it equally among all persons. Recall my example, where all matters of luck are the same for A and B, and are also the same for C and D, but A and B are luckier than C and D. In this case, for all factors that are matters of luck, we would estimate the difference between the monetary value of the factors that apply to A and B and the monetary value of the factors that apply to C and D. This amount would then be redistributed equally among A, B, C and D. But this proposal in effect returns to a version of the equal baseline assumption, which I criticized earlier on the grounds that there is no reason to assume there is some equal distribution that is not a matter of luck, for which people are responsible. It may be replied that no such assumption is needed to underwrite the judgment that differences that are a matter of luck should be neutralized; this judgment may itself be basic. Thus, it may be basic not just that different distributions are permitted if people are responsible for them. It may also be basic that different distributions are *not* permitted if people are *not* responsible for them, regardless of whether there is some equal distribution they *are* responsible for. That a difference in distribution between two persons is a matter of luck, of course, does not entail that some equal distribution between them would not be a matter of luck; equal distributions as well as different distributions may be matters of luck. But on the view suggested, only *differences* that are matters of luck would be of concern. In this sense equality would be a default position not based on judgments of responsibility, and judgments of nonluck would only be needed to justify differences, not to justify equalities. But since equalities that are matters of luck would not be of concern to such a view, and would not be included in its luck-neutralizing aim, such a view would not offer a thoroughgoing luck-neutralizing account of egalitarianism. It would remain to account for equality as a default position.[11]

The aim of sections 1 and 2 has been to induce some critical distance from the responsibility-tracking or luck-neutralizing conception of egalitarianism, and indeed of distributive justice in general. Whether or not one formulates the luck-neutralizing aim in a way that embodies the regression principle, the influence of Kantian thinking can make a responsibility-tracking conception of justice seem natural and inevitable. But we should widen our view; theories of justice need not be (and have not always been) preoccupied with responsibility in this way. To see this it will help to have an attractive alternative conception on offer.

There is evidently much more to be said on this topic than can be said here. This article presents arguments that are only one part of a larger project, a book. The larger project describes more fully a conception of egalitarian distributive justice that is explicitly not a responsibility-tracking conception. It also includes a critique of the neo-Kantian concept of luck and of the regression principle, and a discussion of incentives, which are omitted here. What I will try to do below is to sketch a part of my alternative cognitivist approach to distributive justice.

3. A sketch of a cognitivist alternative

I have argued above that the luck-neutralizing aim provides a problematic basis for egalitarianism. I now want to go on to argue

[11] While I am certain he would not agree with what I say in this paragraph, I am indebted to G. A. Cohen for discussion of these matters.

that we can make a stronger case for egalitarianism from a different fundamental aim. Instead of aiming to neutralize luck, egalitarians should aim to *neutralize bias*. Biases are influences that distort the relationship of our beliefs about what should be done to any truths there may be about what should be done. Biases are cognitive distortions: they distort the relationship of belief to truth in a way that prevents belief from attaining the status of knowledge. For example, a personal desire to believe that something is true is a biasing influence on belief. If you believe something because you want to believe it, then even if your belief happens to be true, it isn't knowledge; and your beliefs in this area wouldn't be a reliable source of input to deliberation about the truth. Many but not all desires distort the formation of beliefs and thus are biasing influences. The aim to neutralize bias plays a central role in a broadly cognitivist approach to political theory.

The cognitive approach to political theory considers how we may achieve knowledge of the answers to political questions, and in particular how we may avoid biasing influences that make knowledge impossible. Elsewhere I have sketched a cognitivist approach to democracy in terms of bias-avoidance in institutions of public deliberation. The aim to neutralize bias also provides a way to develop and support an egalitarian position about distributive justice.[12] I shall argue that aiming at *knowledge* provides a reason to adopt a perspective of *ignorance* in thinking about distributional questions: because ignorance of ourselves would rule out many biasing influences, such as those deriving from self-interest. Egalitarianism can be supported from such a perspective in a way that does not depend on the luck-neutralizing aim. I do not claim that the bias-neutralizing aim identifies a distinctively egalitarian motivation; rather, I employ it quite generally within a cognitive approach to political theory and consider its consequences for various areas. Here I claim that, applied to issues of distributive justice in the way I shall go on to describe, it supports egalitarianism better than the luck-neutralizing aim does.

Consider a generalized Rawlsian framework for thinking about distributive justice. We describe some normatively significant, fictional point of view—such as Rawls' original position—from which principles of justice are to be derived, under certain constraints. The idea is that, if we specify the right, normatively significant constraints on such a point of view, principles derived from it will be fair, will be principles of justice. (I do not here defend this claim, but consider it to have sufficient currency to

---

[12] See Hurley, 1989, part IV.

merit discussion even in the absence of defense. Issues about its justification are of course also of interest, but are not my topic here.) I'll call such a point of view a *perspective of justice*. I want first to distinguish two ways of setting up the perspective of justice. One, often appealed to by utilitarians, involves assuming you have an equal chance of being anyone in society. That assumption, among others, acts as a constraint on the reasoning to principles of justice. I'll call this the *equal chance characterization* of the perspective of justice. The other way of setting up the perspective of justice is Rawls' way: to assume instead a different constraint, namely, that you are radically ignorant of who and what you are. I'll call this the *ignorance characterization* of the perspective of justice.

Having distinguished the equal chance and ignorance characterisations, I first want to connect them to several other distinctions. In particular, I will discuss their relationships to the luck-neutralizing aim and the bias-neutralizing aim, and also to the distinction between risk aversion and uncertainty aversion. I'll interpret the ignorance characterization in a way that Rawls does not, that is, by dissociating it from the luck-neutralizing aim and associating it instead with the bias-neutralizing aim.

Second, I'll ask which is a better way of characterizing the perspective of justice, and will give some reasons favouring the ignorance characterization over the equal chance characterization.

Third, I'll compare the consequences of the ignorance characterization, understood to express the bias-neutralizing aim, with those of the equal chance characterization, understood to express the luck-neutralizing aim. I'll explain why the bias-neutralizing aim does a better job of supporting egalitarianism than the luck-neutralizing aim does. Now Rawls characterizes his original position in terms of ignorance. Moreover, he wants it to yield a maximin principle of distributive justice: that is, to yield a principle that maximizes the position of the worst off members of society. But he also seems to understand the normative significance of the original position at least partly in terms of the luck-neutralizing aim. I will argue, by contrast, that in order to see how an egalitarian maximin principle can be supported, we do better to understand the perspective of justice in terms of the bias-neutralizing aim.

4. Risk aversion vs. uncertainty aversion

My first task, then, is to draw some distinctions and consider how they relate to one another.

Begin by considering the difference between uncertainty, or ignorance, and known risk. (I'll use the terms *ignorance* and *uncertainty* interchangeably.) If I know that there are 50 red balls and 50 black balls in an urn, then I know the risks I run if I gamble on drawing a red ball. But if I know only that there are 100 balls in the urn which are red or black but in completely unknown proportions, then I am in a situation involving what's called uncertainty, or ignorance, as distinct from risk.

Now Rawls insists that his original position should be characterized in terms of ignorance of identity and *not* in terms of having an equal chance of being anyone. Some economists would insist that ignorance or complete uncertainty as between certain possibilities justifies assigning these possibilities equal chances. If our ignorance gives us no sufficient reason to assign them different probabilities, we should assign them the same probability, they think. On this view, ignorance of my identity should be translated into an equal chance of being anyone. But Rawls explicitly resists this move. He's committed to the distinctness of complete uncertainty and known equal risk.

In fact, as economists know, most people do distinguish between uncertainty and known risk. Many people prefer to avoid known risk—they are risk averse. This means that they prefer to get the actuarial value of a gamble, or even less, for certain, to the gamble itself. But even so, most people prefer to act in situations involving known equal risks rather than in situations of complete uncertainty. This is revealed in experiments of a type pioneered by Daniel Ellsberg.[13]

Here's an example. Suppose again that there is an urn known to contain 50 red and 50 black balls. The game is that you bet on drawing either red or black out of the urn, and then you draw. You win $100 if you bet correctly and you lose nothing if you bet incorrectly. So it's worth something to play this game. You are then asked how much you'd be willing to pay to be allowed to play this game. Most people are risk averse to some degree, so they offer to pay an amount below the actuarial value of the game, which is $50. Say the average offer is about $30 or so: the amount the offer falls below the actuarial value reflects aversion to risk.

But now change the urn to an urn of unknown composition— where the red and black balls may be in any proportion—and ask the same question. Offers now drop dramatically lower; it would

[13] See Ellsberg, 1961, 643–669. See also Howard Raiffa's comments on Ellsberg's paper (Raiffa, 1961, 690–694) (the example in the text comes from Raiffa), and my discussion of Raiffa's argument (Hurley, 1989).

be typical for someone who offered $35 to play the first game to offer only $5 to play the second. Aversion to risk has already been taken into account in the first round of offers; the second, lower round of offers reflects an even stronger aversion to uncertainty. Experimental results like these are robust and demonstrate widespread aversion to uncertainty. Uncertainty aversion can be thought of as a widely shared preference to act with more information rather than less, where known risk counts as information.

Moreover, as a matter of logic at least, such aversion to uncertainty is independent of the degrees of risk aversion of the people involved; so even risk-neutral or risk-prone people may be averse to uncertainty. Someone could offer the actuarial value of a game or even more when the risks are known, but still display aversion to unknown risks.

Now the rationality of distinguishing uncertainty from known risk in this way is controversial, and I can't go into that rather technical controversy here.[14] But even having put the technical controversy aside, we can compare the status of attitudes to uncertainty or ignorance and attitudes to risk. As an empirical matter, people show different degrees of risk aversion and indeed different attitudes to risk: some are not risk averse but rather risk neutral or risk prone. There is no conceptual difficulty about general risk proneness, or love of gambling; attitudes to risk are an empirical matter, not conceptually constrained. Now aversion to uncertainty may also be more or less strong. However, there is a conceptual difficulty about general uncertainty proneness (unlike general risk proneness). This is because of the *a priori* connections between action and belief. To prefer quite generally to act in ignorance, that is, without beliefs about the context and consequences of your acts, would be to prefer to act without reasons in an important sense. But it is doubtful that we can make sense of the notion of intentional action without reasons, i.e., action that bears no rational relationship to beliefs about consequences, and via beliefs to desires. It seems to be essential to intentional action that it normally does bear at least weak relations of rationality to beliefs and desires; we make sense of cases of irrationality against a background of such normal relations. To prefer to act without information and hence without reasons would be to prefer not to act intentionally at all, but rather merely to react or lurch blindly. So long as we are talking about preferences that relate to prospective inten-

---

[14] For discussion of and references to the controversy, see Hurley (1989, especially chs. 4 and 15). See also Bacharach and Hurley, 1991, Introduction, sections 2 and 3.

tional actions, there is *a priori* reason to rule out a general prefer-ence for uncertainty. Similar considerations make it reasonable to assume a weak general aversion to ignorance on the part of inten-tional agents—or at least on the part of those intentional agents not discontent with their own intentional agency itself. Other things equal, it's reasonable to assume that intentional agents pre-fer more information to less. As we shall see later, though, a little uncertainty aversion may go a long way from the perspective of justice characterised in terms of radical ignorance.

5. Equal chance vs. ignorance, and luck vs. bias

This brings us to the second task. What reasons are there for and against characterizing the perspective of justice in terms of igno-rance or equal chance to begin with? What is the normative signifi-cance of each characterization, which might make it an appropriate constraint on reasoning from the perspective of justice? After all, if we were convinced the equal chance characterisation in itself had normative significance, it would not be necessary to attack the dis-tinction between uncertainty and known risk, or to argue, against Rawls, from ignorance to equal chance. Instead, we could just start out with the equal chance characterization.

The equal chance characterization seems to owe what normative significance it has to its expression of the luck-neutralizing aim understood to encompass constitutive luck and applied to the pro-ject of deriving principles of justice from something like a perspec-tive of justice. A literal reading of the mysterious idea that we are lucky to have the constitutions we have is in terms of each of us having an equal chance, from some relevant perspective, of having any particular constitution, hence of being any particular person. After all, you are said to be lucky when you had an equal chance of getting many different outcomes, and chance determined, arbitrar-ily, that you got the most desirable one. Or when everyone has the same chance of winning a prize and you win it. So the most imme-diate and literal way of giving expression to the luck-neutralizing aim and to a view of natural endowments as arbitrary, a matter of constitutive luck, would be to characterize the original position in terms of an equal chance of being any person in society, or of occupying any position, where one's position includes one's con-stitution. On this reading, the perspective of justice would derive normative significance from its expression of our *ex ante* equality in relation to various possible constitutions and of the 'moral arbi-trariness' of the outcome of the 'natural lottery'.

However, this literal reading of the notion of constitutive luck is hopeless. The reason is that it requires us to make sense of the nonsensical idea of a constitutionless self. The supposition that 'I' have an equal chance of having any of the possible constitutions seems to require, for its sense, a subject, not yet identified as having any particular constitution, to whom probabilities of being particular persons with particular constitutions can be attached. A person's constitution reflects his constitutive or essential properties, properties without which he would not be that person, and hence his identity. When essential properties and constitution are in question, what I am and who I am cannot be separated. The 'I' who does have a certain constitution, hence certain essential properties, could not have a different constitution and different essential properties, so we must be talking about some constitutionless 'I'. This seems to be a case in which language carries us along into assuming we can make sense of a construction because there is grammatical space for it, when it doesn't actually make sense. It doesn't make sense, that is, unless we postulate a 'bare', metaphysical or noumenal self of Kantian provenance. But such a self makes no sense either. People are not such selves.[15]

The preceding paragraph assumes that constitutive luck is a matter of luck in one's constitutive or essential properties, whatever those may be (of that I hazard no account). If one objects to the operation of constitutive luck in the context of distributive justice in the first place, one presumes that there are constitutive properties of persons that are relevant to issues of distributive justice, in the sense that having some such properties rather than others has distributional consequences. I have gone along with this presumption for the sake of argument. This presumption may itself be questioned: perhaps there are no essential properties of persons, or none that have distributional consequences. If so, however, then constitutive luck is hardly going to be relevant to distributive justice in the first place. There is no difficulty about constitutionless selves, of course, if we are talking about nonconstitutive properties that may be a matter of luck; but then we are not talking about constitutive luck. I take it that a typical luck-neutralizer would not be happy to exempt personal characteristics from his project just because they were constitutive properties, and indeed wants the luck-neutralizing aim to extend to constitutive luck. If so, however, 'constitutive luck' should not be understood literally, as in the assumption that persons have an equal chance of various different constitutions.

[15] These large claims are not argued for here. They are in another piece of work in progress, *The Reappearing Self*.

Now Rawls makes various remarks about the moral arbitrariness of social contingencies and natural endowments and the Kantian interpretation of the original position as the point of view from which noumenal selves see the world. These remarks suggest that his original position should be interpreted to express the luck-neutralizing aim. But he does not characterize the original position in the way that would most immediately and literally express the luck-neutralizing aim, that is, in terms of equal chances of being anyone. Indeed, he resists this characterization and offers what he regards as the distinct ignorance characterization.[16]

Someone might be motivated to resist the equal chance characterization, despite friendliness to the luck-neutralizing aim, by reservations about the Kantian metaphysics of the self. In contrast to the equal chance characterization, the ignorance characterization carries no implications about constitutionless selves.

But, more importantly, the ignorance characterization carries no commitment to the luck-neutralizing aim at all. Veil-of-ignorance devices may be appropriate for modelling the perspective of justice, not because it is 'morally arbitrary' or a matter of luck that you are constituted as you are, but because uncertainty about who and what you are can have an essentially epistemic function in relation to deliberation about the right distributive principles. Such radical uncertainty rules out many biasing influences on deliberation and on the formation of beliefs about what should be done. These include the influence of desires to believe that are triggered by knowledge about your own abilities or disabilities combined with self-interested desires.

Biasing influences on beliefs are influences such that it is antecedently unlikely that beliefs so influenced will constitute knowledge—unlikely, that is, quite independently of any view about the truth or falsity of the beliefs in question. For example, consider a relevant issue about incentives: would it be possible to achieve a state of society in which most of the most talented members of society work at some high, socially beneficial level in the absence of certain incentives? Now if I know that I am talented and I strongly want to believe that the most of the talented *could not* work to this very high level without large incentives, then it is antecedently unlikely that my belief to that effect constitutes knowledge. I'm biased. But by the same token, if I am less talented and I strongly want to believe that most of the talented *could*

[16] See especially Rawls, 1971, sections 12, 24, 28 and 40. For a relevant and interesting discussion, see Barry, 1989, 217–234. Cf. also Parfit, *Equality* (Oxford, typescript).

work to that high level without large incentives, but rather to benefit the less talented, like me, then it is also antecedently unlikely that my belief constitutes knowledge. I'm also biased in this case. We can often identify bias without knowing the truth or falsity of the beliefs in question. I suggest that the normative significance of the ignorance characterization of the perspective of justice should be understood to derive from its expression of this bias-neutralizing aim rather than of the luck-neutralizing aim. This suggestion locates the perspective of justice within a cognitive conception of political theory of the kind I mentioned earlier; it invites us to reconceptualize concerns of substantive justice as flowing from more general epistemic concerns.

I am suggesting, then, that the issue between the equal chance and ignorance characterizations of the perspective of justice is not independent of another issue, between the luck-neutralizing aim and the *bias-neutralizing aim*. These two aims provide the most natural ways, respectively, to understand the normative significance of the two characterizations. The ignorance characterization has, despite Rawls' apparent sympathies with the luck-neutralizing aim, a more natural affinity with the *bias-neutralizing aim*. Moreover, the bias-neutralizing aim provides a way to free egalitarianism from the problems generated by the luck-neutralizing aim.

So we've got two distinctions in play now: luck- vs. bias-neutralization, and equal chance vs. ignorance. I don't claim that they necessarily coincide, though I do claim that equal chance is most naturally interpreted to express the luck-neutralizing aim and ignorance the bias-neutralizing aim. But we should consider the other two possibilities also: (A) that the ignorance characterization might express the luck-neutralizing aim, and (B) that the equal chance characterization might express the bias-neutralizing aim.

(A) First, could the ignorance characterization alternatively express the aim to neutralise the effects of luck? This seems to be the situation we find in Rawls. However, in trying to explain how ignorance neutralizes luck as opposed to bias we would come up against the difficulties of finding a coherent and appropriate reading of luck, which doesn't implicitly appeal to constitutionless selves in the manner of the equal chance assumption taken literally. (I elaborate these difficulties in the larger project.) We'll also come up against the practical and theoretical difficulties with the luck-neutralizing aim that I've already explained, in sections 1 and 2. These include the way in which the aim to neutralize the *effects* of luck incorporates the regression principle and the way in which, even given a reformulation that avoids appealing to the effects of luck, the judgments needed to apply the luck-neutralizing aim outrun our determinate judgments about responsibility. We do better simply to let luck go and understand the normative significance of ignorance in terms of bias-neutralization. The ignorance characterization does better than the equal chance characterization partly *by avoiding* the difficulties about luck.

Given the aims of reflective equilibrium, a reason to reject an equal chance characterization might be that it does not yield egalitarian results. I shall argue as much on behalf of egalitarianism shortly. Could someone pursuing the luck-neutralizing aim adopt the ignorance characterization instead of the equal chance characterization, on the grounds that it leads to better results *in luck-neutralizing terms*? Perhaps it should not be assumed that neutralizing luck in the real world is to be accomplished by arguing from a perspective prior to the operation of constitutive luck, in which we all stand in the same relation of equal chance to the various possible outcomes of the natural lottery. Perhaps we do better to neutralize realworld luck by arguing from a position of ignorance.

However, this suggestion assumes that the luck-neutralizing aim has determinate content when applied directly to the real world, apart from some argument from a perspective of justice characterised in terms that derive normative significance from the luck-neutralizing aim, such as in terms of equal chance. I have registered reasons for doubting that the luck-neutralizing aim has such determinate content in section 2 above, in arguing that our real-world judgments of responsibility do not extend as far as would be required in order to neutralize just differences due to luck and not others. In the absence of such determinate content, there is no basis for judging an ignorance characterization to do better than an equal chance characterization just by reference to their respective luck-neutralizing consequences.

(B) The other possibility is that the equal chance characterization might itself be taken to express the bias-neutralizing aim. I'll return to this possibility in the next section, when I'll be better placed to address it.

The first reason I gave against the equal chance characterization was that its literal reading of the idea of constitutive luck involved us in nonsensical suppositions about constitutionless selves. But an egalitarian has further reasons for rejecting the equal chance characterization. These concern the role of attitudes to risk in reasoning from a perspective of justice characterized in terms of equal chance. I shall mention two such further reasons.

One reason for rejecting the equal chance characterization concerns the basic idea of using attitudes to risk to model distributive justice. The supposition that I have an equal chance of being anyone is a decision theoretic device that trades on a certain analogy. The analogy is between different possibilities, only one of which is realized, and different people, only one of which is me. This analogy may be theoretically fruitful, in that it may provide a way of reducing interpersonal problems to individual decision problems in which there are equal chances of various mutually exclusive outcomes. But the very analogy itself is disturbing, because of the way in which it induces us to model attitudes to the distribution of goods across person in terms of attitudes to risk. Attitudes to risk are attitudes to the distribution of goods across possible states of affairs, *only one of which will be actual*. When we think about such states of affairs, it is appropriate to think 'it (some accident, e.g.) may never happen; the chances are small'. We think this way, for example, when we decide whether or not to take out insurance. But why should we use such attitudes to model our attitudes to the distribution of goods across persons, *all of whom are or will be actual*? When all of the people in question are real, living persons, it is not obvious that any thought analogous to the thought that 'it may never happen; the chances are small' can do justice to their situations. For example, 'the chances that I get a handicapped constitution in the natural lottery are small' is not obviously appropriate to thinking about the just distribution of goods over persons, all of whom are actual and some of which are actually handicapped, in the way that 'it may never happen; the chances are small' is obviously appropriate to thinking about the distribution of goods over possible states of affairs in deciding whether to insure. 'So what if the chances of it being *your* handicap are small?', we want to ask. 'It's still *somebody's* real handicap; the relevance of some actual person's actual handicap to considerations of justice just doesn't depend on the chances that it might have been yours.' This challenge is damaging to the normative significance of the equal chance characterization.

It is a further question whether the merely epistemic supposition, that I do not know who I am, avoids what is disturbing about the formal parallel between a life being mine and a possibility being actual. I claim that it does, to the extent that attitudes to ignorance do not reduce to attitudes to risk. Intuitively, the question 'Should I insure my child against a 10 per cent chance of a handicap?' is not the same question as this: 'One of the ten children in that ward I am about to enter is actually handicapped and can be helped at a cost, and one of them is mine; if I know nothing else, what should I do?' Such ignorance, understood to serve bias-neutralization, can function precisely to render inappropriate the 'it may not be the case; the chances are small' style of thinking: one knows that one's ignorance does not affect reality—or the objective risks. The point of imposing ignorance is to get the deliberative decision maker to focus on the actuality of the handicap or other relevant circumstance, and its attendant suffering, to avoid the bias or cognitive distortion that goes with knowing that one is safe—*or probably safe*, in an objective sense of 'probability'. I'll later suggest, for related reasons, that the bias-neutralizing aim, though it is served by the ignorance characterization, cuts against the equal chance characterization.

The preceding argument against the equal chance characterization, in a nutshell, is that this characterization assumes that it is appropriate to model attitudes to the distribution of goods across actual persons in terms of attitudes to the distribution of goods across possible states of affairs, only one of which will be actual. But, for the reasons given, this assumption is unwarranted.

The other reason for rejecting the equal chance characterization requires us to understand the way it would make the question of what distributions are justified depend on what attitudes to risk are assumed. If I have an equal chance of being anyone and I act to maximise my expected utility, then I should distribute goods in a way that maximizes the average utility of people in society. That is, I should weight the utility of each possible outcome equally, since the probability of my being each person is the same under the equal chance assumption. Then I should design institutions so as to maximise the sum of these weighted utilities, or the average utility in society. But maximizing average utility is compatible with great disparities in utility and resource levels between the best and worst positions: for example, if I am risk neutral. The aim to maximise average utility has no greater egalitarian tendencies than are imposed by aversion to risk; moreover, these may be very weak.[17] If I am risk averse, I will maximize average utility by designing institutions that distribute resources more equally. But we would have to assume extreme risk aversion in order to reach the egalitarian maximin principle of maximising the resource level of the worst off members of society. Otherwise I might be tempted to trade risk-avoidance off against my chances of great wealth by allowing further inequalities. Such trade-offs may be tempting even when I have an equal chance of being anyone, if wealth levels go high enough. There is no evident way of getting from an equal chance characterization to an egalitarian maximin principle of distribution without assuming extreme risk aversion.

[17] See Sen, 1982, for compelling examples.

However, Rawls offers good reasons not to make any particular assumption about attitude to risk in his original position. No particular attitude to risk should be assumed in the original position because people's attitudes to risk vary considerably and should be respected as part of each person's own conception of the good. If no particular personal conception of the good is supposed to determine the choice of the principles of justice, then no one attitude to risk, such as risk aversion, should be assumed as rational or allowed to determine the choice of the principles of justice.

So the resulting egalitarian objection to the equal chance characterization, then, is just this: It's objectionable to make any particular assumption about attitudes to risk in the perspective of justice. But if we do not assume risk aversion, the equal chance characterization does not support egalitarianism. This means that the luck-neutralizing aim interpreted literally in terms of equal chances of being anyone does not support egalitarianism either.

Considerable criticism of Rawls' attempts to derive an egalitarian maximin principle from the original position has focused on the apparent need to assume risk aversion in order to reach a maximin principle, despite Rawls' insistence that risk aversion need not and should not be assumed (Rawls, 1972, section 28). Such criticisms assume that Rawls' ignorance characterization is either equivalent to or entails the equal chance characterization. But the criticism that risk aversion needs to be assumed can be resisted by insisting that equal chance and ignorance are distinct and by rejecting the equal chance characterization, as Rawls does. So these criticisms of Rawls are misplaced; the real issue is over the distinction between the equal chance and ignorance characterizations. If we respect Rawls' claim that the equal chance characterization of the original position is not appropriate to begin with, and does not follow from the ignorance characterization that he favours, then risk aversion is not relevant to the derivation of principles of justice at all. Risk aversion needs a characterization in terms of risk in order to get a grip. Given the logical independence of attitudes to risk from attitudes to uncertainty, risk aversion gets no such grip from the radical ignorance characterization. The question now naturally arises of what assumptions would be needed to derive a maximin principle from a position of radical ignorance, but that is different from the question of what assumptions are needed to derive maximin from a position of equal chance.

The equal chance characterization does not support egalitarianism because it would require an objectionable assumption of risk aversion to yield an egalitarian principle. But the parallel point for the ignorance characterization has much less force: it requires an assumption of uncertainty aversion to yield an egalitarian principle. Objections to the assumption of risk aversion needed to get an egalitarian result from equal chance do not apply to the assumption of uncertainty aversion needed to get an egalitarian result from ignorance. In order to show this I need to move on to my third task and consider the consequences of the ignorance characterization.

6. The consequences of the ignorance characterization

Like Rawls, we need to have in the background some general assumptions about fundamental goods, or more generally, about the well-being values and other values that can be assumed from perspective of justice. (I cannot elaborate these assumptions here, but do in the larger project.) We then suppose that the bias-neutralizing aim is expressed by assuming radical uncertainty about who and what one is; this ignorance eliminates many biasing influences on deliberation, such as desires to reach a certain conclusion triggered by information relating to self-interest. We assume also that the uncertainty characterization of the perspective of justice does not entail the equal chance characterization, and that uncertainty aversion is logically independent of attitudes to risk.

Should we further characterize the perspective of justice by assuming aversion to uncertainty? We've already seen that aversion is the normal and very widespread attitude to uncertainty. And while attitudes to risk vary widely, characterizing the original position in terms of uncertainty aversion would not logically constrain attitudes to risk.

It may be objected that most people are also risk averse; variation among attitudes to risk is largely variation in degree of risk aversion. So if it is wrong for the egalitarian to assume risk aversion even though it's widespread, why isn't it equally wrong to assume uncertainty aversion even though it's widespread? Perhaps uncertainty aversion is even more widespread than risk aversion. But this is a difference of degree, not a difference of kind, which is what seems to be needed.

Note, however, that not merely the presence of risk aversion to some degree, but extreme risk aversion, is needed to get a maximin principle from the equal chance characterization. One of the objections to assuming risk aversion in order to derive maximin is that it needs to be extreme. It has to be extreme in order to rule out

trade-offs between risk avoidance and chances of gain that would
lead to relaxing maximin. Perhaps most people are risk averse to
some degree or other, but the variation is still sufficient to make it
wrong to assume extreme risk aversion.

The question then arises what the consequences would be of
assuming not extreme uncertainty aversion but merely uncertainty
aversion to some degree, other things equal. Given that uncertainty aversion to some degree is widespread, this weaker assumption
might be justifiable even if the more extreme assumption were not.
(I do not suggest that Rawls would support the uncertainty aversion characterization, or indeed my other characterizations of the
perspective of justice.) What principles of justice will result from
the perspective of justice if we further characterise it by assuming
the presence of a mild degree of uncertainty aversion? I'll argue
that uncertainty aversion is in a sense more efficient than risk aversion for an egalitarian: you can reach an egalitarian result from an
unobjectionable assumption of only weak uncertainty aversion,
given ignorance, while you need an objectionable assumption of
extreme risk aversion to reach egalitarian results, given equal
chance.

We've admitted that it would be unreasonable to assume that
uncertainty aversion is so extreme as to override all other motivations. But we have also assumed radical ignorance of identity, and
that this is not to be translated into known chances of gain or loss.
Under these assumptions about the perspective of justice there is
no way to trade uncertainty avoidance off against chances of gain.
Hence there's no need for uncertainty aversion to be extreme in
order to rule out such trade-offs.[18]

In a sense this should not be surprising, if we understand the
ignorance characterization of the perspective of justice in terms of
the aim to neutralize bias. The bias-neutralizing aim is precisely
an aim to remove information that would allow potentially biasing
desires to affect deliberation about what should be done. Bias is
understood as a distortion of the ideal relation between truth and
belief that makes for knowledge. I may not be able to tell you
exactly what that ideal relation is, but I know that some things
interfere with it. Desires relating to your own chances of gain may
in this sense be just as biasing as desires relating to your own certainty of gain. And this remains true even when everyone's
chances of gain are the same, so long as desires relating to your
own chances of gain are influential. It may be incidental to the

[18] The claim that radical ignorance renders unavailable the basis for
trade-offs that leads to a softening of maximin, is implied by Ellsberg
(1961, 662–664).

biasing effect of desires relating to your own chances of gain that everyone else's chances of gain are the same; such desires may still distort the relationship between beliefs about justice and the truth of the matter. So, desires relating to your own chances of gain don't cease to bias deliberation just by being filtered through an equal chance assumption.

The kind of bias in question is in the first instance cognitive: a distortion of the ideal relationship between truth and belief, introduced by desire. Such a distortion impugns affected inputs to deliberation. It is only derivatively bias in the sense of differential orientation to and concern for one person as opposed to another. The assumption of ignorance serves the bias-neutralizing aim because it eliminates many of the distorting effects of desire on deliberation and the formation of belief. These include effects that operate via information about one's chances of gain. To repeat: bias in the primary sense of cognitive distortion may be produced if one's beliefs are influenced by desires that operate via calculations of one's chances of gain, even if everyone's chances of gain are equal. The ignorance assumption, unlike the equal chance assumption, gives no scope to such calculations of chances of gain, or to trade-offs between risk avoidance and chances of gain: that is part of the point of imposing ignorance, according to the bias-neutralizing aim. Ignorance thus combines with even mild uncertainty aversion in a way that does not admit the distorting influences of desires that latch onto information about one's chances of gain.

However, the ignorance assumption does allow certain desires to operate: the desire to avoid uncertainty, as well as the general desire for well-being as reflected by the assumed well-being values. Why? A desire to avoid ignorance or uncertainty, unlike desires relating to one's own chances of gain, cannot be regarded as biasing in the sense of cognitive distortion. An aversion to ignorance is a desire for knowledge. Perhaps sometimes a desire for knowledge can operate as a cognitive distortion, but we can assume that a desire for knowledge will be effective on balance more often than it will be self-defeating, and so will not produce net cognitive distortion.

What about the 'Pareto preference': an impersonal and general desire that people be better off in terms of basic well-being rather than worse off, other things equal? This desire seems to do nothing more than reflect our assumption of some fundamental well-being values. We must assume some such values for the perspective of justice, and the Pareto preference merely reflects this assumption. We cannot both assume such values and allow that a

Pareto preference that merely reflects them introduces cognitive distortion: if the preference is distorting then the values were the wrong ones to assume. But no such retort is available to the charge that calculations of one's chances of gain may introduce cognitive distortion. It may be argued that Pareto improvements that admit inequality are inconsistent with the luck-neutralizing aim.[19] But even if we admit this for the sake of argument, it of course would not follow that such Pareto improvements are inconsistent with the bias-neutralizing aim.

Thus uncertainty aversion and the Pareto preference are compatible with the bias-neutralizing aim in a way that concerns about one's chances of gain, licensed by the equal chance assumption, are not.

Here then is a fundamental difference between the perspective of justice when conceived in terms of the bias-neutralizing aim, and when conceived in terms of the luck-neutralizing aim. A device that arguably serves the luck-neutralizing aim, such as the assumption of equal chances, may conflict with the bias-neutralizing aim. But the assumption of ignorance of identity does express the bias-neutralizing aim. The latter, unlike the luck-neutralizing aim, reflects an essentially cognitive approach to justice, which is facilitated by the device of the veiled perspective of justice. It does not lend itself to noncognitive conceptions of the perspective of justice as yielding expressions of constrained self-interest, to the extent the constraints in question still admit cognitive distortion. The exercise of constrained self-interest must be denatured sufficiently to eliminate cognitive distortion.

So, from the perspective of justice, there are no known chances of gain to set against the mild aversion to uncertainty. This is what I meant when I said earlier that, under certain assumptions, a little bit of uncertainty aversion might go a long way. In this situation, choice of the egalitarian principle that the worst off should be as well off as possible can be seen as the closest one can reasonably come to avoiding uncertainty with respect to fundamental goods. We can reach this conclusion in several steps, by exploiting the connection between uncertainty and distribution.

First: If you are given no information at all about what position

[19] Gerald Cohen, 'The Pareto Argument for Inequality' (Oxford, 1992, typescript) argues that anyone who believes that, because the possible sources of inequality are morally arbitrary, an initial equality is *prima facie* just, has no reason to believe that justice is preserved by inequality-admitting Pareto improvements that cause everyone to be better off, including those who end up worst off (section 1).

you occupy, then if you were to distribute a fixed amount of goods absolutely equally this would nevertheless avoid uncertainty: if you know that each position you might occupy is the same because of the equal distribution and you know the total amount of goods to be distributed, then you know exactly what everyone can expect. Even though you don't know who you are, you avoid uncertainty with respect to the distribution of those goods altogether. And there are no known chances of gain to set against this avoidance of uncertainty.

Second: Now relax the assumption of a fixed total amount of goods. If goods are nevertheless to be distributed absolutely equally, then even though you don't know what the absolute common level of goods will be, at least you have avoided as much uncertainty as it is possible to avoid. It is not possible to avoid uncertainty as to absolute level, but at least you have avoided uncertainty as to relative level.

Third: But now you remember that uncertainty avoidance is not extreme and you consider setting against it not any known chances of gain for yourself, but rather increases for some unknown members of society with respect to the basic well-being values so long as the level of the worst off is kept as high as it can be. That is, it now occurs to you that maximin is superior to absolute equality. It does strictly speaking admit additional uncertainty and thus compromise uncertainty avoidance, but at least the only surprises it allows are bonuses, not penalties. Moreover, at this point your Pareto preference engages. In fact there is a conflict between the Pareto preference and uncertainty aversion, in that allowing the Pareto preference to operate means admitting uncertainty as to relative as well as absolute level.

(We may be unused to thinking of uncertainty aversion as weighing at all in favour of dominated alternatives, hence as needing to be outweighed by anything. But strictly speaking, we do admit uncertainty when we move, for example, from (A) a known equal distribution to (B) an unequal distribution where we know everyone will be better off but we do not know which position will be occupied by which persons. If our only concern were knowing exactly who would get what and we had no concern at all with people getting more rather than less, we would prefer (A) to (B). But given that we do have the latter concerns, in the shape of what I have called a 'Pareto preference', pure uncertainty-avoidance reasons to prefer (A) to (B) are outweighed, and reasonably so. To hold otherwise would involve uncertainty aversion of an unreasonably extreme kind.)

So, despite the conflict between uncertainty aversion and the

Pareto preference at step three, you still do know at least that the unknown equal absolute level of step two provides a floor. Uncertainty as to who will receive a bonus is a tolerable deviation from the certainty of an unknown minimum, given only mild uncertainty aversion. Here you are indeed engaging in a trade-off. You trade away some uncertainty avoidance: the difference between certainty of an unknown floor and uncertainty as to who will get a bonus. But you are not trading uncertainty avoidance to increase your own chances of well-being, since there are no known risks under an assumption of radical ignorance. Rather, you trade it for increases in some unknown persons' level of well-being, which leave no one worse off. You judge that their improvement outweighs the additional uncertainty. This is not because you calculate that you have some chance of being them. Their additional well-being, whoever they are, engages the Pareto preference directly. You are not using your concern for yourself and your own chances of gain as a filter for your respect for the wellbeing values. Recall that your aversion to uncertainty is not assumed to be extreme or overriding. Under bias-neutralizing ignorance it doesn't need to be in order for trade-offs against chances of gain to be ruled out; but nothing similarly rules out trade-offs of uncertainty avoidance against Pareto improvements. The Pareto preference does not depend on the calculations of chances of gain that are ruled out by the bias-neutralizing aim. And it only permits inequalities that make no one worse off.

There is a further question as to exactly where the compromise between uncertainty avoidance and Pareto improvements should be struck. Should weak Pareto improvements be permitted, which benefit some and make no one worse off, including of course the worst off? Or should only strong Pareto improvements be permitted, which make everyone better off—again, including the worst off? The first view would admit more relative uncertainty for the sake of Pareto improvement than the second view would. If we keep the assumption of uncertainty aversion very weak, so that uncertainty should be avoided only other things equal, the first view will emerge and weak Pareto improvements will be permitted. A stronger assumption of uncertainty aversion will move us in the direction of permitting only strong Pareto improvements. But neither view will permit inequalities that involve anyone's being worse off than they would be if we stopped with the unknown total amount distributed equally at step two. If the worst off are as well off as possible at step two, they remain as well off as possible under both of these ways of striking a compromise between uncertainty avoidance and Pareto improvement.[20]

Notice the way in which, in step three, the ignorance constraint and the aversion to ignorance work together. It is only in the context set by the ignorance constraint that aversion to ignorance drives us toward equality: if we knew too much to begin with, aversion to ignorance might not have this effect. But aversion to ignorance itself supports the ignorance constraint, just because the constraint rules out biasing influences, cognitive distortions. Ignorance may thus serve knowledge. Given the ignorance constraint, we would still (other things equal) like to know as much as possible, and by keeping everyone at the unknown equal absolute level, we do. If we allow some people to rise above this level but do not know who they are, we sacrifice some knowledge. In particular, we do not know which people will be above this level or even the chances that particular people will be above this level. But it is precisely this knowledge that the ignorance constraint has denied us, in the interests of avoiding cognitive distortion. The trade-off we make at step three between uncertainty avoidance and Pareto improvement is in harmony with the underlying aim of bias-neutralization. Ignorance of the identity of those persons who will be above the floor of stage two is precisely the kind of ignorance that avoids cognitive distortions: such as those of self-interest, or envy, that would be introduced if we considered the chances that we would be, or that we would not be, among those persons.

By means of these three steps, then, an egalitarian maximin principle emerges from the perspective of justice, quite independently of risk aversion. Radical ignorance of identity plus weak uncertainty aversion has yielded a maximin principle, which we assume to apply to a range of goods specified by the basic well-being values of the society.

Moreover, the reasoning from the perspective of justice characterised in terms of radical ignorance of identity plus uncertainty aversion owes nothing to neo-Kantian views about constitutive luck or the aim to neutralize its effects. Nor does the reason to reason from such a position owe anything to neo-Kantian views or the luck-neutralizing aim. Rather, the normative significance of the perspective of justice thus described is found in the aim to avoid the biasing influences that inevitably go with information, even

---

[20] In the full-length treatment of justice without luck, I discuss arguments of Gerald Cohen's about incentive seeking that are relevant at this point. But there is not space to address them here. See Cohen, 1992, 263–329.

probabilistic information, about who one is and what one is like, one's talents and handicaps. More generally, it is found within a cognitive conception of the device of the perspective of justice.

As a result, the ignorance characterization has more secure egalitarian consequences than the equal chance characterization. This is the case even though, and indeed because, I have associated the ignorance characterization with the bias-neutralizing aim and dissociated it from the luck-neutralizing aim. Hence my claim that the bias-neutralizing aim provides a more secure basis for egalitarianism than the luck-neutralizing aim. In this way we can take a lead as egalitarians from Rawls even if we do not share his Kantian sympathies.

Who Needs Ethical Knowledge?

BERNARD WILLIAMS

An old question, still much discussed in moral philosophy, is whether there is any ethical knowledge. It is closely related, by simple etymology, to the question of cognitivism in ethics. Despite the fact that the terms 'cognitivism' and 'objectivism' seem sometimes to be used interchangeably, I take it that the question whether there can be ethical knowledge is not the same as the question whether ethical outlooks can be objective. A sufficient reason for this is that an ethical outlook might be taken to consist of rules or principles, which do not admit of truth or falsehood and so cannot be objects of knowledge, but which can be seen as having an objective basis.[1]

However that may be, it is usually thought that cognitivism is the form that objectivism should take if ethical claims can be true or false. Why should we think this? It may be said: if ethical claims can be true, then the most desirable state one can be in with regard to them is knowledge. By itself, that argument comes close to a simple assertion—it is, at least, very short. However, the argument may perhaps be given a rather richer content, on the following lines. A desirable state for one to be in with regard to one's ethical views is confidence. If one's state is not confidence, then it is doubt, and, at the limit, scepticism; and while it is no doubt a good thing that people should be to some degree open to doubt about their ethical convictions, general doubt can hardly be desirable. But we do not want the confidence of bigotry—if there is to be confidence, it should be reasonable confidence. But reasonable confidence in what is indeed true is knowledge.

This is, at any rate, an argument, and that is already something with regard to an assumption which, so far as I can see, is usually

---

[1] With some qualifications, this is Kant's position. I take it that it also represents Hare's later theory, though Hare himself has, reasonably, been sceptical about distinctions between the 'subjective' and the 'objective'. In a theory such as Hare's, moral principles and their particular consequences are taken to be prescriptions, and hence not possible objects of knowledge; their objectivity consists in their passing a certain test, which is itself said to be grounded in the nature of the moral point of view (in Hare's case, moral language). This raises, of course, a question of the relation between, on the one hand, a moral principle P, which cannot be an object of knowledge, and a claim of the form 'P passes the test', which presumably can be.

Bernard Williams

unargued. However, the argument's conclusion can be challenged by a set of considerations suggesting that the concept of knowledge has only a limited usefulness in ethical matters (more limited than this argument would imply). It is these considerations that I want to examine. In doing so, I am going to sustain the assumption that ethical claims can be true or false. A serious problem in doing this is that it is unclear how large an assumption one is sustaining, and this itself bears on the question of ethical knowledge. If the concept of truth itself has epistemic implications, then the two matters cannot ultimately be kept apart.[2] However, I think that there is something to be learned from keeping the matters apart for as long as possible. For the purposes of this discussion, I shall leave the account of truth itself to one side and shall try to see, rather, what may be learned from considering ethical matters in the light of characteristics possessed by the concept of knowledge in general.

Philosophy's engagement with knowledge has taken at least two different forms. One, the Cartesian form, is not so much concerned with what knowledge is; rather, it makes some assumptions (usually rather demanding assumptions) about the conditions that knowledge has to satisfy, and asks whether we have any. The other approach, familiar in the recent literature, asks for the truth-conditions of 'A knows p'.[3]

In concentrating on the truth-conditions of that particular statement, the second approach implies what is in fact a peculiar stance to the person A. It is not merely that we are asking whether that person knows something which (it is implied) we already know ourselves. In addition to that, the question does not even have the force that it usually has when we ourselves have the knowledge in question, namely whether the truth has got to A, whether he even

[2] A focus for recent discussion of these questions has been provided by ideas of convergence: see notably 'Truth as predicated of moral judgments' in Wiggins (1987). Wiggins' view is criticised by Crispin Wright (1992, Ch.3), though it is unclear how far the notions of normativity that he uses avoid similar ideas. Contrary to some things that I have said earlier (particularly in 'Consistency and Realism' in my *Problems of the Self* (1972b)), I am now in sympathy with the aim of Wright's book, to give an account of truth itself that will have minimal substantive implications and will, so far as possible, leave epistemic and metaphysical issues to be discussed later. An adequate 'minimalism', as Wright argues, will need more than is offered by the 'redundancy theory'; for a recent discussion of this, see Horwich (1990).

[3] Both approaches go back to Plato, the first to the *Republic* and the second to the *Theaetetus*. For the criticism of 'the examiner's stance', which follows, see my 'Knowledge and reasons' (1972a).

believes it. Rather, we are asking whether the true belief we know him to have has adequate warrant; our stance towards A is that of an examiner. The point of concentrating on the examiner's stance is, of course, precisely to isolate the question of warrant, but isolating the question in this way is not in fact the best way of answering it, because it does not help us to grasp the point of the demand for warrant. More generally, the method of starting from the examiner's stance conceals the point of our having a concept of knowledge at all. The point of the concept of knowledge comes out better if we start from questions such as 'who knows whether p?'— questions implying the more basic situation in which a questioner needs information that someone else perhaps has. Starting from this situation will not only give us a more realistic conception of knowledge, but will in particular shed light on the vexed question of warrant (the so-called 'third condition' on knowledge), by setting it against helpful ideas of what the point of imposing such a condition might be. To proceed in this way is to take up what E. J. Craig has called 'the practical explication' of knowledge, an undertaking which he summarizes as follows: 'We take some prima facie plausible hypothesis about what the concept of knowledge does for us, what its role in our life might be, and ask what a concept having that role would be like. . .'[4]

The third condition has its roots in the fact that 'we need some detectable property to lead us to informants with true information'. It is important, as Craig emphasizes, that we are being led to informants, not just to sources of information; we are dealing with other people, people who themselves know and do not merely record and display information. A useful informant on a given question must be reliable, and our ideas of what contributes to reliability are naturally shaped by various constructions of the division of labour. There are varying opportunities to acquire information at different places and times; in relation to these opportunities, we form the idea of a witness. Again, there are differential investments in inquiry, which produce various kinds of expert. (There is also the ideal of a good journalist, who is— though not in the forensic sense—an expert witness.)

If these are, in their most basic form, the kinds of consideration

[4] Craig, 1990, 2. I put forward a sketch in this style in *Descartes: the Project of Pure Enquiry*, 1978, ch.2, having got the idea from the Australian philosopher Dan Taylor, who may have been influenced in this direction by John Anderson. Craig's rich and helpful development of the approach includes a convincing demonstration that attempts to define the third condition so as to produce sufficient and necessary conditions of knowledge are bound to fail.

that provide the roots of the third condition, and hence of knowledge, then it may seem immediately clear that the notion of knowledge does not apply to the ethical, since there are, notoriously, no ethical experts, and, we may add, it is not in the least clear how there could be ethical witnesses. This familiar point has considerable weight, but it needs more careful handling than it sometimes gets. Many of the most convincing arguments on this subject show only that there are no *theoretical* experts in ethics or morality, that these are not sciences. This is indeed a plausible conclusion, and anyone who is tempted to take up the idea of there being a theoretical science of ethics should be discouraged by reflecting on what would be involved in taking seriously the idea that there were experts in it. It would imply, for instance, that a student who had not followed the professor's reasoning but had understood his moral conclusion might have some reason, or the strength of his professorial authority, to accept it; or that someone who did not entirely understand what was involved in some set of ethical sentences might (as with certain formulae of physics) know at least this much, that they expressed some ethical truths.

These Platonic implications are presumably not accepted by anyone, but something like the view that leads to them is implicit in one (it is only one) interpretation of 'applied ethics', in particular medical ethics. This interpretation takes expertise in ethical theory as a qualification for assisting in decisions about such matters as terminating supportive treatment of a comatose patient. It is clear why there is a social need for some kind of authority to help in legitimating ethically controversial policies in publicly answerable institutions, and clear also why this should, in a technical and secular context, be thought to take the form of an expertise. But the readily comprehensible reasons for introducing such a practice hardly lessen the paradox, that it invites us to appeal in matters of life and death to someone who has a PhD in ethical theory but whose judgment, quite possibly, we would not trust on any serious practical question.

All of this shows only that the model of a theoretical expert does not apply to the ethical case. But this is not the only model. Perhaps the idea of a reliable ethical informant should be construed rather in terms of practical experience and judgment. Indeed, Aristotle's famous description of such a person offers a hint of the other basic form of the division of epistemic labour, the idea of a witness. The valuable informant can be seen as one who, so to speak, has been down this road before:

> So we should attend to the undemonstrated sayings and opinions of people with experience, and older or sensible people, no

less than to demonstrations; from their experience they have the eye, and so they see aright. (EN 1143b 11–14)

There are some emphases in this that belong to a traditional society (though it is worth saying that the reference to age is not unqualified, and also that Aristotle suggests only that one should attend to these people's sayings, not that one should always accept them). We can, in any case, lay aside the suggestion of a traditional authority figure, together with Aristotle's inevitable assumption that such a figure must be male. If we do this, who would such a person be? What is our relation to him or her? He or she is, paradigmatically, an advisor, someone who may see better than you do how things stand and will help you to see them aright. An advisor, above all, helps you to understand. This process can express and perhaps impart knowledge.

We should resist the temptation to think that this will be only nonethical knowledge. It is true of some advisors, financial or legal for example, that they primarily offer straightforwardly empirical information, which they possess in terms of an expertise. An all-round advisor, however, who is prepared to help you to decide what is the best thing to do *period*, may well contribute some ethical insight to this, and that insight may take the form of certain kinds of knowledge under ethical concepts—that a certain course of action would be cowardly, for instance, or would count as a betrayal, or would not really be kind, and contributions of this kind can offer the person who is being advised a genuine discovery.

So here there is, in a sense, some ethical knowledge, it seems: knowledge of truths under 'thick ethical concepts'.[5] We have, then, advisors, who may be better than others in helping us to see how things stand under ethical concepts, can assist us in understanding the situation and in making, perhaps, a certain kind of discovery. We have also some 'marks of reliability'. However, these are not best characterised in terms of possessing information, but rather in terms of certain capacities, such as judgment, sensitivity, imagination and so forth. There is a question of how exactly such capacities are related to distinctively ethical knowledge. They can be applied to practical issues more broadly, and also can yield interpretations which, although they may deploy ethical concepts, shade into the psychological, as that a certain person cannot be trusted because of her vanity. Such a judgment can reasonably be

---

[5] I have discussed such concepts, and, to some extent, their possible relations to knowledge, in *Ethics and the Limits of Philosophy*, 1985, ch. 8.

called an ethical judgment, but is knowledge of it an example of ethical knowledge?

This matters less than the question of how much these structures, and these kinds of knowledge, do for the larger concerns of cognitivism. The question becomes very pressing when we consider that a good advisor of one person need not be a good advisor of another—and not merely in the sense that there are some people who cannot be advised by anyone. An advisor, and the person seeking advice, may not share the same presuppositions. Someone could be a capable and insightful advisor, to Catholics, for instance, who accepted the value of chastity, but be no use to someone who did not; in the opposite direction (so to speak) a seeker after advice might think that some well-regarded and shrewd advisor displayed a louche and opportunistic consequentialist outlook. In these ways, ethical knowledge, to the extent that it is identified through the advisor model, remains local. Moreover, the advisor model itself cannot be extended to identify a kind of knowledge that could itself overcome these difficulties. You cannot identify an advisor by marks that do not already include the degree of ethically shared outlook that would enable the person seeking advice to trust and understand the potential advisor. (This is concealed in Aristotle's account, because he speaks from a society which he pretends to be homogeneous and to concede authority to a certain kind of advisor.)

The point that the authority of a potential advisor must depend in part on the degree to which he or she shares the presuppositions of the person seeking advice should not be confused with a well-known argument against moral authority, which invokes the idea of autonomy: that nothing can be a moral belief of mine unless I have freely adopted it. This is no more true of moral beliefs than of any others. What is true is that I cannot reasonably, perhaps even intelligibly, come to accept an ethical belief just because I know that some reputably informed person holds it. We have already considered this in dismissing the idea that a model of theoretical expertise could apply to the ethical. But a similar point applies also to the model of the advisor. There are indeed situations in which one may reasonably take someone's word for it on an ethical matter although one lacks complete insight into the grounds of his judgment. But for that to be so, one has to trust his judgment, and not only in the sense that one can trust him, and regard him as an honourable person, although one disagrees with him on some important ethical matters. To take his word on an ethical question, one has to trust his ethical judgment as applied to oneself, and this requires that there should be enough ethically in common for one to be assured that when he uses the basic formula of advice, 'if I were you', it does not mean 'if you were me'.

Even if the advisor model provides a structure analogous to the practical explication of knowledge, and if the grasping of truths under thick ethical concepts provides some content for that structure, it still remains, as things are, to a considerable extent local. This means that the model does very little for the larger concerns of cognitivism. Cognitivism's question has often been expressed simply by asking whether there is any ethical knowledge or not, but in fact it has typically been concerned with the hopes of resolving the kinds of disagreement that separate from one another the local practices of advice under shared ethical presuppositions. (There are many limiting assumptions that encourage the idea that the answers to the two questions must go together.) The ideal of ethical knowledge was meant to offer the hope that such disagreement should be revealed as involving error.

Since local ethical knowledge fails to meet the larger demands of cognitivism, it might be wondered whether it is really knowledge at all. The question can be related to the argument which I considered at the beginning of this paper (as at least *an* argument) for the view that if ethical claims can be true or false, then the desirable state of mind with respect to those claims would be knowledge. The argument distinguished between reasonable and unreasonable states of confidence, said that the former are what we need, and identified those states with knowledge. Does the advisory model, as developed in its local form (the only available one), meet the demands of this argument? The good advisor, master of the local thick concepts, indeed has a reasonable confidence in their application. That implies a confidence in using these rather than some other ethical concepts, but it is not clear that this confidence itself is reasonable in a sense that meets the demands of knowledge as expressed in this argument. The confidence is not necessarily *unreasonable*. But one thing that we have learned from the attempts to give conditions for knowledge is, surely, that if an alternative which rules out a given judgment has been *actually presented*, then if one is to know the first judgment one should have reason to rule out the alternative.[6] (The practical account of knowledge will, I believe, deliver this conclusion, and also explain why merely con-

---

[6] There seems to be a serious problem in this area for the idea that David Wiggins has advanced in several publications (e.g. Wiggins, 1990), to the effect that with regard to some straightforward ethical judgments, as with some plain mathematical and factual judgments, 'there is nothing else to think but that p'. Nothing else to think about what? If the question about which we are to have something to think is whether setting fire

219

ceivable alternatives do not count.) In the modern world, at least, alternatives are presented to particular thick ethical concepts, and indeed thick concepts more generally are often replaced by the thinner resources typical of some modern ethical outloooks such as contractualism and Utilitarianism. Nothing in the advisory model, the only model we so far have for ethical knowledge, gives us grounds for applying the notion of knowledge to discriminations made at that level, between one set of thick ethical concepts and another, or between thick ethical concepts and their replacement by the thin. One can conceive of a reflective advisor and a reflective advisee arriving at some particular conclusions of that order: to the effect, say, that vanity is a failing, conceit is a vice, and humility is not a virtue. But more generally, there seems no reason to think of the local advisory model as capable in itself of offering us knowledge at such a level. I do not think that this conclusion should lead us to deny that the local practices can offer knowledge, but we shall have to accept the strongly anti-foundationalist consequence that ethical knowledge may rest simply on confidence, and not on a broader knowledge. (We should also consider how strong the original argument, from truth to the aim of knowledge, really is.)

Might we extend the practical explication of ethical knowledge so as to get beyond the local advisory model? The only way that I can see of doing so would lie in the Millian idea that the variety of human cultures, with their various thick concepts and ethical practices, should itself be understood in terms of an epistemic division of labour, as a kind of spontaneous and poorly co-ordinated research programme into the best way for human beings to live. (The unfortunate inhabitants of the previously Communist world, for instance, were no doubt taking part in an ethical experiment, among other things, though the description of it and of its results would certainly differ between different points of view on it.) As things are, our best candidates for ethical knowledge are local, and this fails to match up such ethical knowledge to the ambitions of cognitivism. The further proposal tries to overcome this limitation through interpreting the division between the various local ethical

---

to the cat was cruel or not cruel, then we must think that it was cruel. But people need not have this thought if they are asked 'is it all right to set fire to the cat?' or 'what did they do?' Wiggins' argument assumes that the concept of cruelty is always ethically to hand, but the problem is that it is not. With arithmetical examples and also, differently, plain factual examples, it is not like this.—I hope to discuss this matter more fully in a later paper.

practices in terms appropriate to knowledge, as a version of the division of epistemic labour.

It may seem natural to test this suggested model by asking whether it fits the subject matter of ethical judgments, as understood in terms of metaphysics or the philosophy of language. There is certainly much more to be learned about the subject matter of ethical judgments, as an object of knowledge.[7] But I doubt in fact that the question of this model's ultimate appeal can be answered now, *a priori*, by the unaided resources of these areas of philosophy. What the extended model would need would be a plausible account of how the variety of different human cultural circumstances could be assimilated to the sorts of differences that intelligibly ground an epistemic division of labour: differences of location, for instance, or of subject-matter, or of method, or of specialised observational skill. None of these in itself, it must be said, does offer a very convincing analogy. But in order to say that there could not be any adequate analogy, we would need a better understanding than we have of cultural variety, and of how it is related to what used to be called a theory of human nature. Some philosophers' theories imply that we understand more about this than we do. They suggest, for instance, that anything we can recognise as ethical value must be capable of being mapped on to a structure in which it will be intelligibly related in ethical terms to values we ourselves accept (as an application, extension, limitation or so forth of them),[8] much as anything we could understand as a colour perception would have to be related to the dimensions of colour that we recognize. This demand is too strong, and certainly cannot be established *a priori* from, say, the theory of interpretation. We simply do not know how we may come to understand the relations between the various local practices which offer, as things are, the most convincing models of the practical explication of knowledge in ethical matters. We correspondingly do not know to what extent it may turn out that the differences between local practices can be assimilated to differences in fields of enquiry, so

[7] As I implied in referring to the outstanding problems of truth (note 2) and of plain truth (note 6).

[8] Susan Hurley, in *Natural Reasons* (1989), seems to be committed to this view.—The qualification 'in ethical terms' is important here. If there were a theory that understood cultural variety in terms of basic needs and physical circumstances, it would relate to that variety of human nature, but it would hardly advance the interests of a larger cognitivism, because the difference in circumstances would bear too remote an analogy to conditions of enquiry.

that the whole of human ethical experience might look more like an epistemic undertaking.

Whether or not it turned out to be so, there are two considerations that we are in a position to register now. One is that an interest in the ethical uniformity or otherwise of human nature has been a persistent concern for many centuries, and it would be a little naive to suppose that some new turn of the social sciences was going definitively to answer it. It is more likely that it will always remain a matter for scepticism, or else that the question itself will be swallowed up by global developments in human ethical life. Indeed, even if an answer seemed to emerge, the answer itself might well be a product of developments in human life. Human beings might arrive at a point where it seemed best to understand the process that led to that point in terms (for instance) of a convergent epistemic endeavour, but this impression itself might be a function of the social state that they had reached, an understanding caused by history rather than explanatory of it.

The second consideration is that if the hopes of a larger cognitivism are, in this way at best in the hands of future historical interpretation—interpretation, moreover, the direction of which may well be indeterminately shaped by the same forces that it will be trying to interpret—the status of the claim that such a cognitivism is (so to speak) already true is unclear; it is even less clear that its truth could make any important ethical difference in the world we actually have now. As the practical explication of knowledge reminds us, we are interested in knowledge because we are interested in finding helpful knowers, and cognitivism's best hopes give us no way of doing that in ethical connections except the ways we are already familiar with. Perhaps a hopeful cognitivism, imaginatively construed, may encourage us to make the best sense we can of ethical variety. If so, well and good, but we have many reasons anyway for trying to do that; it is fair to say, too, that in the past outlooks calling themselves cognitivist have not always done much to encourage us to make good sense of ethical variety.

Institutional Ethics*

MARCUS G. SINGER

I

My title may generate some perplexity. It is certainly not a familiar one. So I should make it plain at the outset that I shall not be talking about the ethics of organizations or associations or groups. I want to direct attention to the ethical and valuational questions associated with social institutions, and I distinguish institutions from associations and organizations. One question I am aiming at is whether the principles and standards applicable to moral judgments of actions (either tokens or types) and of persons—call them individual principles—are also applicable, or applicable with only minor changes, to the judgment and critique and evaluation of institutions and practices. This is not the sole question of institutional ethics, but it is a main one.

Consider the following passage from R. H. Tawney's *The Acquisitive Society*:

> An appeal to principles is the condition of any considerable reconstruction of society, because social institutions are the visible expression of the scale of moral values which rules the minds of individuals, and it is impossible to alter institutions without altering that valuation. (Tawney, 1921, ch. 1, para. 4, p. 3)

Tawney's statement may seem unduly optimistic. We have seen institutions altered, valuations changed. societies reconstructed— at least fundamentally changed–without any appeal to principles whatever, certainly not any appeal to rational considerations, although there may have been the illusion of such an appeal. It is, nonetheless, worth taking as a point of reference. For it is a good account, in my judgment, of the basis on which critiques and evaluations of societies and social institutions ought to rest.

*An earlier and abbreviated version of this paper was presented at the XII InterAmerican Congress of Philosophy in Buenos Aires, 28 July 1989, and was published in Spanish, translated by Roberto de Michele, technical revisions by Eugenio Bulygin, under the title 'Etica Institucional', in *Analisis Filosofico*, vol. 10, no. 2 (November 1990), pp. 123–138. This is its first appearance in its author's native language; it has been considerably revised for its appearance here, as a result of discussion on several occasions at different places.

Consider now the following example from an ethics text of some years back:

As I make out the grades for a logic class, I am tolerably sure of the following facts. Student No. 1 will not get into law school next fall unless he receives a *B*. He has earned a *C*. To miss entering in the fall means having to wait another entire year. Student No. 2 will be dropped from college by the dean if he fails to get a *C* in each of his courses. He has earned a *D*. The logic course was not in any sense necessary to him in his future work; he registered for it because he had heard that it was interesting and not too difficult. Student No. 3 will be able to graduate if he receives merely a *D*. If he receives an *F*, he will not. He has earned an *F*. His low mark was probably due to a combination of laziness and indifference. What ought I to do in each case? (Castell, 1954, 5)

I could add further examples with individual variations, to sharpen and further refine the moral judgment that needs to be made, but I shall mercifully refrain. As it stands, each question, and even the general question, is a question of individual ethics, not of institutional ethics. Should all of these students be treated in the same way? That is to say, should the grade be changed in each case, in accordance with the specified need of the student? Or should the grade rather be determined in each case by the instructor's judgment of what grade the student has earned? If one is to distinguish one case from another, and determine that the grade should be raised in some cases and not in others, on what standard should the distinction be made? At this point we come up against what I have called the Generalization Principle[1], but we still do not have a question of institutional ethics.

Such questions as these are perfectly familiar; many teachers as well as others are called upon, more or less often, to make such judgments and evaluations as are called for in the grading of exam-

---

[1] 'What is right (or wrong) for one person must be right (or wrong) for any (relevantly) similar person in (relevantly) similar circumstances.' Discussed in *Generalization in Ethics* (Singer, 1961), esp. chs. 1 & 2. This corresponds in a number of respects, but not in all, with what R. M. Hare and others have called 'universalisability'. I have discussed these differences and some confusions about the Generalisation Principle in 'Universalisability and the Generalization Principle' in Potter and Timmons, 1985, 47–73; in 'Imperfect duty situations, moral freedom, and universalizability' in Starr and Taylor, 1989, 145–169; and in 'Universalizability', forthcoming in *The Cambridge Dictionary of Philosophy*, ed. Robert Audi.

inations and papers and of candidates for prizes and positions and degrees. But what is of special interest about this particular problem is the way it tends almost inexorably to raise questions about the relevant or related institution, in this case the institution of grading. In a system—an institution in another sense—in which the institution of grading did not exist, no such problems could arise. Where the institution operates under radically different rules—where, for example, there is only a Pass/Fail option—the only question that can arise is about student No. 3. Is this a reason for changing or abolishing the institution of grading? Someone who, confronted with a problem of grading such as has been described, asks such questions as 'What are grades for, anyhow? What does a grade mean? How are grades used?' is raising questions about the institution of grading, not about a particular case— even if one is impelled to raise such questions as a consequence of considering a particular case. This may be perfectly sensible and appropriate. Then again it may not. For if one is operating within the confines of the institution of grading as it is determined in a particular institutional setting—that is, in a particular school or college—it may not be open to one, in those circumstances, to raise the question about the appropriateness, fairness, or reasonableness of the institution of grading. One might of course decide to subvert the institution—or 'the system', as it is so quaintly called—by giving everyone A's, or most A's and the rest B's. Such a person would not, and could not, have any of the particular problems detailed. For one who does not accept or is in rebellion against the institution as it exists, there can be no moral problems arising *within* the institution. But another question arises, though our subversive grader might not recognize it, and that is whether anyone has the right to subvert the institution of grading in this way. Does the power to grade convey the right to grade in any way one pleases? Is this right or even sensible?

These last questions are institutional questions, and they arise for anyone with a moral sense in a setting in which the institution exists or is in operation, and who therefore comes within the scope of the institution, whether that person accepts the rules of the institution or not. Because others accept the rules, act on them, and expect others to act on them; otherwise there could be no such institution.

Contrast the grading example with one taken from baseball, suggested by John Rawls. Though good reasons might be given for changing any rule of the game, such as the rule that three strikes are out, it is not open to a player in a particular game (unless, perhaps, it happens to be a pickup game, and this particular player owns the bat and ball) to argue that he ought to be allowed four strikes, even though it may be—supposing omniscience for a moment—that his having four strikes would have best results. Somehow, we feel, there is a difference, that it is absurd even to imagine the player pleading for another chance to hit, even though he has had three strikes already, whereas it is not absurd, or not as absurd, to imagine a student pleading to have his grade raised on the ground that this would get him something he needs or wants very badly, or even on the ground that this would have best results. What, if there is this difference, explains it?

In his earlier writings on this theme Rawls used the term 'practice' as a surrogate for 'institution'. Rawls defined 'practice' as 'a sort of technical term meaning any form of activity specified by a system of rules which define offices, roles, moves, penalties, defenses, and so on', and he gave 'as examples . . . games and rituals, trials and parliaments . . . markets and systems of property'.[2] In this sense, a technical sense, the existence of a practice implies the existence of rights and duties and of rules for determining them. But one ordinary sense of 'practice' that is worth noting is 'a regular, habitual, or customary doing', as in 'the practice of law', 'the practice of medicine', or 'the practice of one's religion', or even 'practising the piano' or 'practising swimming'. In this sense of 'practice' the existence of a practice does not imply the existence of rights and duties. There is no question that there are practices in this sense, in which practices are regular, habitual, or customary activities. There is also no doubt that this is not a primary sense; three of the examples I just used actually presuppose institutions—law, medicine, and religion.

What, then, is an institution? And what is the relevance of institutions to morals and moral philosophy? The latter question is more easily answered than the former.

Their relevance is two-fold. First, in virtue of the existence of an institution in a given society, an act can have a moral quality that it otherwise might not, would not, or could not have. Some actions could not exist, could not be performed, could not be what they essentially are apart from some appropriate institution that defines them, that constitutes them as being what they are. I shall call an action 'defined by' or 'falling under' an institution (to use

[2] Rawls, 1955, 3n; 1958, 164n. Pincoffs, (1966, ch. 3, sec. 2, pp. 53–56), provides an especially intriguing analysis of the distinction between practices and institutions. Although in the end I was not persuaded by Pincoffs's arguments to shift my use of the term 'institution', these arguments are not only worth considering, they need to be considered.

some expressions commonly used in this context) an 'institution-constituted action'. No act could be the breaking of a promise unless there were the institution of promising. There could be no theft without (the institution of) property, no adultery without (the institution of) marriage, no divorce either, though there could be murder, assault, viciousness, and kindness apart from any specific institutions. To understand better the character of the moral judgments that can be made about such institution-constituted actions, one must have an understanding of the presupposed institution.

Second, the character and quality of a society—of a culture, if you will—is determined by the character and quality of its characteristic institutions, which also play a role in moulding the character of the people of the society. Some institutions are common to all societies—are universal—some are common to most, some exist only in some societies and not in others. Criticism and evaluation of a society is criticism and evaluation of its characteristic institutions, as well as of the character of its inhabitants. How can institutions themselves, as distinct from individual actions or kinds or actions, be judged and evaluated?

This is one basic question of institutional ethics, but it cannot be answered or even approached without getting straight on what institutions are, their essential nature and character. Hence this task is fundamental.

An institution is not the same as an organization, nor is it the same as an association, though a number of organizations and associations are also institutions. 'Cricket, five-o'clock tea, the House of Lords, Eton, the Workhouse, a hospital, the National Gallery, marriage, capital punishment, the Law Courts', to cite a list presented by Fowler (1926, 278), 'are all institutions'. So they are, but they are, many of them, institutions of quite different kinds, and in many different senses of the term, and the fact that most of the ones listed exist only in Britain should help bring this out. The term 'institution' is one of those special terms whose importance is matched only by its ambiguity and the complexity of its conception.

I shall now set forth two definitions of 'institutions'. These are two alternative accounts of what is intended to be the same concept, not two different concepts. I am not altogether satisfied with either of these accounts, and put them forward only as an aid in organising the subject, as hypotheses to be tested.

An *institution* can be thought of as (1) a relatively permanent system of social relations organized around (that is, for the protection or attainment of) some social need or value; or as (2) a recognized and organized way of meeting a social need or desire or of satisfying a social purpose.[3]

What both these definitions do is bring out the conception of an institution as an abstraction, as a complex of rules defining rights and duties, roles, functions, privileges, immunities, responsibilities, and services, and this is the main subject of institutional ethics, though it is not the sense of 'institution' that is at the forefront of ordinary, or even ordinary sociological, discourse about institutions. Neither the University of Wisconsin nor the First National Bank nor *The New York Times* is an institution in the sense intended. They are all, to be sure, institutions, but in some other sense of the term or on some other conception of an institution. They are what I call *concrete embodiments* of the institutions of the university, banking (or finance), and the press. Similar things can be said about the House of Lords, the National Gallery, Eton, and the Law Courts, even though it may not always be possible to specify the abstract institution that some more concrete institution is a concrete embodiment of—and I am actually not certain that there need be an abstract institution corresponding to every more concrete one (though there would have to be for every one that is a concrete embodiment).

Thus the sense of 'social institution' primarily relevant to this subject is the sense in which property, punishment, marriage, the family, industry, money, advertising, religion, and promising are institutions. Even here, there are differences among the institutions listed that may or may not correspond to differences of meaning and may or may not correspond to differences in the relevant and appropriate criteria of evaluation. For example, though the family—more precisely, a family—is an association of persons, property is not, even though it necessarily involves relations among persons. A stockbroker who handles institutional accounts may handle accounts for universities, corporations, unions, foundations, and other organizations, all of which are institutions in a perfectly proper and legitimate sense of this elusive term, but does not thereby handle accounts for *the* university, *the* corporation, *the* union, which are of necessity incapable of buying or selling or having accounts though they are none the less still institutions.

There are four or five different conceptions of an institution to be distinguished. There is, first, the sense in which marriage, property, money, and the press are institutions. This is the *abstraction* sense. Second, there is the sense in which corporate

---

[3] I presented a preliminary and much abbreviated account of this conception of institutions in *Morals and Values* (1977), 341ff.

bodies, organizations, groups, or associations, such as Harvard University, *The Washington Post*, Sing Sing, the Mayo Clinic, and the Philadelphia Orchestra are institutions. This is the *concrete embodiment* sense. Third, there is a sense related to the influence and relative permanence or importance of the institution in the society. In this sense, only institutions in the concrete sense that are regarded as somehow more permanent, important, or influential are called institutions, and in this sense *The New York Times* is an institution while the local *Daily Bugle* is not, and Carnegie Hall is an institution while the hall in which the local civic orchestra plays is not. I shall call this the *importance* sense. Fourth, there is a metaphorical sense in which some person of considerable fame, influence, importance, or reverence comes to be regarded as an institution; for example, Bernard Baruch, Bertrand Russell, Sol Hurok, Casey Stengel, Eleanor Roosevelt, Arturo Toscanini, and possibly John Wayne, while they were alive. Fifth, certain buildings or complexes of buildings are sometimes referred to as institutions. The Flat Iron Building, the Empire State Building, the Eiffel Tower, and the Tower of London will serve as examples. But this, I think, is not a separate sense of 'institution'. It seems to be some combination of the third, the importance sense, with the fourth, or *person* sense, and seems also to involve often a confusion of *institution* with *institute*. On this, Fowler has another interesting observation:

> *institution* has seized, as abstract words will, on so many concrete senses that neatness is past praying for. . . An *institute* is deliberately founded; an *institution* may be so, or may have established itself or grown. A man leaves his fortune to institutions, but perhaps founds a parish or a mechanics' institute, i.e. an institution designed to give instruction or amusement to a special class of people. Whether a particular institution founded for a definite purpose shall have *institute* or *institution* in its title is a matter of chance or fashion. (Fowler, 1926, 278)

I am inclined to think that all institutions in the importance sense (sense 3) are institutions in the concrete embodiment sense (sense 2). But it seems evident that only the first two conceptions have relevance to ethics, and that the first, the abstraction sense, is primary. I proceed to give further examples, repeating some from before, of the sense or kind of institutions I have in mind. It should be evident that this set of institutions, far from complete, comprises an intersecting and overlapping network, but I must save specific observations on these interrelations for another occasion.

II

Examples of Institutions [with concrete embodiments bracketed]

Government, The State [The Presidency, the Legislature, Congress are concrete embodiments] [But 'the Presidency' is still an abstraction]

Elections, The Constitution [The Constitution of the United States is a concrete embodiment of the institution of the constitution]

Law, the legal system [The Supreme Court, District Courts]

Punishment, Capital Punishment, Imprisonment [The electric chair, Leavenworth]

Property, Money, Private Property [The dollar, the pound, the yen are not concrete embodiments, only less abstract]

Business, Industry, Finance, the Credit System, Debt, Money, Advertising, Propaganda

Education, The School, The University, Scholarship, Science

Marriage, the Family, Monogamy, Divorce, Annulment, Adoption

Religion, The Church, Monotheism [the church in a concrete embodiment sense]

The Press, The Media, 'The Free Press'

'Freedom of Speech'

Promises, Contracts, Covenants, Treaties

Language, Writing, The Book, The Dictionary

War, Conflict, The Strike

Negotiation, Bargaining, Arbitration, Mediation, Conciliation, Litigation

III

Note the following. First, promises (and promising) and language seem, at least arguably, to have a special status, that of being necessary institutions, institutions necessary for there to be any society at all. This does not seem true of property or punishment. Second, institutions overlap: some are included in others, as sub-institutions. Thus monogamy is included in marriage, as a form of marriage. Others are not included as subsets, but are presupposed, as divorce presupposes marriage but is not a form of marriage.

In addition to overlappings and intersectings, and different senses and levels of institutions, we should notice that institutions are of different kinds: Legal, Political, Economic, Cultural, Civic,

Aesthetic, Religious, Educational, Military, and Sporting, and still more. But *social* is not a species of institutions; it is the genus. There is plenty of overlapping here as well. Thus property is an economic and a legal institution; marriage is a religious, cultural, and legal institution. The museum can be both a cultural and a civic institution. War is a political and, obviously, a military institution, but also an educational and civic and technological one. Money is an economic, and also a political and legal institution. Here again, though, there is no need to multiply examples.

None the less, I want to point out two senses of '*legal* institution'. In one sense, it is an institution defined or determined by the law, such as property, marriage, contract, torts, and crime. In another sense, it is an institution necessary for the law to operate, such as courts, the trial, legislature, adjudication, etc. (In still a third sense, on which I do not dwell here, it can mean a lawful institution, and in this sense conforms to the systematic ambiguity of the expression 'legal rule', which can mean either a rule of law or a lawful—that is, not unlawful—rule.) One question that arises in the study of institutions is this: if an institution, say property, is an instance of different kinds of institutions—in this case, legal and economic, perhaps also political—does it take on different import or meaning when viewed separately as an instance of these different kinds? (If so, how can it be determined which kind is predominant, and what difference would it make? But I shall not stay for an answer.)

Even though a number of the examples I have supplied may ambiguously fall either into the abstraction sense or the concrete embodiment sense (and perhaps some do not belong on the list at all), there is none the less a precise ground of distinction between these two categories. In the abstraction sense, an institution cannot act; it does not and cannot *do* anything; in the concrete embodiment sense, an institution can act. Concrete embodiments are always associations, organizations, groups, or corporations, all of which, as we know, are capable of acting (though not necessarily of taking responsibility.) (The law, especially the common law, often has trouble determining, especially in the case of a corporation, how or on whom sanctions are to be levelled, a problem on which some progress could be made by statutory means, though a further problem is that drafting the appropriate statutes precisely and fairly is a task that is notoriously difficult.) But it makes no sense to speak of property doing something, or the family, or law, or government as distinct from *the* government. And it is in the abstraction sense that actions are or can be institution-constituted (that is, fall under or presuppose an institution). (Yet it should be noted, if only in passing, that institutions in the abstract sense can in a complicated way have effects—or what we would think of as effects. Thus power can corrupt, as can money; property can demean, and convey power, and so forth. But the complicated way in which institutions can have effects, and hence serve as causal agents, needs analysis. There is certainly no mechanical cause and effect relationship operating.)

IV

I suggested before two definitions of institutions: (1) a relatively permanent system of social relations organized around some social need or value; or (2) a recognized and organized way of meeting a social need or desire or of satisfying a social purpose. Although I am not altogether satisfied with these accounts, they seem to me to bring out the abstraction sense I am after and to do a better job than some others I have seen. Consider, for instance, the following alternative accounts:

> [i] An institution is a pattern or framework of personal relationships within which a number of people co-operate, over a period of time and subject to certain rules, to satisfy a need, fulfil a purpose, or realise a value. (MacBeath, 1952, 73)

There are some interesting points here, and I have learned a lot from contemplating this account, but it fails to fit property or law; it seems modelled on the family or an organization of some sort.

> [ii] 'Institution' . . . stands . . . for a form of social union . . . for the modes of organs through which forms of Society operate. . . An institution is a special society. . It is an organization, created and sustained by individual wills, and equally creating and sustaining them. . . *A* family, *a* church, *a* trade union, *a* University, *a* social club, *a* State—each of these is an institution. (Hetherington and Muirhead, 1918, 119–120)

Again, this is instructive, but on this account law and government, property and punishment, would not be institutions. (Furthermore, it has the somewhat awkward consequence that each and every family is a distinct institution; thus my family is an institution, your family is another, her family is a third, his is a fourth, and so on. Although the number of institutions is probably beyond counting, this conception does seem to multiply institutions well beyond necessity.)

One other alternative account is worth a brief look:

[iii] One general characteristic of complex societies is the development of a number of *institutions*—relatively self-contained social groups within which a number of different social careers are organised into a system. The term 'institution' . . . here . . . refers to actual social groups (such as governments, churches, and military organizations) which play important parts in the structure of largescale societies. Institutions (in this sense) tend to be at least semi-permanent; they are quite formally organized, often in a hierarchical manner. Within the institution is found a large variety of social roles which are linked into careers and authority relationships. (Bock, 1969, 157)

Although this is a perfectly legitimate sense of 'institution', and certainly an important one, it involves the sense of institution in which it means a group or organization or corporation, a concrete embodiment of an institution in the abstraction sense. And again, such major institutions as punishment, property, and money would not count, on this account, as institutions, since none is a 'social group', actual or potential. And, while social groups can act, institutions, in the abstract sense, cannot. Their role is much more subtle. (I do not disparage any of these other accounts. Each has merits for certain purposes. I have highlighted them here to bring out the sense of institutions on which I want to concentrate, which I regard as more central to ethics, and also incidentally to illustrate some of the fascinating complexity of the subject.)

V

I referred just now to money as an instance of an institution. An especially intriguing account of money is provided in the following passage:

The money illusion is ancient and universal, present in every transaction and absolutely necessary to every exchange. Money is worthless unless everyone believes in it. A buyer could not possibly offer a piece of paper in exchange for real goods—food or clothing or tools—if the seller did not think the paper was really worth something. This shared illusion is as old as stone coins and wampum—is a power universally conferred by every society in history on any object that has ever been regarded as money: clamshells, dogs' teeth, tobacco, whiskey, cattle, the shiny metals called silver and gold, even paper, even numbers in an account book.

Modern money . . . requires the same leap of faith, the same social consent the primitive societies gave to their money. Modern money, in fact, is even more distant from concrete reality. Over the centuries, the evolution of money has been a long and halting progression in which human societies have hesitantly transferred their money faith from one object to another, at each step moving farther away from real value and closer to pure abstraction.[4]

What I am interested in here is not so much the specific account given of money—as fascinating as it is—but in the idea that 'money is an illusion', that 'money is worthless unless everyone [more accurately, I should think, *nearly* everyone] believes in it', that it is a 'shared illusion' and 'requires . . . [a] leap of faith'. (The idea of 'real value' that occurs in the passage, and its contrast with 'pure abstraction' and the attendant implication that money has no 'real value' and that 'pure abstractions' are not real, are ideas that in another context I should want to argue with, but I here bypass them.) The question this passage raises for institutional ethics is whether all institutions (abstract sense) are 'shared illusions', or whether money is special or distinctive or unusual in this respect. I here point out only that this characteristic of money, so eloquently and dramatically described in this passage, is not shared by such institutions as punishment, imprisonment, or advertising. (Advertising comes close, but it is not so much shared illusion as something that generates illusion.) But it appears true of property (unless property is identified with land, yet that is obviously error). I do not think it is true of marriage, or of promising, which marriage presupposes. It may be taken as applying to punishment, especially legal punishment such as imprisonment, in so far as in the so-called civilized world the system of punishment tends to operate largely with threats, which are often illusory.[5] The central

---

[4] William Greider, *The New Yorker*, 16 November 1987, p.68, published since (1989), as *Secrets of the Temple: How the Federal Reserve Runs the Country*; wherein the ideas in the passage quoted may be found in and around pp. 226–229. It is interesting that the book does not, in its later accounts, adhere consistently to the idea of money as an illusion. Cf., e.g., pp. 242, 265, 453, 620, 673, 685, 688, and 714. Discussion of the consistency of Greider's ideas, however, is more appropriately reserved for a discourse explicitly on money. I have quoted his striking account of money because it is an observation on an especially interesting and certainly abstract institution, which may have application to other institutions as well.

[5] I owe this point, or the thought behind it, to my colleague Claudia Card.

characteristic of institutions that this account points to is the characteristic of shared beliefs and values and social purposes. And the concept of social relations, which is involved in the concept of an institution, though not an illusion by any means, is still something very difficult to characterize.[6]

VI

The question to be faced now is whether there really is a distinct branch of ethics to be called institutional ethics, which is what I am claiming. If the same principles that apply to actions (which I am calling individual principles) can apply to institutions, even in the most abstract sense, one incentive to the project at hand would seem to be removed. So is this so?

It is in some instances. Consider slavery, certainly an example of an institution even if not one that is current, approved of, or operative in this society (though it has unfortunately not been altogether eradicated from the world). Surely the ground—or a ground—for condemning slavery can be found in The Categorical Imperative, in either its Universality form or its Humanity form. Slavery is to be condemned (1) because its maxim could not be willed to be universal law, and also (2) because it involves treating human beings merely as means to ends in which they cannot share and to which they cannot consent, and therefore not as ends in themselves. So even though slavery is an institution, and not either an action or a kind of action, it looks as though this individual principle of action more than suffices in application to it. And I am sure a similar argument could be propounded using the Principle of Utility, though I am not about to propound it. No doubt a similar argument could work in application to a number of similar arrangements that can be called institutions. However, I do not think it would work for all. I do not see any parallel argument either for or against or even with respect to advertising, industry, property. (Punishment, of course, is an old figure in this game, since it has been the favourite institution exercising the ingenuity of moral philosophers for decades.) What we need to look for are principles, or simply considerations, that apply to, throw light on, and serve as a basis for criticism and improvement of an institution—say education or the university or marriage or law—and not

[6] At least I find it difficult to characterize. An interesting discussion, almost the first word on the topic, is provided by Winch (1958). But of course there are valuable discussions by Durkheim and Weber and others.

simply as a basis for a judgment that it ought or ought not to exist, be practiced, or be tolerated. This sort of search will bring us into somewhat closer contact with our subject. The application of a moral principle ought not to be regarded as an automatic matter in any case.

Consequently, even if individual principles, whatever they are, could be applied as they stand or with a minimum of modification to institutions, they would not meet the requirements of the problem. Intelligent appraisal and evaluation and critique and modification of an institution—of the sort exemplified by Tawney's work, whatever one thinks of his conclusions—requires more than merely applying an external standard to it, on a sort of litmus paper model. It requires understanding the institution on its own terms.

VII

Let us consider now the criteria or standards for evaluation of institutions. These standards—the first three at least—will on the surface appear similar to if not identical with some standard principles of individual ethics. I mention four.

1. *A utilitarian or consequentialist type.* This involves considering the consequences of an institution and its various alternative arrangements—including the alternative of not having anything like it at all—and judging which alternative has results that are best on the whole. This is an important consideration and I do not denigrate it. Indeed, I think utilitarianism understood this way makes better sense in application to institutions or practices than it does in application to actions. It is, however, terribly difficult to apply, if only because we lack the requisite knowledge, and because of the fairly external view it takes of the workings of an institution. By itself I should not think it would be anywhere near adequate.

2. *A functional evaluation* relates to the institution's end or purpose or function. This requires dealing with a number of questions. Does it meet its purpose? Does it meet it efficiently? What other consequences does it have—that is, what are its side effects? This involves something like a cost-benefit analysis, only it involves in addition the difficult task of figuring out what benefits and costs are, and this itself requires normative evaluation and can be done effectively only in the light of a knowledge of sensible alternatives and standards. Further questions present themselves.

Just what is the function or purpose of the institution? Is this function itself good or worthwhile? We must, furthermore, distinguish between what the function or purpose *is* and what it *ought to be*. With an institution this is neither easy nor obvious. Indeed, it may be that when we consider the purpose or function or ends of institutions the distinction between *is* and *ought* begins to break down, since they so readily merge into each other. Tawney says that

> the purpose of industry is obvious. It is to supply man with things which are necessary, useful, or beautiful, and thus to bring life to body or spirit. In so far as it is governed by this end, it is among the most important of human activities. In so far as it is diverted from it . . . it possesses no more social significance than the orderly business of ants and bees, the strutting of peacocks, or the struggles of carnivorous animals over carrion. (Tawney, 1921, 9, n.2)

But this sounds to me, especially given Tawney's target in *The Acquisitive Society*, more an account of what the purpose of industry ought to be, or would be in a better arranged or functional society, than what it *is* in fact in the 'acquisitive society' Tawney was castigating, and in which we still to a great measure live. Tawney also says that it 'is patent' that 'the purpose of industry is to provide the material foundation of a good social life', so that, consequently, 'any measure which makes that provision more effective, so long as it does not conflict with some still more important purpose, is wise, and any institution which thwarts or encumbers it is foolish . . .', and he goes on to say that 'It is foolish . . . to cripple education . . . for the sake of industry; for one of the uses of industry is to provide the wealth which may make possible better education' (Tawney, 1921, 96; 97; cf. 179). But *is* it patent or obvious? In 'the acquisitive society' the purpose of industry *is* to increase the monetary returns to shareholders; that is precisely Tawney's complaint against it.[7]

So the functional or Tawneyesque criterion is more complicated than it at first appears. In addition, given the definition of an insti-

[7] The following statement by A. J. Liebling helps illustrate the complexity of these terms: 'The function of the press in society is to inform, but its role is to make money' (Liebling, 1964, Foreword, p. 7, par. 22). Suppose 'role' and 'function' were interchanged, to give: 'The role of the press in society is to inform, but its function is to make money.' This doesn't fit as well, and certainly would not say what Liebling wanted to say. Why not, and how are 'role' and 'function' to be defined?

tution as a recognized and organized way of meeting a social need or desire, with respect to any institution the question arises what social needs or desires it meets and whether these are worth meeting. What needs does it organize and satisfy, and do these needs deserve satisfaction? It is better not to try to finesse this question by definition or by the acclamation of something as obvious.

3. This teleological or functional standard actually merges with a *deontological* standard based on considerations of equity, justice, or fairness. Is the institution fair? Given that fairness can be a matter of degree, how fair, and how unfair? Even if needs are satisfied efficiently, are they being satisfied fairly? Some such principle as the Principle of Humanity comes into play here. The main objection to slavery is not that it was inefficient—that it may or may not have been, and efficiency is not an altogether useless test in appraising institutions. But the major, and sufficient, objection to slavery is that it was unjust, on grounds that this principle makes manifest.

4. Rawls's two principles of justice should perhaps be mentioned at this point, since they emphasize justness as fairness. In their first approximation they state:

> First: each person is to have an equal right to the most extensive basic liberty compatible with a similar liberty for others. Second: social and economic inequalities are to be arranged so that they are both (a) reasonably expected to be to everyone's advantage, and (b) attached to positions and offices open to all. (Rawls, 1971, 60)

I mention these, though without going into their further refinements and qualifications, for two reasons. One is that Rawls emphasises that these principles apply 'to the basic structure of society' (p. 61), 'to institutions' (p. 63), and insists that 'The principles of justice for institutions must not be confused with the principles which apply to individuals and their actions in particular circumstances' (p. 54). The second is that Rawls insists at the outset that 'Justice is the first virtue of social institutions . . . laws and institutions no matter how efficient and well-arranged must be reformed or abolished if they are unjust' (p. 3). One might say that Rawls's theory of justice is an institutional ethics, except that it is much more than that, and also that there are questions of institutional ethics it does not touch on.

5. The relations among these various modes of institutional critique and evaluation need to be studied; in the tradition they are usually taken to be competing and at odds and irreconcilable. I

think the tradition is mistaken. A society is a network of inter-
related interlocking and interacting institutions and institutional
arrangements, and responsible appraisal must consider the relation
of this set of interrelations to institutional criticism. A change in
one institution in a society—much like a change in one feature of a
legal system—will almost inevitably bring about a change in others, and so on, indefinitely; these institutional consequences need
to be taken into account and evaluated on sensible standards of
evaluation, for in dealing with something as complex as a society
or as a social system what we face is *interaction*, not just cause and
effect, even social cause and effect. And just as the distinction
between *is* and *ought* tends to break down or merge when considering the functions of institutions, so too do the distinctions and
supposedly sharp divisions between (or among) teleological, consequentialist, and deontological theories.

VIII

We come now to what I call the problem of the inference gap, a
central though certainly not the only problem of institutional
ethics. What I am calling the inference-gap thesis states that no
moral judgment of an institution-constituted action follows from a
moral judgment of the related institution. The converse thesis is
that no moral judgment of an institution follows from a moral
judgment of a related institution-constituted action. Is this thesis
sound, and is it sound in all its multifarious forms?

Let us put to one side a question about a 'moral judgment following from' something. If something is genuinely a moral *judgment*, then, although inference enters into it—for where there is
judgment there is always inference—it cannot strictly speaking be
a deduction from anything, for if it is a deduction it is not a matter
of judgment. But, as I said, let us put this to one side—and leave it
there.

Example 1. Consider the institutional judgments (a) that slavery
is unjust, or (b) that slavery ought to be abolished, and imagine we
are living in a place where slavery is legal and in operation.
Suppose you come to agree with one of these institutional judgments, yet find that you are the owner of slaves, perhaps by inheritance. What ought you to do? In particular, what ought you to do
with your slaves? The inference-gap thesis states that no answer to
this individual question can be deduced from the judgment of the
institution. You might think, at first, that you ought to free them.
But whether this is what you ought to do depends on a number of

factors, including the other laws of the society in which you live—which may not make provision for freeing slaves, for instance; on the disposition of other 'free' people in your society—you might free your slaves only to have them in turn enslaved by Simon Legree; and on the condition, including the educational condition, of your slaves.

It might be thought that there is a difference between the judgment (a) that slavery is unjust and the judgment (b) that slavery ought to be abolished, on the ground that the second judgment implies that there is something that ought to be done, namely abolish slavery, whereas the first judgment, that slavery is unjust, does not imply that there is anything that ought to be done. I agree that there is a *prima facie* difference. But it is my considered judgment that this difference is illusory and amounts to nothing. Normally the judgment that some arrangement is unjust implies, everything else equal, that it ought to be either changed or abolished. It should be especially noticed that slavery cannot be so changed as not to be unjust, so that with respect to slavery there is no point in talking about changing it though not abolishing it, but this is almost certainly a special case, not applicable to all institutions. So the institutional judgment that slavery is unjust, *tout court*, all things considered, implies that slavery ought to be abolished, and judgment (b), therefore, has no implications not possessed by judgment (a), since judgment (b) is implied by judgment (a). (The logical principle here is that whatever implies a given proposition implies everything implied by that proposition, an implication of the transitivity of implication.)

It is, I think, manifest that no answer to the individual question follows from the adverse judgment of the institution. All that follows is that one has a problem, of the form, What ought I to do, given that I have slaves and have arrived at the opinion that slavery is unjust (or that slavery ought to be abolished)? It does not even follow that you ought to work against or vote against slavery. If your society does not have the institution of voting, you cannot vote against it; if it lacks the institution of free speech, you might be endangering yourself as well as your slaves by working against slavery. Something ought to be done—that is plain. But *what* ought to be done is a problem, one not solvable by deduction from the negative premise about the institution. This serves only to generate the problem, not to solve it.

Example 2. Consider again the grading case. Suppose you conclude that grading is unjust or is an inefficient and not very useful educational device. Does that determine what you should do if you are called upon to turn in grades? No, it does not. For it does not follow that you ought not to turn in any grades at all. That would, in any educational institution with a grading requirement, be equivalent to turning in an *F* for all. And that would be to grade, in an especially harsh manner.

Similarly, to take the positive rather than the negative case, if you judge that the institution of grading, despite its defects, is in general fair and useful, that by itself does not determine how you ought to act with respect to any of the supplicants in the grading case earlier presented. You still have the original problem. However, reflection on the purpose and function of grading might enable you to arrive at a more enlightened way of dealing with the matter than you could arrive at without such reflection.

Example 3. From (1), Boxing ought to be abolished, it does not follow that (2), Michael Spinks and Mike Tyson ought not to have boxed. In general, no statement like (2) follows from any statement like (1). A statement like (2) can follow only from some such statement as (3), No one ought to engage in or participate in boxing. But (3) is not an institutional judgment simply because an institution is mentioned in it. It is a general or universal individual judgment. And (3), No one ought to engage in or participate in boxing, does not follow from (1), Boxing ought to be abolished.

Example 4. Let us go back a few years, to the period before the so-called 'Tax Reform Act' of 1986. Let us suppose that I am of opinion that the lower capital gains tax rate ought to be eliminated and that capital gains ought to be taxed at the same rate as ordinary income. Yet it would be foolish of me, if I have capital gains, not to declare them as such and take the lower tax rate on them. In any case, that I ought not to take the lower tax rate does not *follow* from, is in no way supported by, the adverse judgment of the institution.

Example 5. Consider the judgment (a), This is a bad law and ought to be repealed. Does it follow that (b), The judge ought not to apply this law in deciding this case? It seems plain that it does not. (a) might provide a reason for (b), but it certainly does not entail it. Nor does (b) imply (a). Consider now (c), No judge ought to apply this law in deciding *any* case. (c) also does not follow from (a). Now consider (d), No judge ought to apply *any* law in deciding *any* case. (d) is incoherent. Yet (d) implies (c), that No judge ought to apply this law in deciding any case, which in turn implies (b), that The Judge ought not to apply this law in deciding this case, so (d) implies (b). But this does not breach the inference-gap thesis. For (a) [This is a bad law] does not imply (b) [The judge ought not to apply this law in this case], and (b) does not imply (a). From 'The judge ought not to apply this law in deciding this case' it does not follow that this is a bad law and ought to be repealed.

Example 6, which I provide at the risk of breaching Ockham's razor and multiplying examples beyond necessity, is this. In the United States in recent years a movement has arisen for imposing term limits on occupants of certain elected offices, such as terms in Congress. Now imagine a Senator Hypothetical who is in favour of instituting term limits by having a law passed that would limit members of the Senate to no more than two consecutive terms, who has served two terms and is running for a third. Does the judgment that term limits should be mandated by law imply that Senator Hypothetical ought not to run (in the United States one cannot *stand* for office, or one would be bowled over by those running) for a third term. No, it does not. To be in favour of the institutional change, which, if it were in effect, would preclude Senator Hypothetical from running for a third term, in no way implies that in the absence of such a law, which would apply to all senators alike, Senator Hypothetical is bound by an individual judgment that precludes running again. For Senator Hypothetical's original judgment was about an institution, and was not the self-referring individual judgement, 'I, Senator Hypothetical, ought not to serve more than two terms.' That Senator X ought to be limited to two terms because there ought to be a law limiting all senators to two terms as senator, is not in any way a necessary statement. However, the institutional judgment can easily be confused with the general judgment that 'No senator ought to serve more than two consecutive terms.' This last is not an institutional judgment, it is a general moral judgment that clearly applies to all individuals within its scope. The fact that it makes reference to an institution in no way implies that it is a judgment about an institution, that is to say, an institutional judgment. I incline to think that those who fallaciously infer individual judgments from institutional judgments are confusing a general moral judgment with an institutional one. I hereby dub this move 'the institutional fallacy', and hazard the prediction that it will have a longer and less turbulent life than the naturalistic fallacy. (It is, actually, a form of the fallacy of misplaced concreteness.)

Example 7. I cannot resist adding one more example, Ockham's razor be hanged, because it has just come to hand, and illustrates the institutional fallacy so aptly. A reader of *The New Republic* writes, in a letter to the editor: 'not so long ago Michael Kinsley . . . wrote that he didn't support the federal tax deduction for mortgage interest, but none the less he took the deduction. Judging himself, Kinsley did not find his action . . . "hypocritical".[8] Nor is there any reason why he should have, since there is nothing hypocritical about it. The deduction is legally available, why not take it? One is under no legal or moral obligation not to (though if one were running for office on a platform of repealing that deduction it would be politically impolitic to take it, so there might be a 'political', that is to say, prudential, obligation not to take it). The example speaks for itself as an example of the institutional fallacy, and is an instance of a wide-spread kind, infecting the world of politics and journalism. Yet there is no moral or logical inconsistency, or even any incoherence, in condemning an institution and at the same time acting under it.

Let us determine now what these examples illustrate and in the process demonstrate. Example 5, the judge example, illustrates both the inference-gap thesis and its converse. And on the basis of such examples as these I am convinced that its breach is a recurrent source of fallacious moral reasoning. So we are now in a position to state the inference-gap thesis more generally and precisely (which shows, incidentally, that generality is not always tied to vagueness):

(A) *Negative version*: From the 'fact' or judgment that some institution is immoral, unjust, or wrong, nothing follows about what one should do in connection with it or even about whether one should or should not perform an act constituted by the institution.

(B) *Positive version*: From the truth or judgment that some institution is moral or just or justified, nothing follows about whether one should or should not perform an act constituted by the institution.

(C) *Converse negative version*: From the judgment that one ought not to act in a certain way that is constituted by an institution, it does not follow that there is anything wrong or immoral about the institution. Take an example from baseball: from the specific judgment that the player on first base ought not to steal second it does not follow that base-stealing—a technical term from the game of baseball—is wrong or that a rule should be adopted prohibiting it. Again (and perhaps more intelligibly for a British audience, despite the fact that there is no death penalty in Britain), from the judgment that the judge ought not to sentence this defendant, who has been proved guilty, to death, it does not follow that the death penalty is wrong, odious, or immoral, or that it ought to be abolished.

[8] *The New Republic*, vol. 208, no. 9, issue no. 4076, 1 March 1993, p. 5.

(D) *Converse positive version*: From the judgment that the judge ought to sentence the defendant who has been duly found guilty to death it by no means follows that the death penalty is a good thing, that it is just, morally justified, or admirable.

These examples alone seem to me to show that the inference-gap thesis holds in its converse versions, so I will say no more about them. They do not, in any case, occur with any great frequency. The positive, non-converse, version, also seems almost self-evident, as illustrated by the grading example (example 2). The first—negative non-converse—version is the one that generates the greatest difficulties, and I shall say only this about it on this occasion.

One possible and actually plausible response to Version (A) of the inference-gap thesis is that the premise that, say, slavery is unjust or ought to be abolished generates a presumptive or *prima facie* reason—not a conclusive reason—to conclude that one ought to do one thing or another, depending on the circumstances, free one's slaves if one has some, or work to eliminate slavery, speak or write against it, vote against it if voting is an option, and so on. In general, on this view, an adverse judgment of an institution would provide a presumptive but not a conclusive reason for or against performing any one of a number of actions constituted by or defined by the institution—just which, would depend on the filling in of the concrete details. On this view, such a premise would have the same relation to a practical conclusion that any consideration would have in practical or concrete moral reasoning. And, on this view, the inference-gap thesis would have no special relevance to institutional ethics, since a similar gap—if it is a gap—prevails in all or nearly all reasoning to a practical moral conclusion.

But I must leave further exploration of this matter to some future occasion. I conclude with the observation that the inference-gap thesis, if sound, is the first principle of institutional ethics. However, as I hope to have brought out, it is not the only principle of institutional ethics and the problem of determining its soundness is not the only problem connected with this topic. I am pleased to commend the subject to students of moral philosophy as a rewarding object of study.

APPENDIX

As mentioned above (section IV), there are a number of competing accounts and conceptions of institutions. Two others, not heretofore listed, are worth mentioning, especially since it is my guess that they are not well known in Britain. Indeed, it is probable that they are not well known in philosophical circles in the United States.

One is *How Institutions Think*, by Mary Douglas (1986). From the title alone it is clear that Mary Douglas's conception of *institution* is quite different from mine. I mention the work because it is very astute and important in further inquiry on this matter—see esp. pp. 46–47 and 124–125.

The other is *The Institutions of Society*, by James K. Feibleman (1956). This is a very long book (389 pages) containing a number of interesting ideas. 'Institution' is defined as:

> that subdivision of society which consists in human beings in groups established together with their customs, laws and material tools, and organized around a central aim or purpose. More briefly, an institution is an established social group working in customary ways with material tools on a common task.

Feibleman comes close to an important part of the conception advanced herein in part of the above definition and also when he goes on to recognise 'as institutions two levels of social organization, the level in which "education" is an institution, and the level in which "Oxford University" is an institution. The family is an institution, and the Medici in Renaissance Italy may be said to have been one as well. Thus we are ordaining that the genus and the species of institutions shall share the classification' (pp. 20–21; see also p. 23). I first became acquainted with this book in 1981, when the main ideas of this paper had already been largely formed. But the present paper is intended as an organizing study for a book, which I still have some hope of completing, and there is much to be gained from each of the works just mentioned.

References

Aristotle. 1972. *De Partibus Animalium*, trans. D. F. Balme. Oxford: Clarendon Press.

Aristotle. 1984. *Complete Works of Aristotle*, ed. J. Barnes after Ross. Princeton: Princeton University Press, Berlin: Becker.

Augustine. 1923. *Confessions*, trans. R. Matthew, ed. R. Huddleston. London: Burns & Oates.

Augustine. 1968. *The Teacher, The Free Choice of the Will and Grace and Free Will*, trans. R. P. Russell. Washington: Catholic University of America Press.

Bacharach, M. and Hurley, S. 1991. *Foundations of Decision Theory: Issues and Advances*. Oxford: Blackwell.

Barry, B. 1989. *Theories of Justice*. London: HarvesterWheatsheaf.

Bartky, S. 1990. 'Feminine Masochism and the Politics of Personal Transformation', in *Femininity and Domination*. London: Routledge.

Berlin, I. 1980. 'From Hope and Fear Set Free', in *Concepts and Categories*. Oxford: Oxford University Press.

Bernard, C. 1949. *Introduction to the Study of Experimental Medicine*, trans. H. C. Greene. New York: Shuman.

Blair, Hugh. 1801. *Sermons: To which is annexed a short account of the life and character of the author, by James Finlayson*. 5 vols. Edinburgh: Wm. Creech; London: W. Strachan and T. Cadell; 1797–1801.

Blake, W. 1966. *Complete Works*, ed. G. Keynes. London: Oxford University Press.

Blish, J. 1968. *Black Easter*. London: Faber.

Blish, J. 1974. *The Day after Judgment*. Harmondsworth: Penguin (1st publ. by Faber, 1972).

Bock, P. 1969. *Modern Cultural Anthropology*. New York: Alfred A. Knopf.

Boethius 1973. *Tractates and Consolation of Philosophy*, trans. H. F. Stewart, E. K. Rand and S. J. Tester. London: Heinemann, Loeb Classical Library.

Brandt, R. B. 1959. *Ethical Theory*. Englewood Cliffs: Prentice-Hall.

Brandt, R. B. 1979. *A Theory of the Good and the Right*. Oxford: Clarendon Press.

Brink, D. 1989. *Moral Realism and the Foundations of Ethics*. Cambridge: Cambridge University Press.

Burnet, J. (ed.) 1900. *The Ethics of Aristotle*. London: Methuen.

Campbell, T. 1975. 'Perfect and Imperfect Duties', *The Modern Schoolman*, **102**, 195–204.

Carritt, E. F. 1935. *Morals & Politics: Theories of their relation from Hobbes and Spinoza to Marx and Bosanquet*. Oxford: Clarendon Press.

Carritt, E. F. 1947. *Ethical and Political Thinking*. Oxford: Clarendon Press.

Castell, A. 1954. *An Elementary Ethics*. Englewood Cliffs: Prentice-Hall.

References

Chandrasekhar, S. 1987. *Truth and Beauty*. Chicago: University of Chicago Press.

Chesterton, G. K. 1961. *Orthodoxy*. London: Fontana (1st publ. 1908).

Chroust, A. (ed.) 1964. *Aristotle's Protrepticus: A Reconstruction*. Indiana: University of Notre Dame press.

Clark, S. R. L. 1985. 'Slaves and citizens', *Philosophy* **60**, 27–46.

Clark, S. R. L. 1990. *A Parliament of Souls*. Oxford: Clarendon Press.

Clark, S. R. L. 1993. 'Natural Goods and Moral Beauty', in D. Knowles and J. Skorupski (eds) 1993. *Virtue and Taste, Essays in Memory of Flint Schier*. Oxford: Blackwell.

Cohen, G. 1992. 'Incentives, Inequality and Community', in Petersen, 1992.

Cohen, J. 1989. 'On the Currency of Egalitarian Justice', *Ethics*, 99.

Copp, D. and Zimmerman, D. (eds.) *Morality, Reason and Truth*. Totowa, New Jersey: Rowman and Allanheld.

Craig, E.J. 1990, *Knowledge and the State of Nature*. Oxford: ????

Dancy, R. M. (ed.) 1993. *Kant and Critique*. London: Kluwer.

Daniels, N. 1979. 'Wide Reflective Equilibrium and Theory Acceptance in Ethics', *Journal of Philosophy*, 76.

Davidson, D. 1980. *Essays on Actions and Events*. Oxford: Clarendon Press.

Diogenes Laertius. 1925. *Lives of the Philosophers*, trans. R. D. Hicks. London: Heinemann, Loeb Classical Library.

Dostoyevsky, F. 1962. *Letters to Family and Friends*, trans. E. C. Mayne. London: Chatto & Windus.

Douglas, M. 1986. *How Institutions Think*. Syracuse: University Press.

Dummett, M. 1991. *The Logical Basis of Metaphysics*. London: Duckworth.

Dunne, J. S. 1965. *The City of the Gods*. London: Sheldon Press.

Eco, U. 1986. *Art and Beauty in the Middle Ages*, trans. H. Bredin. New Haven and London: Yale University Press.

Ellsberg, D. 1961. 'Risk, Ambiguity, and the Savage Axioms', *Quarterly Journal of Economics*.

Epictetus. 1926. *Discourses and Encheiridion*, trans. W. A. Oldfather. London: Heinemann, Loeb Classical Library.

Feibleman, J. 1956. *The Institutions of Society*. New York: Humanities Press, 1968 (1st publ. 1956).

Feldman, F. 1978. *Introductory Ethics*. Englewood Cliffs: PrenticeHall.

Fishkin, J. 1982. *The Limits of Obligation*. New Haven: Yale University Press.

Fowler, H. 1926. *A Dictionary of Modern English Usage*. Oxford: Clarendon Press.

Freud, S. 1957. *Civilization and Its Discontents*. London: Hogarth Press.

Freud, S. 1979. 'A child is being beaten', in *Selected Writings*, vol. 10. Harmondsworth: Pelican.

Frey, R. (ed.) 1984. *Utility and Rights*. Minneapolis: University of Minnesota Press.

Gardner, P. 1992. 'Propositional Attitudes and Multicultural Education, or Believing Others are Mistaken', in J. Horton and P. Nicholson (eds) *Toleration: Philosophy and Practice*. Aldershot: Avebury Press.

Gibbard, A. 1990. *Wise Choices, Apt Feelings*. Oxford: Oxford University Press.

Greider, W. 1989. *Secrets of the Temple: How the Federal Reserve runs the Country*. New York: Simon & Schuster.

Griffin, J. 1986. *Well-Being: Its Meaning, Measurement and Moral Importance*. Oxford: Clarendon Press.

Hare, R. M. 1952. *The Language of Morals*. Oxford: Oxford University Press.

Hare, R. M. 1963. *Freedom and Reason*. Oxford: Oxford University Press.

Hare, R. M. 1967. 'Some Alleged Differences between Imperatives and Indicatives', *Mind*, **76**, 309–326.

Hare, R. M. 1971. 'The Argument from Received Opinion', in *Essays on Philosophical Method*. London: Macmillan.

Hare, R. M. 1981. *Moral Thinking: Its Levels, Method, and Point*. Oxford: Oxford University Press.

Hare, R. M. 1985. 'A *reductio ad absurdum* of Descriptivism', in S. Shanker (ed.) *Philosophy in Britain Today*. London: Croom Helm. Reprinted in Hare, 1989.

Hare, R. M. 1989. *Essays in Ethical Theory*. Oxford: Oxford University Press.

Hare, R. M. 1993. 'Could Kant have been a Utilitarian?', *Utilitas*, 5. Also in Dancy, 1993.

Hart, H. 1963. *Law, Liberty and Morality*. London: Oxford University Press.

Havel, V. 1992. *Selected Plays*. London: Faber.

Hetherington H. and Muirhead, J. 1918. *Social Purpose*. London: George Allen & Unwin.

Hintikka, J. (ed.) 1967. *The Philosophy of Mathematics*. Oxford: Oxford University Press.

Hofstadter, D. and Dennett, D. (eds) 1982. *The Mind's I*. Harmondsworth: Penguin.

Honoré, A. 1988. 'Responsibility and Luck', *Law Quarterly Review*, **104**, 530–553.

Horwich, P. 1990. *Truth*. Oxford: Blackwell.

Hospers, J. 1982. *Human Conduct*. London: Harcourt Brace Joyanovich.

Hume, D. 1948. *Dialogues Concerning Natural Religion*, ed. H. D. Aiken. New York: Hafner.

Hume, D. 1729. *A Treatise of Human Nature*.

Hurley, S. 1989. *Natural Reasons*. New York: Oxford University Press.

James, W. 1890. *The Principles of Psychology*. London: Macmillan.

Jeffreys, S. 1990. *Anti-Climax: A Feminist Perspective on the Sexual Revolution*. London: The Women's Press.

Joad, C. E. M. 1938. *Guide to the Philosophy of Morals and Politics*. London: Gollancz.

References

Kant, I. 1928. *Critique of Judgement*, trans. C. J. Meredith. Oxford: Clarendon Press.

Kant, I. 1929. *Critique of Pure Reason*, trans. N. Kemp Smith (*KrV*.) London: Macmillan.

Kant, I. 1948. *The Moral Law* (*Grundlegung zur Metaphysik der Sitten*), trans. H. Paton (*Gr*.). London: Hutchinson.

Kant, I. 1964. *Doctrine of Virtue*, trans. M. Gregor (*Tgl*.). New York: Harper and Row.

Keats, J. 1956. *Poetical Works*, ed. H. W. Garrod. London: Oxford University Press.

Klein, M. 1990. *Determinism, Blameworthiness and Deprivation*. Oxford: Clarendon Press.

Lakatos, I. 1964. 'Proofs and Refutations', *British Journal for the Philosophy of Science*, 14.

Leicester, M. 1986. 'Multicultural Curriculum or Anti-racist Education: denying the gulf', *Multicultural Teaching to Combat Racism in School and Community*, **4**, 4–7.

Levinas, E. 1969. *Totality and Infinity*, trans. Alphonso Lingis. Pittsburgh: Duquesne University Press.

Levinas, E. 1972. *Humanisme de l'autre homme*. Montpellier: Fata Morgana.

Levinas, E. 1976. *Difficile liberté*. Paris: Albin Michel.

Levinas, E. 1981. *Otherwise than Being or Beyond Essence*. The Hague: Martinus Nijhoff.

Levinas, E. 1982. *De Dieu qui vient à l'ideé*. Paris: Vrin.

Lewis, H. D. 1976. (ed.) *Contemporary British Philosophy*, Series IV. London: George Allen & Unwin.

Liebling, A. J. 1964. *The Press*. New York: Ballantine Books.

Lyons, D. 1976. 'Mill's Theory of Morality', *Nous*, **10**, 101–120.

MacBeath, A. 1952. *Experiments in Living*. London: Macmillan.

MacDonald, I. 1991. *The New Shostakovich*. Oxford: Oxford University Press.

MacIntyre, A. 1985. 'Relativism, Power and Philosophy', *Proceedings of the American Philosophical Association*, 59.

Mackie, J. L. 1946. 'A Refutation of Morals', *Australian Journal of Philosophy*, **24**, 77–90.

Mackie, J. L. 1977. *Ethics: Inventing Right and Wrong*. Harmondsworth: Penguin.

Malebranche, N. *The Search after Truth*, trans. T. M. Lennon and P. J. Olscamp. Columbus: Ohio State University Press.

Mayo, B. 1986. *The Philosophy of Right and Wrong*. London: Routledge & Kegan Paul.

McGhee, M. 1993. 'Chastity and the Male Philosopher', *Journal of Applied Philosophy*, 10.

McMurrin, S. (ed.) 1988. *The Tanner Lectures on Human Values*. Salt Lake City: University of Utah Press.

Mill, J. S. 1879. *System of Logic*. London: Longmans Green.

Mill, J. S. 1965. *Collected Works*. London: Routledge; Toronto: University of Toronto Press, 1965–.

Moore, G. E. 1903. *Principia Ethica*. Cambridge: Cambridge University Press.

Mothersill, M. 1984. *Beauty Restored*. Oxford: Clarendon Press.

Murdoch, I. 1970. *The Sovereignty of the Good*. London: Routledge.

Nagel, T. 1979. 'Moral luck', in *Mortal Questions*. Cambridge: Cambridge University Press.

Newman, J. H. 1985. *The Grammar of Assent*, ed. I. J. Ker. Oxford: Clarendon Press.

Newton-Smith, W. 1981. *The Rationality of Science*. London: Routledge & Kegan Paul.

Nozick, R. 1974. *Anarchy, State and Utopia*. New York: Basic Books.

Nozick, R. *Philosophical Explanations*. Oxford: Clarendon Press.

Nussbaum, M. 1986. *The Fragility of Goodness: Luck and Ethics in Greek Tragedy and Philosophy*. Cambridge: Cambridge University Press.

O'Neill, O. 1989. 'The Great Maxims of Justice and of Charity', in *Constructions of Reason: Explorations of Kant's Practical Philosophy*. Cambridge: Cambridge University Press.

O'Neill, O. 1992. 'Theories of Justice, Traditions of Virtue', in H. Gross and R. Harrison (eds) *Jurisprudence: Cambridge Essays*. Oxford: Clarendon Press.

Parfit, D. 1984. *Reasons and Persons*. Oxford: Clarendon Press.

Petersen, G. (ed.) 1992. *The Tanner Lectures on Human Values*, vol. 13. Salt Lake City: University of Utah Press.

Pincoffs, E. 1966. *The Rationale of Legal Punishment*. New York: Humanities Press.

Plotinus, 1956. *Enneads*, trans. McKenna. London: Faber.

Pojman, L. 1990. *Ethics: Discovering Right and Wrong*. Belmont: Wadsworth.

Potter, N. and Timmons, M. (eds) 1985. *Morality and Universality: Essays on Ethical Universalizabilty*. Dordrecht: Reidel.

Quine, W. V. 1953. *From a Logical Point of View*. Cambridge, Mass.: Harvard University Press.

Raphael, D. 1981. *Moral Philosophy*. Oxford: Oxford University Press.

Rawls, J. 1951. 'Outline of a Decision Procedure for Ethics', *Philosophical Review*, 60.

Rawls, J. 1955. 'Two Concepts of Rules', *Philosophical Review*, 44.

Rawls, J. 1958. 'Justice as Fairness', *Philosophical Review*, 47.

Rawls, J. 1972. *A Theory of Justice*. Oxford: Clarendon Press.

Rawls, J. 1975. 'The Independence of Moral Theory', *Proceedings and Addresses of the American Philosophical Association*, 48.

Rawls, J. 1980. 'Kantian Constructivism in Moral Theory', *Journal of Philosophy*, 77.

Rawls, J. 1985. 'Justice as Fairness: political not metaphysical', *Philosophy and Public Affairs*, 14.

Roemer, J. 1985. 'Equality of talent', *Economics and Philosophy*, 1.

References

Roemer, J. 1986. 'Equality of Resources Implies Equality of Welfare', *Quarterly Journal of Economics*, CI.

Roemer, J. 1987. 'Egalitarianism, Responsibility, and Information', *Economics and Philosophy*, 3.

Roemer, J. 1993. 'A Pragmatic Theory of Responsibility for the Egalitarian Planner', *Philosophy and Public Affairs*, 22.

Rorty, R. 1980. *Philosophy and The Mirror of Nature*. Oxford: Blackwell.

Rosenzweig, F. 1925. 'The New Thinking' ('Das neue Denken. Einige nachträgliche Bemerjungen zum Stern de Erlösung'), *Der Morgen*, Vol. 1.

Ross, W. D. 1930. *The Right and the Good*. Oxford: Oxford University Press.

Roth, J. K. (ed.) 1969. *The Moral Philosophy of William James*. New York: Crowell.

Sartre, J.P. 1965. *L'Existentialisme est un humanisme*. Paris: Nagel.

Sartre, J.P. 1969. *Being and Nothingness*, trans. H. Barnes. London: Methuen.

Scanlon, T. 1988. 'The Significance of Choice', in MacMurrin, 1988.

Scanlon, T. 1990. 'The Aims and Authority of Moral Theory', Hart Lecture in Jurisprudence and Philosophy, University College, Oxford.

Schneewind, J. B. 1990. 'The Misfortunes of Virtue', *Ethics*, **101**, 42–63.

Sen, A. 1982. 'Equality of What?', in *Choice, Welfare and Measurement*. Oxford: Blackwell.

Singer, M. 1961. *Generalization in Ethics*. New York: Alfred A. Knopf. London: Eyre & Spottiswoode, 1963.

Singer, M. 1977. *Morals and Values*. New York: Charles Scribner's & Sons.

Singer, P. 1974. 'Sidgwick and Reflective Equilibrium', *The Monist*, 58.

Sircello, G. 1975. *A New Theory of Beauty*. Princeton & London: Princeton University Press.

Skorupski, J. 1985. 'Objectivity and Convergence', *Proceedings of the Aristotelian Society*, LXXXVI, 1985/6, 235–50.

Skorupski, J. 1992. 'Liberal elitism', in D. Milligan and W. Watts-Miller (eds.) *Citizenship and Autonomy*. Aldershot: Avebury Press.

Skorupski, J. 1993. 'Anti-realism, Inference and the Logical Constants', in J. Haldane and C. Wright (eds.) *Realism and Reason*. Oxford: Oxford University Press.

Snitow, A. 1979. 'Mass Market Romance: pornography for women is different', *Radical History Review*, 20.

Solzhenitsyn, A. 1990. *One Day in the Life of Ivan Denisovitch*, trans. R. Parker. Harmondsworth: Penguin.

Starr, W. and Taylor, R. (eds) 1989. *Moral Philosophy: Historical and Contemporary Essays*. Milwaukee: Marquette University Press.

Stevens, P. S. 1976. *Patterns in Nature*. Harmondsworth: Penguin.

Strawson, G. 1986. *Freedom and Belief*. Oxford: Clarendon Press.

Strawson, P. F. 1950. 'Truth', *Proceedings of the Aristotelian Society*, supp. vol. 24.

Tawney, R. H. 1921. *The Acquisitive Society*. London: G. Bell & Sons.

Theweleit, K. 1987. *Male Fantasies*, Vol. 1. Cambridge: Cambridge University Press.

Warnock, G. J. 1967. *Contemporary Moral Philosophy*. London: Macmillan.

Warnock, G. J. 1971. *The Object of Morality*. London: Methuen.

Weber, R. 1986. *Dialogues with Scientists and Sages*. London: Routledge & Kegan Paul.

Weil, S. 1959. *Waiting on God*, trans. E. Crawford. London: Fontana.

Westermarck, E. 1932. *Ethical Relativity*. London: Kegan Paul, Trench, Trubner.

Wieland, G. 1982. 'Happiness: the perfection of man', in N. Kretzmann, A. Kenny, and J. Pinborg (eds.) *Cambridge History of Later Mediaeval Philosophy*. Cambridge: Cambridge University Press, 673–686.

Wiggins, D. 1987. *Needs, Values, Truth, Essays in the Philosophy of Value*. Oxford: Blackwell.

Wiggins, D. 1990. 'Moral Cognitivism, Moral Relativism and Motivating Beliefs', *Proceedings of the Aristotelian Society 1990–91*, 91.

Williams, B. 1972a. 'Knowledge and Reasons', in G. H. Wright (ed.) *Entretiens de Helsinki* (I.I.P). The Hague: Martinus Nijhoff.

Williams, B. 1972b. *Problems of the Self*. Cambridge: Cambridge University Press.

Williams, B. 1978 *Descartes: The Project of Pure Enquiry*. Harmondsworth: Penguin.

Williams, B. 1981. *Moral Luck*. Cambridge: Cambridge University Press.

Williams, B. 1985. *Ethics and the Limits of Philosophy*. London: Fontana.

Winch, P. 1958. *The Idea of a Social Science*. London: Routledge & Kegan Paul.

Windelband, J. 1921. *An Introduction to Philosophy*, trans. J. McCabe. London: T. Fisher Unwin.

Wittgenstein, L. 1953. *Philosophical Investigations*. Oxford: Blackwell.

Wittgenstein, L. 1967. *Zettel*. Oxford: Blackwell.

Wittgenstein, L. 1969. *On Certainty*, ed. G. Anscombe and G. von Wright. Oxford: Blackwell.

Wright, C. 1992. *Truth and Objectivity*. Cambridge, Mass.: Harvard University Press.

WynneTyson, J. (ed.) 1985. *The Extended Circle*. Fontwell: Centaur Press.

Zaehner, R. C. 1974. *Our Savage God*. London: Collins.

Notes on Contributors

Renford Bambrough of St. John's College, Cambridge, is the editor of *Philosophy*.

Stephen R. L. Clark is Professor of Philosophy at the University of Liverpool.

Catherine Chalier is the author of many books, her latest being on Spinoza, *Pensées de L'éternité* (Paris: Rosenzweig).

James Griffin is a Fellow of Keble College, Oxford.

Peter Gardner lectures on the Philosophy of Education at the University of Warwick.

Jean Grimshaw is Principal Lecturer in Cultural Studies at the University of the West of England.

R. M. Hare, formerly White's Professor of Moral Philosophy at the University of Oxford, is now Professor of Philosophy at the University of Florida, Gainsborough.

S. L. Hurley, presently a Fellow of St. Edmund Hall, will be taking up an appointment as Professor of Political and Ethical Theory at the University of Warwick in 1994.

Onora O'Neill is Principal of Newnham College, Cambridge.

Lord Quinton is President of the Royal Institute of Philosophy.

Professor Marcus G. Singer is Professor of Philosophy at the University of Wisconsin, Madison (see also the Preface).

John Skorupski is Professor of Philosophy at the University of Aberdeen.

Professor S. R. Sutherland is at present the Vice-Chancellor of the University of London. He will be taking up a new appointment as Vice-Chancellor of the University of Edinburgh in 1994. He is Chairman of the Council of the Royal Institute of Philosophy.

Bernard Williams is White's Professor of Moral Philosophy at the University of Oxford, and Deutsch Professor of Philosophy at the University of California, Berkeley.